Landmarks in CALL Research

Advances in CALL Research and Practice

Series Editor: Greg Kessler, Ohio University

This series is published in cooperation with the Computer Assisted Language Instruction Consortium (CALICO). Each Spring just prior to the CALICO annual conference the series publishes one volume comprised of articles previously published in *CALICO* journal together with a new Introduction.

Landmarks in CALL Research:

Looking Back to Prepare for the Future: 1995–2015

Edited by Greg Kessler

SHEFFIELD UK   BRISTOL CT

Published by Equinox Publishing Ltd.

UK: Office 415, The Workstation, 15 Paternoster Row, Sheffield, South Yorkshire
      S1 2BX
USA: ISD, 70 Enterprise Drive, Bristol, CT 06010

www.equinoxpub.com

First published in book form with a new Introduction 2016. Chapters 2 to 9 previously published in *CALICO* journal between 1995 and 2006.

ISBN   978-1-78179-360-2 (paperback)

British Library Cataloguing-in-Publication Data

A catalogue record for this book is available from the British Library.

Library of Congress Cataloging-in-Publication Data
Landmarks in CALL research : looking back to prepare for the future, 1995-2015 / Edited by Greg Kessler.
     pages cm. -- (Advances in CALL Research and Practice)
  Includes bibliographical references and index.
  ISBN 978-1-78179-360-2 (pb)
  1. Language and languages--Computer-assisted instruction--Research. 2. Language and languages--Study and teaching--Research. I. Kessler, Greg (Linguist) editor. II. CALICO Journal.
  P53.28.L33 2016
  418.00285--dc23
                         2015033344

Typeset by CA Typesetting Ltd, Sheffield, www.sheffieldtypesetting.com
Printed and bound in Great Britain by Lightning Source UK Ltd., Milton Keynes and Lightning Source Inc., La Vergne, TN

Contents

1   Introduction

Greg Kessler

Welcome to Advances in CALL Research and Practice, the new book series of the Computer Assisted Language Instruction Consortium (CALICO). The previous CALICO Monograph series was published from 1986 to 2015 with some years having no volume and others having more than one, including the 2013 Festschrift volume in honor of Bob Fischer who edited the monograph series from 2006 to 2015. Of course, most readers will know this was only one of the many contributions Bob Fischer made to the organization as he has was the Editor of the CALICO Journal and Executive Director of CALICO during much of this time as well. The many excellent volumes that were released in the CALICO Monograph series are a testament to his hard work! With the CALICO Journal transitioning to Equinox publishing in 2013, it made sense for the book series to follow that path as well. I believe we will benefit greatly from the potential for broader distribution of the important work included in CALICO books.

One condition of working with an outside publishing house is that it now requires more time to produce a volume. That issue of time brought about this initial reflective volume. The editors of the CALICO Journal, Bryan Smith and Mathias Schulze, initially proposed the idea of creating a CALICO book series volume that would include significant articles that have been previously published in the CALICO Journal. When I was selected to take on the role of series editor, they presented this idea to me, along with a number of suggestions for how contributions for such a collection might be identified. They had solicited the input of the editorial board and gathered individual recommendations from a handful of individuals. They gathered data reflecting the 'most influential' and 'seminal' works according to server records for the journal as well as the 'annual best article award.' These are identified and available on the CALICO Journal website at http://www.equinoxpub.com/journals/index.php/CALICO. The editors also collected the CALICO Journal portion of entries from the *Computer Assisted Language Learning: Critical Concepts in Linguistics* collection that Philip Hubbard had compiled in 2009. I found all of these suggestions to be extremely compelling, but having been simultaneously serving as co-editor of a special issue of *Language Learning & Technology* (with Philip Hubbard and Paige Ware) covering previous special issues of that publication, I knew there were many alternate ways to reflect on the influence of these publications. It was obvious that most of these attempts had been subjective in nature. It seemed to me that this collection of CALICO Journal articles could be unique if their selection were wholly based on objective data. I was immediately drawn to the Google scholar metrics. This is the most common means through which academic publishing can gather data about citations today. They also represent the broadest inclusion of citations since they include conventional scholarly articles as well as a number of other types of publications. Other comparable metrics (such as the Thompson Reuters Journal Citation Reports and Microsoft® Analytics) tend to only include citations from a limited set of peer reviewed scholarly journals. As I began to explore the results of Google scholar searches for CALICO Journal, I noticed that there were a number of articles that had been previously identified through the aforementioned approaches, but there were also a handful that had not been identified as 'most influential', 'seminal', or 'annual best article.' This seemed to me to be an intriguing approach. In consultation with the CALICO Journal editors, I decided to rely upon the citation reports provided by Google. Some of the other approaches have clearly achieved a degree of influence in their own way and it felt refreshing to allow the data to reveal itself. Thus, it made sense to me to rely wholly upon an objective means of identifying these entries as a novel way of identifying articles to include.

In consultation with the editors of the journal we agreed to include articles from the past two decades. This period of time covers a significant number of developments in CALL and provides valuable information for those who are new to the field. This period was also intentionally selected due to the influence of the Internet upon our field. 1995 was a pivotal year for Internet access and expansion. Although some of us had been using the world wide web prior to 1995 for a variety of academic purposes, this was the year that saw rapid growth of ISPs and the opening of the commercial use of the Internet which led to extensive network backbone expansion. In fact, the term Internet was officially defined by the Federal Networking Council in October 1995 (Leiner, et al., 2003). Most sources that track the growth of Internet use begin with the year 1995. For example, the Pew Research Center claims that in 1995 14% of American adults had used the Internet. According to the report, by 2014 that had increased to 87%. Worldwide, there are estimates that 0.4% of the population had used the Internet in 1995 compared with 42.4% in 2015. The early Internet was generally

Spartan and very limited in functionality. We have, of course, observed a dramatic evolution of the Internet over this time, including the widespread use of audio, video and other media, the advent of interactive Web 2.0, virtual immersive environments, and the emerging Internet of things. These developments are reflected in the chapters of this volume. We should all anticipate future evolution of the Internet to present us with a breadth of new opportunities. Understanding how the field has evolved alongside the Internet over the past 20 years should guide our future expectations and plans.

With the wealth of citations to each of these entries, I have chosen not to provide a summary of each of these articles as would be conventional. This will most certainly be included in future volumes, but for this volume I would encourage readers to seek out the many articles that have cited these influential contributions to develop a better sense of their contribution. These are available through Google Scholar at https://scholar.google.com. Of course, this approach provides readers with a dynamic, up to the minute perspective of current citations. Any brief and static summary would seem insufficient and a disservice.

References

Pew Internet, Science and Tech. Internet use over time. (Data Trend). Pew Research Center Washington, DC: Pew Research Center, 2004. Web. 28 July. http://www.pewinternet.org/data-trend/internet-use/internet-use-over-time

Leiner, B.M., Cerf, V.G., Clark, D.D., Kahn, R.E., Kleinrock, L., Lynch, D.C., Postel, J., Roberts, L.G., & Wolff, S. (2003). *A Brief History of the Internet.* Internet Society. http://www.isoc.org/internet/history/brief.shtml.

2 Comparing Face-to-face and Electronic Discussion in the Second Language Classroom

Mark Warschauer*

Even before the advent of the personal computer, social scientists were making bold claims about the potential effects on society of new forms of computer-mediated communication. As far back as 1978, Hiltz and Turoff (1978) asserted that computerized conferencing would eventually 'have dramatic psychological and sociological impacts on various group communication objects and processes.'

In the 1980s, computer conferencing began to be used in academia and the business world, both in its asynchronous form (largely through e-mall discussion lists) and its synchronous form (through real-time discussion on local area networks). Since then, social scientists have examined the psychological and sociological impacts of these new forms of communication.

One of their main findings was a strong equalizing effect of computer-mediated communication. In other words, whereas face-to-face discussions tend to be relatively unbalanced, with one or two participants dominating the floor or determining the topics, computer-mediated communication features more balanced participation, with speakers sharing the floor more equally. Sproull and Kiesler (1991) reviewed six studies that compared the equality of participation in electronic discussion to face-to-face discussion and all six studies showed that electronic discussion was decidedly more balanced.

* Mark Warschauer is a researcher at the University of Hawai'i National Foreign Language Resource Center, where he investigates the uses of computer-mediate communication for language teaching. His publications include *E-mail for English Teaching: Bringing the Internet and Computer Learning Networks into the Language Classroom* (TESOL Publications 1995) and *Virtual Connections: Online Activities and Projects for Networking Language Learners* (University of Hawai'i Press 1995).

In addition, they found that it is those who are traditionally at the bottom of the totem pole who benefit most from this increased equality. For example, McGuire, Kiesler, and Siegel (1987) found that women made the first proposal as often as men in electronic discussion, compared to only one-fifth as often in face-to-face-discussion. Huff and King (1988) found that topics proposed by lower-status group members were accepted equally in electronic discussion, but were rarely accepted in face-to-face discussion. Sproull and Kielser found that over time peripheral members of organizations benefited more from the use of electronic mail than did core members of organizations.

Electronic Communication for Teaching Composition

In the 1980s, the use of electronic communication started to become popular in the United States in the teaching of composition. This was based on claims that it (1) provided more writing practice (DiMatteo, 1990, 1991); (2) encouraged collaborative writing (Barker & Kemp, 1990); and (3) facilitated peer editing (Bolarsky, 1990; Moran, 1991).

In addition, composition teachers also found computer-mediated communication to have the same kind of equalizing effects mentioned above. Flores (1990) and Selfe (1990) report that computer networking served to equalize wornen's participation in courses they taught. Mabrito (1992) found that students who were more apprehensive about writing tended to benefit most from peer critique conducted electronically. Harman, et al. (1991) found that electronic discussion helped less able students increase their amount of communication both with the teacher and with other students.

Electronic Communication in the Second Language Classroom

In the late 1980s, second and foreign language teachers began to integrate electronic communication into language teaching. For teachers of second language writing, the rationale and motivation were largely the same as for their first language counterparts. For teachers of general second language classes, there were a number of additional motivations, including the desire to provide authentic communication partners (Cohen & Miyake, 1986; Paramskas, 1993), the recognition of the importance of cultural exchange (Soh & Soon, 1991), and the desire to teach new learning skills to language minority students (Cummins & Sayers, 1990).

Second and foreign language teachers have also claimed that electronic communication has proved an equalizer in their classrooms. Tella (1992) found that Finnish girls, who traditionally have less access to and experience with computers than boys, benefited greatly from their full and equal participation in an international English-language e-mail project. Kelm, citing anecdotal evidence from his own teaching, reports that in his Portuguese classes 'computer-assisted classroom discussions are great equalizers' of student participation (1992: 443). Kern (1995) compared electronic and face-to-face discussions of the same length in his university French class and found that all students participated in two 50-minute whole class electronic discussions but four did not participate at all, while five tended to dominate, in two 50-minute face-to-face discussions. Sullivan and Pratt (in press) conducted a similar study and found that 50% of the students participated in a whole class face-to-face discussion compared to 100% in a whole class electronic discussion.

Thus evidence suggests that electronic communication can bring about more equal participation among second and foreign language students. However, all of the previously reported studies compared whole class discussion, where it is especially likely that shy students would be afraid to participate. No studies yet have attempted to compare systematically student participation in face-to-face and electronic discussions which take place in small groups, where the patterns of interaction might be different.

Language Complexity

A number of researchers have suggested that electronic communication differs linguistically from both traditional written and spoken discourse (Chun, 1994; Ferrara, Brunner, & Whittemore, 1991; Kern, 1995; Murray, 1988; Wang, 1993), and that these differences can be exploited for pedagogical advantage. Chun (1994), for example, contends that electronic discussion is similar to written texts in terms of language complexity, yet resembles face-to-face discussion in terms of functions performed, and thus can serve as an important bridge for transfer of communication skills from the written to spoken domain. Kern (1995) found that students' language electronic discussions in French was more morphosyntactically complex than their face-to-face language. No such study has yet been done with ESL students though.

Research Questions

This study used a controlled experiment to address the following questions regarding student participation and language complexity in face-to-face and electronic discussions:

1. Do second-language students participate more equally in small group discussions held electronically than in those held in a traditional face-to-face manner?
2. If so, who benefits from this more equal participation? In particular, how are differences in participation from a face-to-face mode to an electronic mode related to factors such as gender, nationality, age, and language proficiency?
3. What are students' attitudes toward participating in electronic and face-to-face discussion and how do these attitudes correlate with changes in amount of participation?
4. Does electronic discussion include language which is lexically or syntactically more complex than face-to-face discussion?
5. What other differences are noted in the language use and interaction style in the two modes?

Method

Subjects

The subjects in the study were 16 students out of 20 enrolled in an advanced ESL composition class at a community college in Hawaii. (The other four students were not included because they were absent on the day of the study). The students enrolled in this advanced class on the basis of one of three criteria: (1) an 11.5–12.9 score on the college's general English placement test (indicating 11–12th grade level) with a passing grade on the college's writing sample test, (2) a score of 13.0 (indicating college level reading ability in English) on the Nelson Denney reading test, or (3) a grade of 'C' or better for English 22, a beginning-level writing course.

The students included five Filipinos, five Japanese, four Chinese and two Vietnamese. Two of the students were male and 14 female. The students ranged from 19 to 44 years of age. All had participated in a computer-lab writing class from one-half to one-and-a-half semesters, so they had experience using the **InterChange** computer program described below. In addition, beginning typing skills were a requirement to enter this section of the course.

Materials

Two audio tape-recorders were used to record face-to-face discussions. Electronic discussions were carried out on IBM personal computers which were situated around the classroom and were facing the walls.

Software used for the electronic discussions was **Daedalus InterChange**, a real-time communication component of the **Daedalus Integrated Writing Environment**. Using **InterChange**, students type their messages on the bottom half of a split screen. When they hit 'enter', messages are instantaneously posted (with the name of the writer) on the top half of their own screen and that of everyone else. Messages on the top half are continually posted in chronological order. Users can scroll back and forth to reread previous messages if they wish.

Proficiency levels were assessed using results of the listening comprehension and reading comprehension tests of the Secondary Level English Proficiency Test (SLEP), produced by the Educational Testing Service. As a paper-and-pencil context-reduced test, the SLEP most likely measures the students' academic language skills in English. The SLEP was administered to all the students by the college approximately two weeks before this research study. Unfortunately, it was not possible to take additional time from the students to administer a more communicatively-oriented test of their listening or speaking ability.

Information about personal background and attitudes was gathered by a non-anonymous survey. Although the lack of anonymity might have affected students' willingness to answer honestly, this was a necessary decision in order to allow correlations to be calculated between their answers on the survey and their amount of participation.

The survey included six personal information questions (gender, age, native language, birthplace, length of residence in the US, and number of years studying English) and 19 additional questions answered on a five-point Likert scale. These 19 questions queried students' self-assessment of various abilities – conversing fluently, typing, and using computers – and students' attitudes toward electronic and face-to-face discussion.

Procedures

The study was conducted during a normal 75-minute class-period class period. The 16 students present were randomly assigned to four groups of four students each. Two groups were brought together around separated tables for a face-to-face discussion. Two groups were seated around the room at personal computers for electronic discussion. Using a counterbalanced repeated measures procedure, the groups later changed mode of discussion.

Each group was instructed to discuss two (counterbalanced) questions, one face-to-face and one electronically. The questions, chosen in consultation with the teacher to correspond with the students' current course theme of 'the family', were the following:

1. Who should decide basic things about teenagers' lives-what they major in, how they spend their money, who they go out with-the teenagers themselves or their parents?
2. If a husband and wife each work full-time (40 hours a week), how much and what type of housework should the husband do?

Students were given 15 minutes for each discussion. An outside observer with a tape-recorder sat in on each face-to-face discussion and made notes as to who said what. It should be mentioned that the students were not accustomed to being recorded, so this may have affected their participation; for example, shy students may have been ever more afraid to talk than they normally would be. The classroom teacher sat at her own computer and monitored the electronic discussions, as she usually did. One week later, the classroom teacher administered the surveys to the students during a normal class period.

Analyses

The face-to-face discussions were transcribed and all the transcripts (both face-to-face and electronic) were entered into the Computerized Language Analysis program (CLAN) of the Child Language Data Exchange System (CHILDES), which was used to count the number of words per speaker and to calculate the type-token ratio (see below). The transcripts were then analyzed to calculate the total number of clause coordinations and clause subordinations they contained.

Group comparison

The number of words per speaker was used to calculate the participation percentage per speaker. This was then used to compute the Gini coefficient of participation inequality for each group. The Gini coefficient sums, over all the group members, the deviations of each from equal participation, normalized by the maximum possible value of this deviation (Alker 1965; Welsband, Schneider, and Connolly, in press). The coefficient thus takes values between 0 and 1, where 0 means perfect equality. For a set of observed participation rates, $X_1 X_2 X_3$ and X_4, the Gini coefficient (G) is calculated as:

Increased participation in computer mode (IPC)

All students were assigned an IPC score by subtracting their face-to-face participation percentages from their electronic discussion participation percentages. Students who decreased their participation in computer mode were assigned negative IPC scores. Correlations between students' age, time in the US, SLEP scores and IPC scores were analyzed.

While it was the original intention to examine gender as well, on this particular day several male students were absent and there were only two male students present out of a total of 16 students. Due to the small number of male students and the great imbalance between male and female students, it was decided that it would not be meaningful to include gender as a variable for analysis.

Student attitudes

Mean scores and distributions of survey answers were reviewed to determine which questions students had strong opinions on. In addition, correlations between students' attitudes (as expressed by survey answers) and IPC scores were calculated.

Language complexity

Two analyses were made to compare the complexity of the students' output in the two modes (face-to-face and electronic):

1. Type-Token Ratio (TTF,), as defined by the total number of different words divided by the total number of words. For example, the sentence, 'The boy likes the girl' would have a TTR of 0.8, because there are four different words divided by five total words. A higher TTR is generally considered to indicate greater complexity. –

$$G = \frac{2}{3} \sum_{i=1}^{N} I X_i - \frac{1}{4} I$$

Since TTR varies according to length of passage, excerpts totalling the same amount of total words were taken from the face-to-face and electronic transcripts for this measure.

2. Coordination Index (CI), as defined by the number of independent clause coordinations divided by the total number of combined clauses (independent coordination plus dependent subordination). CI is considered to be inversely proportional to complexity, since more advanced writers or speakers of a language generally use proportionally more subordination than do beginners.

Due to the small number of students involved in the study, statistical results for group comparisons, IPC, and student attitudes were not checked for significance. Any results from these tests should be seen only as indicating trends rather than statistically significant results. Due to the much greater number of total sentences available for comparison, the statistical results for language complexity were checked for significance (at alpha <0.05).

Qualitative analysis

Finally, the transcripts were examined to look for qualitative differences in the language use and interaction style in the two modes.

Results

Group Comparisons

Table 2.1 shows the individual participation percentages of the four groups in face-to-face and electronic mode, as well as the Gini coefficients of participation inequality.

Groups 2, 3, and 4 all showed greater equality of participation in the electronic discussion. Group 1 showed the opposite. The Gini coefficients indicate that the electronic discussions as a whole were twice as equal as the face-to-face discussions (= 0.20 vs. = 0.41).

Correlations with IPC

Table 2.2 shows how the IPC (increase in participation in computer mode) is correlated with the SLEP listening score, SLEP reading score, time in the US and age. The largest correlation, at 0.62, is between SLEP listening score and IPC, thus accounting for 38.4% (0.62^2) of the variance.

Table 2.3 shows the average participation for each main nationality in the study for both the face-to-face and electronic discussion. The Filipino students, taken as a whole, decreased their participation in electronic discussion, while the Chinese, Japanese, and Vietnamese student groups each, on the average, increased their participation.

Student attitudes

On the whole, the students reported feeling that they could express themselves freely, comfortably, and creatively during electronic discussion, that

Table 2.1. Percentage of Participation for Each Student in Face-to-Face Discussion and Electronic Discussion

	Face-to-Face Discussion			
	Group 1	*Group 2*	*Group 3*	*Group 4*
Student 1	29.0%	49.6%	48.0%	49.7%
Student 2	27.8%	35.0%	46.1%	37.0%
Student 3	25.9%	14.5%	2.8%	12.7
Student 4	17.2%	0.8%	3.1%	0.5
Gini Coefficient	0.10	0.46	0.59	0.49
	Electronic Discussion			
	Group 1	*Group 2*	*Group 3*	*Group 4*
Student 1	14.9	25.5	27.2	28.5
Student 2	12.2	21.8	42.7	28.9
Student 3	45.5	26.7	10.5	31.3
Student 4	25.5	27.7	19.7	11.3
Gini Coefficient	0.30	0.05	0.26	0.18

Table 2.2. Correlations with Increased Participation in Computer Mode (IPC)

SLEP Listening	0.620
SLEP Reading	0.214
SLEP Total	−0.499
Age	−0.042
Time in US	−0.319

Table 2.3. Average Percentage of Participation by Nationality

	Face-to-Face Discussion	Electronic Discussion
Filipinos (n=5)	41.7%	30.6%
Japanese (n=5)	11.0%	17.0%
Chinese (n=4)	19.9%	22.6%
Vietnamese (n=2)	28.4%	30.2%

(Numbers do not add up to 100% since students were not spread out equally in groups)

participating in electronic discussion assisted their thinking ability, and that they did not feel stress during electronic discussion. In fact, in all of these areas, their attitude toward electronic discussion was slightly better on the average than that toward face-to-face communication. In addition, they also found the **InterChange** program easy to use (see Table 2.4).

Table 2.4. Student Attitudes Toward Face-to-Face and Electronic Discussion: Average of Likert-Scale Responses, Maximum=5

	In Face-to-Face Discussion	In Electronic Discussion
I can express myself freely	3.53	3.87
I am comfortable in expressing opinions	3.27	3.93
I can creatively express opinions	3.27	3.60
I feel stress	2.80	1.87
Helps improve my thinking ability	4.00	4.07
The InterChange program is easy to use	n.a.	4.00

A simple regression showed the following three factors correlating significantly with IPC (increased participation in computer mode):

I can converse in English fluently. (negative correlation of 0.714)

I am comfortable in expressing opinions during face-to-face discussions. (negative correlation of 0.681)

I can express myself freely during face-to-face discussions (negative correlation of 0.662).

Finally, a multiple regression showed that responses to five questions regarding attitude could, when analyzed together, predict nearly all the increased participation in computer mode (see Table 2.5).

Table 2.5. Correlation of Student Attitude with Increased Participation in Computer Mode (IPC): Multiple Regression Analysis

Survey Question	Total Correlation	Added Correlation
I can converse in English fluently	−0.714	
I am [not] comfortable expressing opinions in electronic discussion	−0.853	(−)0.139
Participating in electronic discussions [doesn't] improve my thinking ability	−0.897	(−)0.044
I'm comfortable expressing opinions in face-to-face discussion	−0.938	(−)0.041
I can express myself freely in face-to-face discussion	−0.965	(−)0.027

The electronic discussions were compared to the face-to-face discussions on two measures of complexity, one lexical (type-token ratio) and one syntactic (coordination index). On both measures, the electronic discussions involved significantly more complex language than the face-to-face discussions (see Table 2.6). Differences were especially pronounced in the syntactic area, with 47.5% of the combined clauses in the face-to-face mode based on coordination (rather than the more complex subordination), compared to just 18.5% of the combined clauses in the electronic mode.

Table 2.6. Complexity of Language in Face-to-Face and Electronic Discussions

Mode	Type-Token-Ratio	Coordination Index
face-to-face	0.262	0.475
electronic	0.301**	0.185**

** Significant difference at $p<0.001$.

Qualitative Analysis

A qualitative analysis of the data indicated two important differences in language and interaction between the two groups, one related to turn-taking and one related to formality.

Turn-taking

The conversational mode was marked by numerous short turns with many confirmation checks and active responses. The following was a typical face-to-face exchange of Group 1:

S4: What about you?
S2: Me?
S4: Yeah.
S2: I make my own decision.
S4: Oh, you make your own decision.
S3: Are you living by yourself?
S2: I live with my parents, but…
S3: Oh, yeah.
S4: You are independent.
S3: Independent.
S2: I do whatever I want to do.
S1: Oh, yeah?

The electronic exchanges were longer. Sometimes the level of interaction was less direct, with people expressing their own ideas as opposed to directly answering questions. This seemed to be due in part to the fact that more than one person could be writing at the same time. The following is a typical electronic exchange from the same group:

S4:   I think both husband and wife should do housework but the husband should pay all bills too.

S3:   The wife and husband, both work full time so the wife and husband should share the bill evently. However, the husband can does the heavy work since he has the ability of strenght. He could can do the house works instead let the wife does.

S2:   Most of the people believe housechore is the type of female, but nowaday since male and female are equal. If the husband and wife are full time workers they should share the housechorse. If the wife cook then the husband do the dishes. Or perhaps the husband could help the wife the prepared for dinner. In order words, both husband and wife have to shared the housechore. Men will be able to do everything that women do. For example, clean, cook, wash, take care children.

S4:   If a working woman want to shift their housework to his husband, how can be fair between mean and women.

S1:   Based on my experience, the husband do share some of the housework with his wife. Once in a while, he must cook for the entire family and do the clearning of the house. The husband should help in taking care of the children, like taking the child to the doctor when the wife is working. Also, the husband should do once in a while the groceries.

Formality of language

The electronic discussion tended to include more formal expressions, such as, 'in my opinion', 'over all', 'based on my experience', 'such as,' and 'therefore' which were virtually absent from the face-to-face discussion. A relatively formal style is seen in this electronic comment made by a Filipino student:

> For example, some of the teenagers are saving money to buy their necessities such as the things they need including clothings and some money to spend with their friends. (S10, in electronic communication)

In contrast, face-to-face comments used more informal expressions as seen in the following example from the same student:

> Because, like, like, for us, it's like eight of us in a family, you know, so I guess my mum has to take care of all of us. (S10, in oral communication)

A similar contrast is seen in these two comments by a Japanese student, the first taken from her electronic discussion and the second taken from her oral discussion:

> I agree with Keiko. When young people graduated high school, basically they can make their own decisions. However they can ask parents about suggest anytime. (S9, in electronic communication)

I'm, so he's not so good. So I do that for him, I did. And he helped me do like Yumiko said, put the garbage out, that kind of stuff. He did. But like paying bills, like we split everything. (S10, in oral communication)

Discussion

First, the study demonstrated a tendency toward more equal participation in computer mode, with three of the four groups substantially more equal in electronic discussion and the overall participation rate twice as equal in electronic discussion as in face-to-face discussion. It is not clear why the fourth group showed no trend toward greater equalization in computer mode, but it could be related to the fact that the three groups, unlike the fourth, all included students from Japan, and it was the Japanese students who barely participated in face-to-face discussions but participated much more equally in electronic mode (see discussion below).

Second, which factors were correlated with individual increase in participation in computer mode (IPC)? One element that could be viewed as a surprise is that the SLEP listening score was correlated with IPC. One might assume the opposite: that greater listening ability would correlate with increase in participation in face-to-face mode. This suggests that other factors such as shyness, rather than failure to understand the discussions, might be causing some students to limit discussion in face-to-face mode but participate more equally in electronic mode.

Perhaps most interesting are the tendencies toward unequal participation due to nationality, with Filipino students tending to dominate the face-to-face discussions and the other students, especially the Japanese, speaking much less. One possible reason is that English is one of the national languages in the Philippines and thus Filipinos have more opportunities for oral practice than most other immigrants. Their greater experience, compared to the other groups, in conversational English may be one reason they tended to dominate the oral discussions. Students of English in Japan, usually get very little oral communication practice, either in the classroom or in society. It is not surprising that they would communicate less in the face-to-face mode and thus register the biggest increase in computer mode.

The differences between the Filipino students and the Japanese students could also be influenced by cultural factors. Japanese schools socialize students to listen quietly, rather than to speak up, and Japanese students in the United States often continue this same pattern. It is thus possible that Japanese students choose not to participate in face-to-face discussions but will participate more readily in electronic discussions, which don't involve having to speak out in class.

One more detail on this aspect is worth noting. Four of the five Japanese students made an average of only 1.8% of the comments in their face-to-face discussions; in other words, they were virtually silent. The fifth Japanese student made 48% of the comments in her face-to-face discussion. In fact, this single student made five times as many face-to-face comments as all four other Japanese students combined. It turns out that this student is married to an American and thus probably has had considerably more opportunities for oral practice than the other Japanese students, and perhaps had more socialization in American culture as well.

The student surveys lend support for the hypothesis that lack of oral fluency (or confidence in oral fluency) and discomfort in speaking out are important factors in determining students' relative participation in face-to-face and electronic mode. As noted above, there was high negative correlation between the students' answer to 'I can converse in English fluently' with IPC. At the very least one can say that students who think they are not fluent tend to participate more equally in computer mode. Also as noted earlier, this correlation becomes extremely strong when one adds factors such as discomfort in expressing opinions during face-to-face discussions.

Finally, the electronic discussion featured language that was both more formal and more complex than the face-to-face discussion. This is not surprising as this is generally true in the case of written communication. Since this particular study did not include other examples of the students' written texts, a fuller comparison is not possible.

Nevertheless, the results do suggest that electronic discussion can be a good environment for fostering use of more formal and complex language, both lexically and syntactically.

At the same time though, the electronic discussion had fewer of the interactional features – such as questioning, recasting, confirmation checks, and paraphrasing – that are often found in face-to-face interaction and which are viewed as important for language learning (Long, 1996; Long and Porter 1985).

Since electronic and face-to-face discussion differ so substantially, they are probably best used with different purposes in mind. Several features of electronic discussion – the longer turns involved, the more equal opportunity for all students to express their ideas, and the fact that electronically-produced texts can be saved for post-hoc review and analysis – suggest that electronic discussion might be used effectively as a prelude to oral discussion. Students could first generate many ideas and then look them over and discuss or debate them orally. In addition, the formality and complexity of language in electronic discussion suggests that it might be an excellent medium for pre-writing work since it could serve as a bridge from spoken interaction to written composition. In other words, face-to-face and electronic discussions could be combined in different ways to highlight the advantages of each.

Conclusion

The findings of this study suggest that electronic discussion may create opportunities for more equal participation in the classroom. Furthermore, this apparently can be achieved without disadvantaging more verbal students. The five most outspoken students in the face-to-face discussions (four Filipinos and one Japanese married to an American) all continued to participate more than 25% of the time in the four-person electronic discussion groups. Thus, while their percentage of participation dropped, they still participated more than their share and may have even benefited from the more balanced discussion, since they had more opportunities to listen to others. On the other hand, the four quietest members of the class in face-to-face discussion (all Japanese), increased their participation almost tenfold (from only 1.8% of comments to a 17.3% of comments) and thus went from almost total silence to relatively equal participation.

At the same time, the more complex and formal language in the electronic discussions was potentially beneficial to all the students, since it may assist them in acquiring more sophisticated communicative skills.

The following are some recommended research studies which might shed more light on the differences between face-to-face and electronic discussion:

1. Studies in which group composition is controlled by nationality (in this study it was not).
2. Studies in which speaking fluency is assessed as a dependent variable (in this study, only written test scores were available).
3. Studies comparing face-to-face and electronic discussion among the whole class or pairs (as opposed to small groups).
4. Studies which measure how participation in both modes might be affected by type of task, for example by including closed tasks (requiring specific solutions) in addition to the relatively unstructured tasks that were part of this study.
5. Studies which evaluate certain sequences of activities, for example electronic discussion followed by face-to-face discussion as compared to the other way around.

Learning more specifics about how electronic discussion differs from face-to-face discussion can help language teachers make informed decisions about how, when, and to what purposes to use these two modes of communication in the classroom.

Acknowledgments

I am grateful to Michael H. Long and James D. Brown of the Department of English as a Second Language at the University of Hawai'i for encouraging this project in part fulfillment of course requirements. I am also grateful to Richard Schmidt for his comments on an earlier draft of this paper and to two anonymous *CALICO Journal* reviewers for their helpful comments. Any errors or shortcomings are my own.

References

Alker, H. R. (1965). *Mathematics and Politics*. New York: Macmillan.
Barker, T., & F. Kemp (1990). Network theory: A postmodern pedagogy for the written classroom. In C. Handa (Ed.), *Computers and community: Teaching composition in the twenty-first century*. Portsmouth, NH: Heinemann.
Boiarsky, C. (1990). Computers in the classroom: The instruction, the mess, the noise, the writing.' In C. Handa (Ed.), *Computers and community: Teaching composition in the twenty-first century*. Portsmouth, NH: Heinemann.
Chun, D. (1994). Using computer networking to facilitate the acquisition of interactive competence.' *System 22*(1), 17–31.
Cohen, M., & N. Miyake (1986). A worldwide intercultural network: Exploring electronic messaging for instruction.' *Instruction Science 15*, 257–273.

Cummins, S., & D. Sayers (1990). Education 2001: Learning networks and educational reform. *Computers in the Schools* 7(1/2), 1–29.

DiMatteo, A. (1990). Under erasure: A theory for interactive writing in real time. *Computers and Composition 7* (S.I.), 71–84.

DiMatteo, A. (1991). Communication, writing, learning: An anti-instrumentalist view of network writing. *Computers and Composition 8*(3), 5–19.

Ferrara, K., H. Brunner, & G. Whittemore (1991). Interactive written discourse as an emergent register. *Written Communication 8*(1), 9–33.

Flores, M. (1990). Computer conferencing: Composing a feminist community of writers.' In C. Handa (Ed.), *Computers and community: Teaching composition in the twenty-first century* (pp. 107–139). Portsmouth, NH: Heinemann.

Hartman, K., C. Neuwirth, S. Kiesler, L. Sproull, C. Cochran, M. Palmquist, & D. Zubrow (1991). Patterns of social interaction and learning to write: Some effects of networked technologies. *Written Communication 8*(1), 79–113.

Hiltz, S. R., & M. Turoff (1978). *The network nation.* Cambridge, MA: MIT Press.

Huff, C., & R. King (1988). An experiment in electronic collaboration.' In J. D. Goodchilds (Ed.), *Interacting by computer: Effects on small group style and structure.* Symposium conducted at the meeting of the American Psychological Association, Atlanta.

Kelm, O. (1992). The use of synchronous computer networks in second language instruction: A preliminary report.' *Foreign Language Annals 25*(5), 441–454.

Kern, R. (1995). Restructuring classroom interaction with networked computers: Effects on quantity and quality of language production. *Modern Language Journal 79*(4), 457–476.

Long, M. H. (1996). The role of the linguistic environment in second language acquisition. In W. C. Ritchie and T. K. Bhatia (Eds.), *Handbook of research on language acquisition. Volume 2: Second language acquisition.* New York: Academic Press.

Long, M. H., & P. A. Porter (1985). Group work, interlanguage talk, and second language acquisition. *TESOL Quarterly 19*(2), 207–227.

Mabrito, M. (1991). Electronic mail as a vehicle for peer response: conversations of high- and low-apprehensive writers. *Written Communication 8*(4), 509–532.

Mabrito, M. (1992). Computer-mediated communication and high-apprehensive writers: Rethinking the collaborative process.' *The Bulletin,* December, 26–30.

McGuire, T., S. Kiesler, & J. Siegel (1987). Group and computer-mediated discussion effects in risk decision making. *Journal of Personality and Social Psychology 52*(5), 917–930.

Moran, C. (1991). We write, but do we read? *Computers and Composition 8*(3), 51–61.

Murray, D. (1988). Computer-mediated communication: Implications for ESP. *English for Specific Purposes 7*, 3–18.

Paramskas, D. (1993). Computer-Assisted Language Learning (CALL): Increasingly into an ever more electronic world. *The Canadian Modern Language Review 50*(1), 124–143.

Selfe, C. (1990). Technology in the English classroom: Computers through the lens of feminist theory.' In C. Handa (Ed.), *Computers and community: Teaching composition in the twenty-first century.* Portsmouth, NH: Heinemann.

Soh, B. L., & Y. P. Soon (1991). English by E-mail: Creating a global classroom via the medium of computer technology. *ELT Journal 45*(4), 287–292.

Sproull, L., & S. Kiesler (1991). *Connections: New ways of working in the networked organization.* Cambridge, MA: MIT Press.

Sullivan, N., & E. Pratt (1996). A comparative study of two ESL writing environments: A computer-assisted classroom and a traditional oral classroom. *System 24*(4), 491–501.

Tella, S. (1992). *Boys, girls, and E-mail: A case study in Finnish senior secondary schools.* Helsinki: University of Helsinki, Department of Teacher Education.

Wang, Y. M. (1993). *E-mail dialogue journaling in an ESL reading and writing classroom.* Unpublished Ph.D. dissertation, University of Oregon at Eugene.

Weisband, S., S. Schneider, & T. Connolly (1995). Electronic communication and social information: Status salience and status differences. *Academy of Management Journal, 38,* 1124–1151.

3 Developing L2 Oral Proficiency through Synchronous CMC: Output, Working Memory, and Interlanguage Development

J. Scott Payne* and Paul J. Whitney**

Introduction

On the applied side of second language acquisition (SLA) theory much of the debate over what promotes competence has focused on the role of input in language learning. It has even been argued that input is the greatest sole determiner of language acquisition (Krashen, 1985). However, there is evidence that input alone is not sufficient to obtain high levels of proficiency in a second language. Language immersion programs in Canada provide students with an input-rich learning environment, but equivalent opportunities to produce the target language are often lacking. Research on these immersion programs depicts the learners as highly developed in their receptive language skills while exhibiting weaknesses in grammatical accuracy (Harley, 1993).

* J. Scott Payne received his Ph.D. from the Individual Interdisciplinary Doctoral Program at Washington State University in 2000. His research interests include psycholinguistics and the impact of individual differences in working memory capacity on learner behavior in computer-mediated learning environments. He is currently collaborating with faculty, conducting research and developing software under the auspices of Project 2001, an initiative funded by the Andrew W. Mellon Foundation to encourage the integration of technology into foreign language instruction in 62 liberal arts colleges.
** Paul Whitney is Professor and Chair of Psychology at Washington State University. He received his Ph.D. in cognitive psychology from the University of Kansas in 1984. His research interests are in psycholinguistics, particularly in individual differences in language and memory processes. Professor Whitney has published over 30 articles dealing with the role of knowledge and ability factors in determining language processing strategies.

Consistent with the hypothesis that output is important for developing competence, Swain (1985, 1993) and Swain and Lapkin (1995) argued that L2 output may trigger certain cognitive processes necessary for second language learning. Swain's proposal of the Output Hypothesis places an emphasis on language learners 'noticing' the gaps in their linguistic knowledge as a result of external feedback (e.g., clarification requests, modeling, and overt correction) or internal feedback (monitoring) of language they have produced. By becoming consciously aware of one's own language production, output can serve the metalinguistic function of helping to internalize linguistic forms, test hypotheses about the language, and increase control over previously internalized forms.

The Output Hypothesis has sparked numerous studies addressing its components. In the interactionist literature, research has found that learners test hypotheses about the target language and modify their output in response to clarification or confirmation requests by their interlocutors (Pica, Holliday, Lewis, & Morgenthaler, 1989). In studying native speaker-nonnative speaker interaction, Linnell (1995) found that clarification requests resulted in more syntax modification on the part of nonnative speakers than modeling correct responses and that those modified (improved) syntactical structures were maintained over time. Findings from research of the construct of 'noticing' suggest that second language learners do notice gaps in their Interlanguage knowledge (Swain & Lapkin, 1995). Further research has investigated whether learner awareness of problems in output can prompt the solicitation of additional input (Izumi, Bigelow, Fujiwara, & Fearnow, 1999).

Unfortunately, process models that could suggest causal mechanisms have not guided research on the role of output in acquisition. Employing process-based working models has the distinct advantage of allowing researchers to make specific predictions about the performance of second language speakers under specific task requirements. In the L1 literature, Levelt's model of language production (1989, 1993, 1995) has received the most empirical attention and is the most widely adapted model for depicting L2 or bilingual language production processes (De Bot, 1992; De Bot & Schreuder, 1993; Poulisse & Bongaerts, 1994). In 1992, de Bot employed Levelt's model together with Anderson's (1982) notions of declarative and procedural knowledge as a means of analyzing the notions of the Output Hypothesis from a psycholinguistic perspective. De Bot limited his discussion to lexical access and how it relates to the shift from controlled (declarative knowledge) to automatic processing (procedural knowledge) – a process referred to as restructuring. The crux of de Bot's argument was that output plays a crucial role in the restructuring of linguistic forms into procedural forms allowing for automatic and efficient performance. However, according to de Bot, output does not play a role in the acquisition of declarative knowledge itself.

The purpose of the present paper, like de Bot's work, is to use Levelt's model as a basis for proposing mechanisms that influence L2 acquisition. However, the authors will attempt to show that Levelt's model (1989, 1995) augmented with other concepts from cognitive psychology, particularly Working Memory theory, can serve as a basis for understanding second language processes beyond those considered by de Bot. Though Levelt's model alone may prove useful for depicting second language production processes, it does not have a way of accounting for individual differences in processing capacity and how they may relate to performance on L2 production tasks.

Levelt (1989) acknowledges the importance of the short-term storage of information in language production, but this aspect of his model has not been fully developed. Working Memory theory provides researchers with models and measurement techniques for determining an individual's capacity for temporarily maintaining verbal and visual-spatial information in memory and for performing judgment or executive functions based on changing conditions in one's immediate environment. First language research suggests that individual differences in Working Memory capacity are closely related to (a) verbal fluency (Daneman, 1991), (b) the ability of individuals to utilize contextual clues in text for learning novel words (Daneman & Green, 1986), and (c) maintaining a representation of language strings for 'offline' processing when language becomes too complex for 'online' processing (Gathercole & Baddeley, 1993). Findings from second language studies indicate that verbal Working Memory capacity serves as an effective predictor of L2 vocabulary development (Gathercole & Baddeley, 1989a; Papagno, Valentine, & Baddeley, 1991), second language proficiency (Service, 1992; Service & Kohonen, 1995), and it appears to play an even more crucial role in L2 than L1 acquisition (Miyake & Friedman, 1998; Geva & Ryan, 1993).

Conversational exchange in a second language requires interlocutors to perform a complex set of cognitive tasks as they attempt to comprehend language input, relate it to what they know about the target language and the world, and then make decisions about whether the new information should be incorporated into their existing knowledge base in some manner. The two Working Memory concepts that appear to relate most directly to this task are executive capacity (as measured by reading span) and verbal span (as measured by nonword repetition). Executive function, or what Baddeley (1986) refers to as the Central Executive, should play a critical role in second language production and comprehension, especially in conversational exchange. Second language learners are constantly comparing what they hear and read to what they know to be true about the target language, based on their current stage of Interlanguage development. The ability to maintain a representation of target language input in memory, retrieve L2 syntactic and semantic information from long-term memory, make judgments and store the intermediate results of these calculations are all tasks of the Central Executive. Measuring an individual's capacity for executive function may provide insight into the acquisition of second language speaking skills.

The Working Memory construct that is most intuitively associated with speaking a second language is verbal span or the ability to temporarily maintain phonological information in memory. Verb Working Memory has been the focus of most empirical studies of Working Memory and second or foreign language acquisition. Exploring the relationship between these two Working Memory constructs and second language oral proficiency development may shed light on the impact of memory limitations on such complex tasks as conversing in a foreign language.

The goal of this article is to augment Levelt's model of language production with Working Memory theory and to use this framework for testing the hypothesis that synchronous computer-mediated communication (CMC) or chatting in a second language can indirectly improve oral proficiency by developing the same cognitive mechanisms underlying spontaneous conversational speech. Within the context of this research question, what is currently known about Working Memory and the role that it plays in learning will make it possible to make predictions about whose L2 development will benefit the most from the chatroom environment and why. Before reporting on this study and its results, an explanation of how Levelt's model and Working Memory theory will support these research goals is in order.

Levelt's Language Production Model

According to Levelt's model (1989, 1995), utterances begin as nonlanguage specific communicative intentions in what Levelt refers to as the Conceptualizer (see Figure 3.1). During production the job of the Conceptualizer is to determine the semantic content of the utterance to be spoken. The preverbal message generated by the Conceptualizer is maintained in Working Memory and fed into the Formulator where the lemmas or lexical items are selected that most accurately represent the semantic content of each chunk of the preverbal message. Lemmas also contain the information necessary for formulating syntax and are used to generate the surface structure of an utterance through a process called Grammatical Encoding. The second task of the formulator is to select phonological representations or lexemes for the selected lemmas. What emerges from the Formulator is the articulatory plan of an utterance. However, prior to entering the Articulator, where the vocal musculature is engaged for producing an utterance, the articulatory plan may be monitored internally with the support of subvocalization. During this internal feedback loop, the articulatory plan is stored in the Articulatory Buffer (Working Memory).

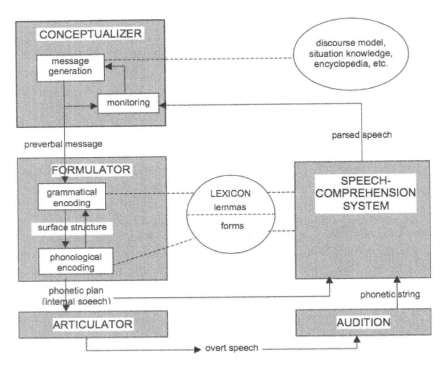

Figure 3.1. Blueprint for the Speaker

Note: Boxes represent processing components; the circle and ellipse represent knowledge stores (Levelt, 1989).

The stages of Levelt's model operate in a modular and incremental fashion. That is, once the preverbal message has entered the Formulator and the lexical access process has begun, it is not possible for the Formulator to check back with the Conceptualizer to verify the intended meaning of the message. Nor is it possible for the Articulator to be alerted about processes that are currently underway in the Formulator. When a lemma and its lexeme have been selected, that information leaves the Formulator where the first opportunity to screen output via internal monitoring is possible. The autonomy of operation (modularity) and consecutive progression is what makes parallel processing within Levelt's model possible. In other words, while one word is being uttered, the lemma and lexeme for another word are being selected, and, in the Conceptualizer, the speaker is still deciding what words will follow. In fact, as speakers, we often begin uttering a sentence even before we have determined how we are going to end it. This is what is meant by *incremental* in the model.

Three adaptations of Levelt's model to illustrate bilingual language production processes have been proposed. De Bot (1992) augmented the model with language-specific Formulators in an attempt to explain fluent code-switching behaviors. A year later, de Bot and Schreuder (1993) introduced an additional component called the Verbalizer, located between the Conceptualizer and the Formulator, which has the function of organizing information in the preverbal message into lexicalizable chunks. In a third effort, Poulisse and Bongaerts (1994) employed spreading activation theory to explain how preverbal concepts can be tagged for language. It was argued that spreading activation theory obviated the need for adding a component to the model and addressed weaknesses in de Bot's (1992) multiple Formulator approach. These modifications have been proposed to account for code-switching among bilinguals. However, as de Bot (1992) suggested, a bilingual production model must also account for cross-linguistic influences, equivalent language processing speed between mono- and multilinguals, unbalanced bilingualism, and the potential to master an unlimited number of languages. These three adaptations of Levelt's model and the additional bilingual phenomena mentioned by de Bot (1992) point to important questions for bilingual language processing research. Unfortunately, these proposals and suggestions fail to address the need to understand how individual differences in Working Memory capacity may boost or constrain the language processing capabilities of second language learners.

Working Memory and Levelt's Model

As Levelt's model suggests, lexical access and articulation in the L1 are automatic. Controlled processing in the model is limited to the Conceptualizer where communicative intentions are generated, and where internal speech is monitored (Levelt, 1989). Second language production, on the other hand, is quite different. Controlled processing appears to play a central role in lexical access and articulation in a second language, at least until a high level of proficiency has been achieved. L2 speech tends to be more hesitant with longer and more frequent pauses, consist of shorter utterances, and contain many more slips of the tongue than L1 speech (Poulisse, 1997; Weise, 1984; Möhle, 1984; Lennon, 1990). As second language speakers become more fluent, speech rate and length of run increase, and the number of filled and unfilled pauses decrease (Lennon, 1990). The assumption is that fluency is a direct function of automatic language processing ability. Since controlled processing implicates Working Memory, limitations in Working Memory capacity should have an impact on L2 performance and consequently acquisition. Not surprisingly, then, many of the same dependent measures used as indices of competence in L2 speech research (e.g. articulation rate, pause length, length of run, and slips of the tongue) have been employed when researchers have tested the role of Working Memory in first language development. Most of these studies have investigated the role of phonological Working Memory capacity in the spoken language and vocabulary development of young children (Adams & Gathercole, 1995, 1996; Gathercole & Baddeley, 1989b). Only a few of these studies have examined second language development in children (Speidel, 1989, 1993; Service, 1992; Service & Kohonen, 1995). Findings from this line of research show that the articulation rate among children between the ages of 4 and 7 is directly related to their phonological Working Memory capacity. In other words, the larger the capacity for temporary storage and maintenance of sound information in memory, the faster a child at an intermediate stage in language development is able to talk. Pauses during speech have also been linked to lexical access in research with adults. These hesitations most often occur before content words and signal the speaker's need to access items from the mental lexicon with the time required to complete the search as a function of the difficulty of the content word and Working Memory capacity (Daneman & Green, 1986).

In a series of studies, the Kassel Group (Dechert, 1980, 1983; Dechert, Möhle, & Raupach, 1984; Dechert & Raupach, 1980a, 1980b, 1987; Raupach, 1980, 1984; Rehbein, 1987) examined pauses in L1 and L2 speech samples of German, French, and English. The major difference between fluent and nonfluent L2 learners of these languages is the type or level of processing that occurs during periods of hesitation. For less fluent learners, the focus is on lower levels of planning, whereas pauses in speech among fluent speakers represent integration and macroplanning processes, much like the pausal behavior of native speakers (Schmidt, 1992). These findings suggest that the demands placed on Working Memory by less fluent L2 speakers may differ qualitatively and most likely quantitatively from more fluent L2 speakers. Less fluent speakers of a second language may expend a great deal of their attentional resources on retrieving appropriate words from their mental lexicon, determining the correct surface structure or syntax, and selecting the corresponding lexemes or phonological units for the words in the utterance. If these processes are not automatic, a burden is placed on the Phonological Loop (Baddeley, 1986) to maintain the intermediate products of calculations as the speaker cycles through Levelt's model, generating communicative intentions in the Conceptualizer, mapping lexical items and their syntactical and phonological components from the preverbal message, monitoring the utterance internally, and making any needed adjustments. While the Phonological Loop is storing and maintaining the utterance under construction, attentional resources allocated by the Central Executive (Baddeley, 1986) are required to make judgments about the correctness of the lemmas selected, the syntax and sound structure of the utterance, what information needs to be retrieved from long-term memory, and what new updated information needs to be put back into the Phonological Loop for storage. For more fluent speakers, many of these processes occur without much conscious attention, leaving attentional resources for contemplating subtleties of expression.

Language Production, Working Memory and Synchronous CMC

Only a handful of studies have systematically examined the impact of chatroom environments on L2 performance (Warschauer, 1996; Kern, 1995; Chun, 1994).

We would expect that chatrooms could provide a useful environment for improving some L2 processes. A few studies have looked at how interlocutors resolve breakdowns in communication through negotiation of meaning, suggesting that synchronous online environments can play a role in Interlanguage development (Linnell, 1995; Pellettieri, 2000; Blake, 2000). In general, studies of L2 chatroom use have found that the dynamics of conversational interaction are altered in an online conferencing environment. Results from these studies have indicated that (a) students tend to produce more complex language in chatrooms than in face-to-face conversational settings (Warschauer, 1996; Kern, 1995), (b) participation increases online with 'quieter' students participating as much or even more than those individuals who normally dominate classroom discussion (Warschauer, 1996; Kern, 1995; Chun, 1994), and (c) attitudes towards the target language were reported to improve (Healy-Beauvois, 1992; Warschauer, 1996; Kern, 1995; Chun, 1994).

Given the theoretical discussion of L2 processes covered above, one effect of chatroom practice may be to automate some language production processes and thereby ease the burden on Working Memory. To date, the impact of individual differences in Working Memory in a synchronous CMC environment has not been explored. Working Memory may prove to be a useful construct for predicting what types of learners will benefit the most from synchronous CMC. Two characteristics of L2 chatroom interaction may have implications for Working Memory. First, the rate of conversational exchange in a chatroom is slower than face-to-face; people simply cannot type as fast as they can speak. Thus, the processing demand is reduced, or, more precisely, the amount of language that an individual has to parse, comprehend, and respond to is lower for a given time period. Second, chatroom exchanges do not have the same ephemeral quality as spoken utterances. When chatting, participants can refresh memory traces by re-reading comments, which is not the case in aural conversation, face-to-face or otherwise. This characteristic would suggest that learners with lower Working Memory capacities would benefit from a conversational environment where processing demands are reduced, but where the tasks and interactions are the same. Thus, another goal of the present study is to determine whether individual differences in Working Memory capacity can effectively predict the rate of L2 oral proficiency development for different types of learners in a chatroom setting.

Research Questions

Based on Levelt's model of language production, synchronous online conferencing in a second language should develop the same cognitive mechanisms that are needed to produce the target language in face-to-face L2 conversation. In fact, the only difference, from an information processing perspective, should be engaging the musculature to produce overt speech. Furthermore, by augmenting Levelt's model with concepts and measurement techniques from Working Memory theory, two major benefits accrue. First, we can gain insight into how individual differences in processing capacity may affect oral proficiency development. Second, if we can predict which learners may benefit from what types of instructional treatments, we can use this information to provide guidance to curriculum developers. With these potential benefits in mind, the present study addresses the following research questions:

1. Can L2 oral proficiency be indirectly developed through chatroom interaction in the target language?
2. Can individual differences in Working Memory capacity effectively predict the rate of L2 oral proficiency development for different types of learners in a chatroom setting?

We predicted that the oral proficiency development of participants in the experimental group would be at least equivalent to that of the control group, and possibly even greater, since the chatroom environment should reduce the burden on Working Memory, thus facilitating the development of low Working Memory span participants.

Methodology

Experimental Design

The study employed a pretest, posttest quasi-experimental design with two sample groups receiving the treatment and two sample groups receiving the face-to-face instruction typical for the language program. The experimental groups participated in two face-to-face and two online class periods per week. A few chatroom days were cancelled during exam periods and to dedicate some extra computer lab time for familiarizing students with an online collaborative research and writing tool used as part of the course. The experimental sections met for a total of 21 times in the chatroom during the 15-week semester. All four days of instruction were face-to-face for the control groups. The instructional content was the same for both the experimental and the control groups, thus the same activities or discussions were held online in the chatroom and in the face-to-face classroom. Levels of the treatment could not be randomly assigned to groups due to scheduling issues for the instructors teaching the four courses. The study lasted 15 weeks (one semester). During the second week of the semester, the computerized versions of the reading span measure, nonword repetition task, and the Shipley verbal intelligence measure were administered in a computer laboratory. During the third week and the beginning of the fourth week of the study, the speaking pretest was administered; during the last week of the study, the posttest was administered. These measures are described below.

Participants

Participants were 58 volunteers from four sections of third semester Spanish courses. Intact groups were used and the treatment was assigned to the groups in a manner that could accommodate the schedules of the participating instructors. (Since computer access for the instructors was located in one specific building it was necessary to avoid forcing them to run back and forth across campus.) However, each instructor taught one experimental and one control group, so the treatment was not confounded by the instructor variable. Participants in all conditions received extra credit totaling a maximum of one third of a letter grade for participating in the study.

Materials

Currently, the most widely recognized instrument for measuring oral proficiency is the oral proficiency interview (OPI) based on the ACTFL Oral Proficiency Guidelines. This scale ranges from 0–5 with 0 representing no proficiency and 5 representing the oral proficiency of an educated native speaker. This scale was not appropriate for use in this study for two reasons: (a) the OPI is not sensitive enough to measure changes in oral proficiency that may occur in a single semester in a course meeting only four hours per week and (b) a significant proportion of the OPI score consists of competencies that are not addressed by this study's research questions (i.e., sociolinguistic competence). It is important to note that the term oral proficiency in this article is a more simplified construct than that used by ACTFL. Oral proficiency in this context refers to an individual's ability to produce language that is comprehensible with syntax and vocabulary appropriate to the task, is grammatically accurate, and is pronounced in a manner that approximates the speech of a native speaker. Therefore, an oral proficiency instrument was developed for this study (see the Oral Production Interview Scale in Appendix A). For the speaking test, participants selected one of four envelopes containing a speaking task written in English (see speaking tasks in Appendix B). The description of the speaking tasks was written in English to ensure that performance on the task was not confounded by reading ability in Spanish. Participants were required to read the instructions and then speak in Spanish for approximately five minutes. If participants ran out of things to say on a particular topic, they selected a new task and began again. The objective was to obtain a five-minute speech sample. The role of the examiner was to listen to, but not interview, the speaker. Two examiners (one native speaker and one nonnative speaker, both female) administered the speaking tests. The examiners were told to think of someone they know who is a very fluent nonnative speaker of Spanish and consider that individual's language ability as a perfect score (the 50 point maximum). This expectation differs from that used in the ACTFL scale, which uses the language skills of an educated native speaker as the highest rating. Clearly, the very high criterion used on the ACTFL scale was inappropriate for a study examining changes in proficiency over the course of a single semester. The examiners received instruction on how to use the scale and compared evaluations for the first two speaking tests on each test day to maintain interrater reliability. For the oral proficiency pretest, interrater reliability on the

50-point scale was 0.86; on the posttest, interrater reliability was 0.94. The examiners were paid $100 each for their efforts.

Working Memory measures consisted of a recognition-based non-word repetition task and a reading span measure. The nonword repetition task measures an individual's capacity to maintain phonological information in Working Memory and is the most widely used test for measuring verbal Working Memory capacity. Several variations of the nonword repetition task have been reported in the literature. In the nonword repetition task developed for this study, participants listened to an audio file of eight pseudowords read with a one-second interval between words. After listening to the audio file, participants clicked on a button to see a screen containing 16 pseudowords, eight of which were articulated in the audio file. Students selected the eight words they believed they heard by clicking on the checkbox next to each word. The participants could take as much time as they needed to make their eight selections. After clicking the submit button, the next audio clip would load, ready to be played. The complete nonword repetition task consisted of three sets of eight pseudowords.

The reading span test used in this study is an adaptation of Daneman and Carpenter's (1980) measure used in numerous studies of Working Memory (see Whitney & Budd, 1999). Reading span assesses two key functions of executive Working Memory: the ability (a) to make judgments and (b) to temporarily store the results of calculations. The reading span test is also considered a good measure of Central Executive capacity (Engel, Kane, & Tuholski, 1999). This version of the reading span presents participants with 15 sets of sentences, the first three sets containing only two sentences each and the final three sets consisting of six sentences. Each sentence in the set is visible for seven seconds. While viewing the sentence, participants are required to make a response indicating whether the sentence makes sense or not and to remember the last word of the sentence. After participants have seen all sentences in the set, they must remember all the sentence-final words. With only two sentences in a set, combining the judgment and memory tasks is relatively easy. However, as set size increases, more memory resources must be allocated to maintaining the final words of each previous sentence in the set, making the task of judging the sensibility of the current sentence while maintaining the last words from the previous sentences much more difficult.

The computer-based delivery of the reading span measure displayed one sentence after another in seven-second intervals until all of the sentences in a set had been viewed. While reading the sentences, subjects selected the radio button corresponding to their estimate of the sentence's sensibility.

After all sentences in the set had been seen, participants clicked on a button to see a screen of words with checkboxes next to the words. For each word to be remembered, there were two distractors (i.e., for sets containing five sentences there was a total of 15 words). Distractors were of two types: (a) the same semantic category (e.g., if the target word was 'girl,' the distractor could be 'woman') or (b) the last words from sentences in previous sets. Subjects selected the words they identified as being final words by clicking the checkbox next to the word. All Working Memory tests were recognition and web-based with a database backend, enabling automatic scoring and calculation of results.

Data were collected on student grades at the conclusion of the third semester Spanish course, overall GPAs, and verbal intelligence scores as measured by the Shipley test. These academic and verbal IQ data were used to account for extraneous factors that could confound the interpretation of results.

Treatment

One of the challenges of conducting research in a natural setting with intact groups is the issue of unequal treatment or of a 'teacher effect.' To ensure that the treatment administered to participants in the experimental and control conditions were equivalent, the curriculum and lesson plans for all four groups were the same. Thus, the students in the experimental groups meeting online in the chatroom engaged in the same activities on the same days as those in the control groups did face to face. The chatroom tool designed for this project enabled the instructors to read and participate in up to four chatrooms simultaneously. During the pilot phase of the project, it was determined that chatroom discussion groups of four to six students were the best. With larger groups, active participation causes the chat window to scroll too fast for students to be able to follow and process the conversation. Foreign language classes at the institution where the study was conducted typically range from 18 to 22 students, so using four chatroom groups per class was optimal. The same activities and group configurations were also used in the face-to-face sessions. In fact, the instructors actually printed out the task description from the chatroom interface for use in their face-to-face groups. Tasks assigned on the days when the experimental groups were online consisted of role plays, discussions of cultural texts or video, and other communicative activities. The first two chatroom sessions were held in the foreign language computer lab giving students the opportunity to familiarize themselves with the chatroom tool and ask any questions that they might have. After these initial training sessions, most participants did not come to the foreign language computer lab but, rather, accessed the chatroom from their home computers or machines in other computer labs on campus. Those participants who continued coming to the foreign language computer lab during the study either did not own a computer or lived too far from campus to return home for a one-hour class. In fact, the participants were encouraged not to be online in the same physical location as their classmates in an effort to make their online 'conversation' the only form of synchronous exchange to occur in the target language during the scheduled class hour. The largest number of students seen at one time chatting in the foreign language computer lab was never more than four and during most sessions only two students were in the same 20 station lab. This location-independent design is important because it represents a significant difference from the majority of studies investigating the intersection of synchronous CMC and second language acquisition.

Another aspect of the treatment employed in this experiment was a curriculum design that sought to control for a possible Hawthorne effect related to technology use by fully integrating technology in the form of learning systems and online course management features into all participating groups. Both experimental and control groups used these tools and completed the following assignments:

1. weekly threaded discussion as preparation for synchronous discussion,
2. weekly online drill and practice exercises with feedback,
3. weekly online quizzes with feedback,
4. independent viewing of the video accompanying the textbook, and
5. a collaborative research and writing project involving a multiple draft word-processed essay.

Scoring and Data Analysis

Scores for all of the instruments consisted of raw scores. The scores from the two examiners on the 50 point oral proficiency scale were averaged for both pre- and posttests. For the nonword repetition task there were three sets of eight words with a perfect performance of 24. The reading span measure awarded one point for the combination of the correct indication of the sensibility of a sentence and recall of its final word. A perfect score on the reading span was 60, based on a total of 60 sentences. The Shipley verbal intelligence measure has a vocabulary and an abstract reasoning score that were combined for a total raw score.

Can L2 Oral Proficiency Be Indirectly Developed Through Chatroom Interaction in the Target Language?

To test the hypothesis above, an ANCOVA was calculated with the pre-test score functioning as a covariate to factor out the participants' level of oral proficiency at the beginning of the course. The rationale for using an ANCOVA instead of repeated measures ANOVA is derived from the mean pre- and posttest oral proficiency scores of the four groups. Looking at the pretest means in Table 3.1, it is apparent that the groups were not equal at the beginning of the experiment.

Table 3.1. Pretest and Posttest Mean Oral Proficiency Scores

	Pretest Mean	Pretest SD	Posttest Mean	Posttest SD	Gain Mean	Gain SD	N
Control 1	18.76	4.27	28.56	5.52	9.79	6.82	17
Control 2	18.74	6.32	28.59	7.92	9.85	6.83	17
Experimental 1	18.23	5.41	32.08	5.12	13.85	4.42	13
Experimental 2	23.64*	7.25	33.32	7.15	9.68	7.80	11

$* p < 0.05$

While the control groups and the first experimental group exhibited very similar means, that of the second experimental group was considerably higher. Because of this difference, a repeated measures ANOVA would not take this pre-existing difference into account. Using the results of the pre-test as a covariate permitted a more accurate analysis of the posttest scores.

The ANCOVA results (see Table 3.2) showed that participants in the experimental condition as an aggregate group outperformed participants in the control condition ($p < 0.05$).

Table 3.2. ANCOVA for Treatment and Posttest with Pretest as Covariate

Source of Variation	Sum of Squares	DF	Mean Square	F	Sig of F
TREATMENT	135.72	1	135.72	3.96	0.05
PRETEST (Covariate)	441.55	1	441.55	12.88	0.001
Residual	1885.26	55	34.28		
Total	2560.12	57	44.91		

Covariate Raw Regression Coefficient PRETEST 0.472

These findings suggest that the participants spending half of their instructional time in a synchronous online environment were advantaged in their oral proficiency development over those meeting face to face in the classroom. The language production processes outlined in Levelt's model imply that language production, whether aural or textual, should develop the same set of underlying cognitive mechanisms. On the basis of Levelt's model alone, the logical prediction would be an equivalent gain in oral proficiency between the control and experimental conditions. Two *t*-tests were run to test this hypothesis as well. The results indicated that both the experimental and control groups demonstrated significant improvement from pretest to posttest (control group, $p < 0.05$; experimental group, $p < 0.05$). The fact that the mean gain score of participants conducting half of their class time in the chatroom was higher than the control condition suggests that synchronous CMC may offer some unique benefits to second language learners that may be difficult to obtain in a conventional classroom setting.

Can Individual Differences in Working Memory Capacity Effectively Predict the Rate of L2 Oral Proficiency Development for Different Types of Learners in a Chatroom Setting?

The first step in analyzing the data addressing this question was to run the correlations between the gains in oral proficiency scores on the posttest and the various psychometric predictor variables (see Table 3.3).

Table 3.3. Correlation Matrix for Predictors and Oral Proficiency Gain Scores

	Oral Proficiency Gain	Nonword Repetition	Reading Span	Shipley Verbal Intelligence
Oral Proficiency Gain	—	—	—	—
Nonword Repetition	0.30*	—	—	—
Reading Span	0.09***	0.33*	—	—
Shipley Verbal Intelligence	0.03***	0.31*	0.63**	—

*$p < 0.05$; **$p < 0.001$; ***not significant

It should be recalled that the composite Working Memory score consisted of a nonword repetition test score, measuring phonological capacity, and the reading span measure, providing a metric for Working Memory function. Based on the correlation of 0.09 between reading span and oral proficiency gain scores, the Central Executive appears to have no real relationship with oral proficiency development. However, this conclusion should be considered tentative based on the present results. A review of the histograms of the frequency distributions for the nonword repetition test and the reading span measure (see Figures 3.2 and 3.3) shows that the scores are much more concentrated than is customary in the production-based reading span and nonword repetition tests.

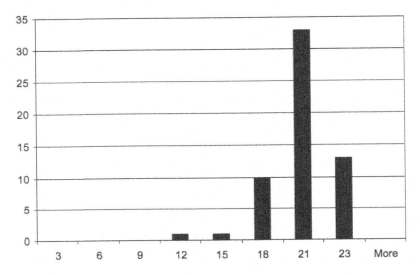

Figure 3.2. Nonword Repetition Scores

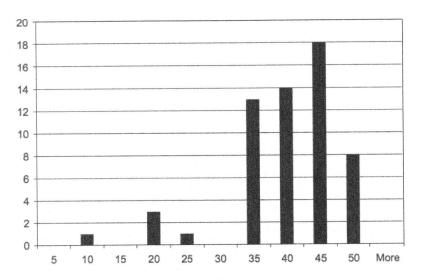

Figure 3.3. Reading Span Scores

There are two potential explanations for this phenomenon. First, it is possible that the participants in this study were a more homogeneous group than previously thought; the fact that subjects were drawn from third semester Spanish courses may have biased the sample. It stands to reason that intermediate level foreign language courses could contain students who have higher cognitive abilities in general, thus causing a truncated range of scores. The second possibility is that the recognition-based tests are not as taxing on memory resources as pure production tasks are. Having to maintain only enough of a memory trace to recognize words previously seen (i.e., reading span) or heard (i.e., nonword repetition task), as opposed to reproducing the word in either a written or aural form, may reduce the memory load. Reducing the burden on Working Memory may produce a facilitating effect for low spans and result in scores concentrated towards the upper half of the scale. The most plausible explanation may in fact be a combination of a more homogeneous sample than expected and the memory load reducing nature of recognition-based tests.

The relationship that stands out the most clearly is the one between the nonword repetition task and the oral proficiency gain scores ($r = 0.30$). This correlation suggests that phonological Working Memory capacity plays some role in oral proficiency development. The lack of a relationship between the Shipley verbal intelligence test and gains in oral proficiency suggests that it is the Working Memory construct measured by nonword repetition (the Phonological Loop) which is related to performance rather than a more global construct like general intelligence.

As previously mentioned, the chatroom environment should reduce the burden on Working Memory by (a) slowing down the pace of discussion and (b) allowing users to refresh memory traces by re-reading previous comments. The ramifications of these differences between synchronous online conversation and synchronous face-to-face conversation should be that learners with lower Working Memory capacity are advantaged in the chatroom setting. To test this hypothesis, the relationship between oral proficiency gain scores and nonword repetition scores was examined. The correlations for the experimental and control participants between oral proficiency gain scores and nonword repetition scores in Table 3.3 show that the correlation was higher for the control group ($r = 0.33$) than for the experimental group ($r = 0.23$). This finding suggests that the learners with lower phonological buffering capacity were disadvantaged relative to others in the control group but were not so disadvantaged in the experimental group. These results give a preliminary indication that the chatroom environment may be especially beneficial for students with lower ability to maintain verbal information in the Phonological Loop.

Discussion

The findings from this study provide evidence that L2 oral proficiency can be indirectly developed through chatroom interaction in the target language. As was suggested by Healy-Beauvois (1992) and Kern (1995), the oral proficiency gains of the experimental group indicate that a direct transfer of skills across modality from writing to speaking does occur. Based on Levelt's production model, it seemed very reasonable to expect equivalent gains on the part of control and experimental subjects. Nevertheless, the magnitude of gain for chatroom users in this study was somewhat unexpected.

These gains are not the result of a teacher effect. An ANCOVA analysis of the posttest as the dependent measure, pretest as a covariate, and the independent variable of teacher with two levels (native speaker and nonnative speaker) showed no effect of the teacher variable ($p = 0.64$).

From a language instruction perspective, even equivalent levels of oral proficiency development (no significant difference) between the groups would have been a desirable outcome. Therefore, these findings suggest causal mechanisms that extend beyond the equivalence that would be predicted by Levelt's model alone. Additional qualitative data collected from this study (Payne, 1999) indicate that most of the participants in the experimental condition were conscious of their subvocalization of the language they produced in the chatroom. Of the 23 experimental participants who responded to a survey questionnaire, five indicated that they overtly vocalized the comments they were composing, and 16 said they spoke silently to themselves as they typed comments in the chatroom. When asked if they read aloud the comments others posted in the chatroom, more than 50% said yes, at least sometimes. These qualitative data suggest that by vocalizing their own output and the input of their classmates, chatroom discourse for many participants incorporated all components of Levelt's model. This extends beyond the hypothesized equivalency that stopped short of the production of overt speech.

The question that presents itself is what are the characteristics of this form of 'conversation' that appear to enhance the development in speaking skills beyond what is possible in the face-to-face setting alone? Several qualities of chatroom discourse can address this question. First, conversational interaction online is not subject to the turn-taking rules that apply to face-to-face discussions. In an IRC style chatroom, where users cannot see each other's comments until they have been posted, there exists a face-to-face equivalent of everyone in a discussion group talking simultaneously. This situation would be disastrous in a classroom, but it works online. Without having to wait for a turn, learners have a greater opportunity to produce much more language in online discussions than is possible in most conventional classroom settings. In a 45–50 minute online session, it is not uncommon for students to generate 50 full sentence comments in a lively, small group discussion.

Language production in a chatroom is also required for a student to be considered 'present.' In a classroom, students can be passive listeners and still be thought of as attending the discussion. In an online environment, nonparticipation equates to nonattendance. If students go for more than a couple minutes without contributing to the conversation, fellow group members often inquire about their whereabouts.

A third interesting difference between online and face-to-face conversation is the requirement to use language for communicating. In a classroom environment, second language learners can resort to a wide range of paralinguistic compensation strategies to get their points across. Even in a classroom where students are encouraged to use the target language for communication, once learners have understood another interlocutor's communicative intentions, the tendency is often to move ahead with the activity instead of helping their partner find the language to express his or her intentions. The necessity of using language, not pragmatics, for communication in a synchronous online environment may push learners to experiment with the language, testing emerging hypotheses about the meaning of lexical items and the application of syntactical patterns not yet mastered (Pica, et al., 1989).

The chatroom requirement of language use may also increase students' monitoring of their own language and the language of others. On a five-point Likert scale, more than 50% of participants in the experimental condition reported that they focused more on the grammatical correctness and the accuracy of what they said in the chatroom than in face-to-face settings (Payne, 1999). Of the participants receiving the treatment, almost two-thirds said that they noticed other people's mistakes more when conversing in the chatroom than face-to-face. Such an increased awareness may push learners to engage in more syntactic processing and 'notice' gaps in their linguistic knowledge, especially since chatroom exchanges occur in written form (Swain & Lapkin, 1995).

Finally, the decreased speed of conversational exchange and the non-ephemeral nature of the medium of chatroom discourse warrant discussion. From a Working Memory perspective these two characteristics should reduce the memory load normally imposed by synchronous communication. Interlocutors can reread comments to refresh their memory in addition to the reduced rate of exchange. The difference in the correlation between oral proficiency gain and nonword repetition across the two groups suggests that this reduced memory load may benefit learners with lower phonological Working Memory capacity. Another advantage of the reduced pace of exchange in the chatroom is that students have the opportunity to engage in a limited amount of pretask planning. The ability to plan for an oral performance task has shown to result in more fluent and syntactically complex output and increased focus on form (Ortega, 1999).

Conclusion

Since we are very early in experimentally examining oral proficiency development as a result of synchronous CMC, these findings need to be replicated with different populations and different instructional treatments. It would be beneficial to study these same variables in an online course where students rarely or never met face-to-face but had access to pedagogically sound self-study pronunciation software (Donahue, 2000). It is important to emphasize that these results do not suggest that speaking skills can be developed in the absence of face-to-face conversational interaction. Clearly, the participants in the experimental groups had opportunities for face-to-face conversational interaction. It may be most useful to view the chatroom as analogous to the flight simulators used by pilots in training; the chatroom sessions may well serve as a *conversation simulator* for foreign language learners. The notion that learners can practice 'speaking' in an environment where affect and rate of speech are minimized is very appealing. Possibly more important is the realization that if we as second language instructors assume that face-to-face speech is the only way to develop conversational ability, we may in fact be disadvantaging a significant portion of our students. For students who find L2 oral production an overwhelming task and tend to tune out when the linguistic data generated in face-to-face conversational settings becomes too great, the online synchronous interaction appears to give them a leg up on developing L2 oral proficiency.

The overarching questions that need to be addressed in light of the current push towards foreign language distance education are:

- When is face-to-face interaction critical for optimal second language acquisition?
- How can technology-mediated learning systems be used to create alternative instructional models that meet the requirements of communicative language instruction, make foreign language instruction available to a greater number of individuals, and encourage us as foreign language professionals to constantly reevaluate our own views of what constitutes teaching and learning a second language?

As distance learning and location-independent foreign language instruction becomes more pervasive, it is important to learn how chatroom use among distributed learners differs from the computer-mediated classroom discussion (CMCD) model. In the CMCD model, students and the instructor share the same physical space (i.e., a computer lab) and interact with each other online. Understanding how the interaction between location-dependent and location-independent learners may differ is a particularly urgent question considering virtually all empirical research to date on second language chatroom use has been based on the CMCD model. (Blake [2000] is an exception.) Furthermore, almost all of these studies have employed the same software program, *Interchange* of the Daedelus Writing System. (Pellettieri [2000] and Blake [2000] are two notable exceptions.) Since *Interchange* is a LAN-based technology and not a web-based or Internet Relay Chat system, using results from a location-dependent writing environment to guide pedagogical decisions about the design and implementation of location-independent instruction seems a bit precarious.

Finally, the utility of Working Memory theory for explaining the underlying mechanisms of second language acquisition clearly needs to be studied in depth. Based on findings in the study presented here, the connection between phonological Working Memory and second language oral proficiency warrants a closer look. The indication that learning environments can, by design, reduce the burden on Working Memory and thereby produce a facilitating effect for low capacity individuals offers a new perspective on how instruction can meet the individual needs of learners.

References

Adams, A. M., & Gathercole, S. E. (1995). Phonological working memory and speech production in preschool children. *Journal of Speech and Hearing Research, 38*, 403–414.

Adams, A. M., & Gathercole, S. E. (1996). Phonological working memory and spoken language development in young children. *Quarterly Journal of Experimental Psychology, 49A*(1), 216–233.

Anderson, J. R. (1982). Acquisition of cognitive skill. *Psychological Review, 89*, 369–406.

Baddeley, A. D. (1986). *Working memory*. Oxford: Oxford University Press.

Baddeley, A. D., Thomson, N., & Buchanan, M. (1975). Word length and the structure of short-term memory. *Journal of Verbal Learning and Verbal Behavior, 9*, 176–189.

Blake, R. J. (2000). Computer mediated communication: A window on L2 Spanish interlanguage. *Language Learning and Technology* [Online], *4*(1), 120–136. Available: llt.msu.edu

Brooks, L. R. (1967). The suppression of visualisation by reading. *Quarterly Journal of Experimental Psychology, 19*, 289–299.

Chun, D. M. (1994). Using computer networking to facilitate the acquisition of interactive competence. *System, 22*(1), 17–31.

Daneman, M. (1991). Working memory as a predictor of verbal fluency. *Journal of Psycholinguistic Research, 20*(6), 445–464.

Daneman, M., & Carpenter, P. A. (1980). Individual differences in working memory and reading. *Journal of Verbal Learning & Verbal Behavior, 19*(4), 450–466.

Daneman, M., & Green, I. (1986). Individual differences in comprehending and producing words in context. *Journal of Memory and Language, 25*, 1–18.

De Bot, K. (1992). A bilingual production model: Levelt's 'Speaking' model adapted. *Applied Linguistics, 13*(1), 1–24.

De Bot, K., & Schreuder, R. (1993). Word production and the bilingual lexicon. In R. Schreuder & B. Weltens (Eds.), *The bilingual lexicon* (pp. 191–214). Amsterdam: John Benjamins.

Dechert, H. W. (1980). Pauses and intonation as indicators of verbal planning in second-language speech productions: Two examples from a case study. In H. W. Dechert & M. Raupach (Eds.), *Temporal variables in speech* (pp. 271–285). The Hague: Mouton.

Dechert, H. W. (1983). How a story is done in a second language. In C. Faerch & G. Kaspar (Eds.), *Strategies in interlanguage communication*. London: Longman.

Dechert, H. W., Möhle, D., & Raupach, M. (Eds.). (1984). *Second language productions*. Tübingen: Narr.

Dechert, H. W., Raupach, M. (Eds.). (1980a). *Temporal variables in speech: Studies in honour of Frieda Goldman-Eisler*. The Hague: Mouton.

Dechert, H. W., & Raupach, M. (Eds.). (1980b). *Towards a cross-linguistic assessment of speech production*. Frankfurt a.M.: Lang.

Dechert, H. W., & Raupach, M. (Eds.). (1987). *Psycholinguistic models of production*. Norwood, NJ: Ablex.

Donahue, S. (2000). Teaching pronunciation online. *ALN Magazine* [Online], *4*(1). Available: www.aln.org/alnweb/magazine

Engle, R., Kane, M., & Tuholski, S. (1999). Individual differences in working memory capacity and what they tell us about controlled attention, general fluid intelligence, and functions of the prefrontal cortex. In A. Miyake & P. Shah (Eds.), *Models of working memory: Mechanisms of active maintenance and executive control* (pp. 102–134). Cambridge: Cambridge University Press.

Gathercole, S. E., & Baddeley, A. D. (1989a). Evaluation of the role of phonological STM in the development of vocabulary in children: A longitudinal study. *Journal of Memory and Language, 28*, 200–213.

Gathercole, S. E., & Baddeley, A. D. (1989b). The role of phonological memory in vocabulary acquisition: A study of young children learning new names. *British Journal of Psychology, 81*(4), 439–454.

Gathercole, S. E., & Baddeley, A. D. (1993). *Working memory and language*. Hove: Lawrence Erlbaum Associates.

Geva, E., & Ryan, E. B. (1993). Linguistic and cognitive correlates of academic skills in first and second languages. *Language Learning, 43*, 5–42.

Harley, B. (1993). Instructional strategies and SLA in early French immersion. *Studies in Second Language Acquisition, 15*, 245–260.

Healy-Beauvois, M. (1992). Computer assisted classroom discussion in the foreign language classroom: Conversation in slow motion. *Foreign Language Annals, 25*(5), 455–464.

Izumi, I., Bigelow, M., Fujiwara, M., & Fearnow, S. (1999). Testing the output hypothesis: Effects of output on noticing and second language acquisition. *Studies in Second Language Acquisition, 21*, 421–452.

Kelm, O. R. (1992). The use of synchronous computer networks in second language instruction: A preliminary study. *Foreign Language Annals, 25*(5), 441–454.

Kern, R. (1995). Restructuring classroom interaction with networked computers: Effects on quality and characteristics of language production. *Modern Language Journal, 79*(4), 457–476.

Krashen, S. (1985). *The input hypothesis: Issues and implications.* New York: Longman.

Lennon, P. (1990). Investigating fluency in EFL: A quantitative approach. *Language Learning, 40*, 387–417.

Levelt, W. J. M. (1989). *Speaking: From intention to articulation.* Cambridge, MA: The MIT Press.

Levelt, W. J. M. (1993). Language use in normal speakers and its disorders. In G. Blanken, J. Dittmann, H. Grimm, J. Marshall, & C. Wallesch (Eds.), *Linguistic disorders and pathologies: An international handbook* (pp. 1–15). Berlin: de Gruyter.

Levelt, W. J. M. (1995). The ability to speak: From intentions to spoken words. *European Review, 3*(1), 13–23.

Linnell, J. (1995). Can negotiation provide a context for learning syntax in a second language? *Working Papers in Educational Linguistics, 11*(2), 83–103. (ERIC Documentation Reproduction Service No. ED 393 305)

Miyake, A., & Friedman, N. (1998). Individual differences in second language proficiency: Working memory as language aptitude. In A. Healy & L. Bourne (Eds.), *Foreign language learning: Psycholinguistic studies on training and retention* (pp. 139–164). Mahwah, NJ: Lawrence Erlbaum Associates.

Möhle, D. (1984). A comparison of the second language speech production of different native speakers. In H. W. Dechert, D. Möhle, & M. Raupach (Eds.), *Second language production* (pp. 26–49). Tübingen: Narr.

Ortega, L. (1999). Planning and focus on form in L2 oral performance. *Studies in Second Language Acquisition, 21*, 109–148.

Papagno, C., Valentine, T., & Baddeley, A. D. (1991). Phonological short-term memory and foreign-language vocabulary learning. *Journal of Memory and Language, 30*, 331–347.

Payne, J. S. (1999, November). *The psycholinguistic and pedagogical implications of integrating technology into the second language curriculum.* Paper presented at the Second Language Acquisition Institute, University of California, Davis, CA.

Pellettieri, J. (2000). Negotiation in cyberspace: The role of chatting in the development of grammatical competence. In M. Warschauer & R. Kern (Eds.), *Network-Based Language Teaching: Concepts and Practice.* New York: Cambridge University Press.

Pica, T., Holliday, L., Lewis, N., & Morgenthaler, L. (1989). Comprehensible output as an outcome of linguistic demands on the learner. *Studies in Second Language Acquisition, 11*, 63–90.

Poulisse, N. (1997). Language production in bilinguals. In A. M. B. de Groot & J. F. Kroll (Eds.), *Tutorials in bilingualism.* Mahwah, NJ: Lawrence Erlbaum.

Poulisse, N., & Bongaerts, T. (1994). First language use in second language production. *Applied Linguistics, 15*, 36–57.

Raupach, M. (1980). Temporal variables in first and second language speech production. In H. W. Dechert & M. Raupach (Eds.), *Temporal variables in speech* (pp. 271–285). The Hague: Mouton.

Raupach, M. (1984). Formulae in second language production. In H. W. Dechert, D. Möhle, & M. Raupach (Eds.), *Second language productions.* Tübingen: Narr.

Rehbein, J. (1987). On fluency in second language speech. In H. W. Dechert and M. Raupach (Eds.), *Psycholinguistic Models of production* (pp. 97–105). Norwood, NJ: Ablex.

Schmidt, R. (1992). Psychological mechanisms underlying second language fluency. *Studies in Second Language Acquisition, 14*, 357–385.

Service, E. (1992). Phonology, working memory, and foreign-language learning. *Quarterly Journal of Experimental Psychology, 45A*(1), 21–50.

Service, E., & Kohonen, V. (1995). Is the relation between phonological memory and foreign language learning accounted for by vocabulary acquisition? *Applied Psycholinguistics, 16*, 155–172.

Speidel, G. E. (1989). A biological basis for individual differences in learning to speak. In G. E. Speidel and K. E. Nelson (Eds.), *The many faces of imitation in language learning* (pp. 199–229). New York: Springer-Verlag.

Speidel, G. E. (1993). Phonological short-term memory and individual differences in learning to speak: A bilingual case study. *First Language, 13*, 69–91.

Swain, M. (1985). Communicative competence: Some roles of comprehensible input and comprehensible output in its development. In S. Gass and C. Madden (Eds.), *Input and second language aquisition.* Rowley, MA: Newbury House.

Swain, M. (1993). The output hypothesis: Just speaking and writing aren't enough. *The Canadian Modern Language Review, 50*, 158–164.

Swain, M., & Lapkin, S. (1995). Problems in output and the cognitive processes they generate: A step towards second language learning. *Applied Linguistics, 16*(3), 371–391.

Warschauer, M. (1996). Comparing face-to-face and electronic discussion in the second language classroom. *CALICO Journal, 13*(2), 7–26.

Weise, R. (1984). Language production in foreign and native languages: Same or different. In H. W. Dechert, D. Möhle, & M. Raupach (Eds.), *Second language production* (pp. 11–25). Tübingen: Narr.

Whitney, P., & Budd, D. (1999). A separate language interpretation resource: Premature fractionation? *Behavioral and Brain Sciences, 22*, 113.

Appendix A

Oral Production Interview Scale
Student Name: _____
ID#: _____

Comprehensibility
_____ 10-9:   for a native speaker: easy to understand without any confusion or difficulty.
_____ 8-6:   for a native speaker: can understand with minimal difficulty.
_____ 5-3:   for a native speaker: can understand with some difficulty.
_____ 2-1:   for a native speaker: can understand with great difficulty.

Fluency
_____ 10-9:   native-like fluency; hesitations only when appropriate.
_____ 8-7:   near native fluency; very few hesitations or pauses.
_____ 6-5:   some hesitations, pauses, but fairly continuous speech
_____ 4-3:   frequent hesitations and pausing, speech is more disjointed.
_____ 2-1:   very disjointed speech with many hesitations and pauses.

Vocabulary Usage
_____ 10-9:   very extensive vocabulary usage.
_____ 8-7:   good vocabulary usage, very few inappropriate terms.
_____ 6-5:   moderate vocabulary, a few inappropriate terms.
_____ 4-3:   limited vocabulary, some inappropriate terms used.
_____ 2-1:   very limited vocabulary, frequent use of inappropriate terms.

Syntax and Grammar
_____ 10-9:   native-like grammar and syntax; used a variety of syntax and tenses.
_____ 8-7:   near-native grammar and syntax; few mistakes.
_____ 6-5:   used few syntax structures, some grammar and syntax mistakes.
_____ 4-3:   very limited in syntax and grammar usage with frequent mistakes.
_____ 2-1:   no systematic use of grammar and syntax rules.

Pronunciation
_____ 10-9:   native-like pronunciation, virtually no discernable accent, no errors.
_____ 8-7:   near-native pronunciation, slight accent, few errors.
_____ 6-5:   some errors; obvious accent, but doesn't interfere with comprehension.
_____ 4-3:   frequent errors; strong accent; some comprehension difficulties.
_____ 2-1:   little effort to use Spanish pronunciation; comprehension impeded.

Appendix B

Speaking Tasks
Pretest
Task 1:   tell us in Spanish about a trip that you took recently.
Task 2:   tell us in Spanish what you did over summer vacation.
Task 3:   tell us in Spanish about your plans for Labor Day weekend.
Task 4:   tell us in Spanish what you do in a normal week.

Posttest
Task 1:   tell us in Spanish about a trip that you took recently.
Task 2:   tell us in Spanish what you did over Thanksgiving break.
Task 3:   tell us in Spanish about your plans for Christmas vacation.
Task 4:   tell us in Spanish what you do in a normal week.

4 Recent Developments in Technology and Language Learning: A Literature Review and Meta-analysis*

Yong Zhao**

Introduction

This review study is intended to address three related issues in technology and language education. First, policy makers and the general public are interested in learning about the effectiveness of using technology in language education because they need that information to help decide future investment decisions regarding technology (President's Committee of Advisors on Science and Technology (Panel on Educational Technology), 1997). Second, researchers and developers are interested in knowing what has been done and what we already know about using technology to enhance language learning. Such knowledge will hopefully guide their further explorations and development. Third, language educators want to know what works and what does not so that they can make informed decisions in selecting the appropriate technology to use in their teaching.

Answering these questions is not easy for a number of reasons. First, technology is an ill-defined concept that encompasses a wide range of tools, artifacts, and practices, from multimedia computers to the Internet, from videotapes to online chatrooms, from web pages to interactive audio

* This study was supported by a contract from the United States Department of Education as part of its E-language initiative. An earlier version of this paper was submitted to the US Department of Education as a concept paper. The author wishes to thank Dr. Alan Ginsburg, Dr. Susan Sclafani, and Adrianna de Kanter for their support and insights. Views expressed in this paper do not necessarily reflect those of the US Department of Education.

** Yong Zhao is an associate professor of educational technology at Michigan State University, where he also directs the Center for Teaching and Technology. His research interests include computer-assisted language learning and online learning.

conferencing. These technologies vary a great deal in their capacity, interface, and accessibility. It is thus misleading to think the effects of videotapes are the same as those of the online chatrooms just because they are all called 'technology.' Second, the effects of any technology on learning outcomes lie in its uses. A specific technology may hold great educational potential, but, until it is used properly, it may not have any positive impact at all on learning. Thus, assessing the effectiveness of a technology is in reality assessing the effectiveness of its uses rather than the technology itself. Since most information and communication technologies (ICTs) can be used in a variety of ways, some more effective than others, it is inappropriate to overgeneralize the effectiveness (or lack thereof) of one way of using the technology to the technology itself. Third, to further complicate things, the effectiveness of an educational approach is highly mediated by many other variables – the learner, the task, the instructional setting, and of course the assessment tool. Thus, even the same use of a particular technology in different instructional settings may result in different learning outcomes.

Clearly it is unreasonable to expect any single study to tell us to what degree technology is effective in improving language learning. However, a comprehensive review of many studies can get us closer to an answer (e.g., Cavanaugh, 2001; Chapelle, 1997; Lou, Abrami, & d'Apollonia, 2001; Salaberry, 2001). With the help of a research method called meta-analysis (Glass, 1977; Hedges & Olkin, 1985; Lyons, 1995a), we can assess the effectiveness of technology uses in language education by analyzing findings of numerous empirical studies. A carefully conducted review can also help us develop a map of past and current work in the field of technology and language education. The map should reveal what we know, what we have done, what works, and what does not. The study in this paper offers such a review.

Focusing on the issues of effectiveness, this review attempts to achieve three goals: (a) assessing the overall effectiveness of uses of technology in language education through meta-analysis, (b) exploring patterns of recent efforts in using technology to improve language learning, and (c) identifying effective ways to use technology in language education.

Method

Selection of Studies

There is a long history of using technology to improve language learning (Salaberry, 2001). The review in this paper is limited to research published in referred journals during the last five years, from 1997 to 2001. The decision to limit the review to this period of time was motivated by the concern for relevance. The primary purpose of the review is to seek evidence and ideas that will guide our future work, rather than paint a comprehensive historical picture of research in computer-assisted language learning, which can be found in many existing publications (e.g., Chapelle, 2001; Levy, 1997; Salaberry, 2001). Thus, it is reasonable to focus on studies of technological applications that have the most relevance. Relevance is considered in two areas: technology and pedagogy. As we know, technology changes constantly and rapidly. The technological innovations that we are most interested in and that will most likely have an impact on language education in the future are: (a) multimedia computing; (b) the Internet, especially the web; and (c) speech synthesis and recognition. These innovations were a fairly recent development, and efforts to apply them in language education occurred even later. Focusing on the research publications over the past five years in this way should give us sufficient insight into the applications of these relatively new technologies.

There was also a major paradigm shift in the pedagogical and research focus of technology applications in language education recently (Chapelle, 1997, 2001; Pennington, 1996; Salaberry, 2001) – a shift away from traditional drill-and-skill computer-aided instruction (CAI) models toward multimedia, intelligent CAI, and integration models. Studies about applications of these newer models appeared more recently as well.

Works included in this review were identified from five representative journals devoted to research on second/foreign language education and technology and language learning.

Selecting Representative Journals

A four-step process was followed to identify the representative journals. First, a key word search using 'computer assisted language learning' was performed on ERIC through FirstSearch. The search was limited by year, document type, and language. Only journal articles published from 1997 through 2001 in English were included. The search resulted in a total of 389 articles. Second, all articles that did not have the key word 'second language' were excluded, which resulted in a total of 355 articles. Third, all articles that appeared in nonpeer-reviewed, irregularly published, or practice-oriented journals or magazines were excluded, resulting in a total of 156 articles. The fourth step was to calculate the distribution of the articles and their sources. These articles were published in 22 different journals. The journals fell into three categories: (a) technology and language learning journals that specifically address issues in applications of technology in language learning and education; (b) language learning and education journals that address issues in language learning and education in general, of which technology application is a subissue; and (c) educational technology journals that address issues in the application of technology in education in general, of which language learning and education is considered a subarea of study. Figure 4.1 shows the distribution of articles by journal categories.

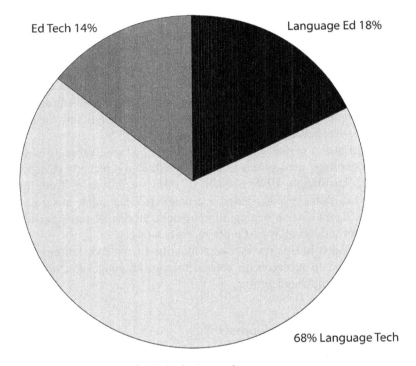

Figure 4.1. Distribution of articles by journal category

However, in many cases, a journal may have had only one or two articles. Nine journals had more than three articles (see Figure 4.2).

As Figure 4.2 shows, most articles appeared in journals devoted to educational technology, especially language educational technology. The three journals devoted to language learning and technology (*System, CALICO Journal*, and *Language Learning & Technology*) published nearly 70% of all the articles.

Further, the articles appeared mostly in two journals: *CALICO Journal* and *Language Learning & Technology* (see Figure 4.3).

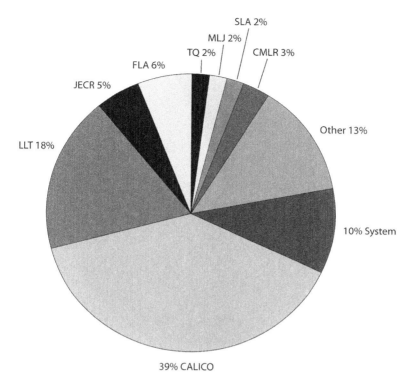

Figure 4.2. Distribution of Articles by Journals

Notes: System = *System: An International Journal of Educational Technology and Applied Linguistics;* CALICO = *CALICO Journal;* LLT = *Language Learning & Technology;* JECR = *Journal of Educational Computing Research;* FLA = *Foreign Language Annals;* TQ = *TESOL Quarterly;* MLJ = *The Modern Language Journal;* SLA = *Studies in Second Language Acquisition;* CMLR = *Canadian Modern Language Review;* Other = other journals.

Based on this analysis, the *CALICO Journal* and *Language Learning & Technology* were first selected to represent studies published in journals devoted to technology and language learning. The *Journal of Educational Computing Research* was selected to represent journals devoted to educational technology. *The Modern Language Journal* and *TESOL Quarterly* were selected to represent journals in language learning and education. These two journals were selected over *Foreign Language Annals* (FLA) because they are generally considered more research oriented than FLA. This selection represents 72% of all articles found to be related to computer-assisted language instruction from the ERIC database during the period of 1997 through 2001. Considering that 13% of the articles are scattered in 12 other journals, the selection should be considered as a reasonable represen-

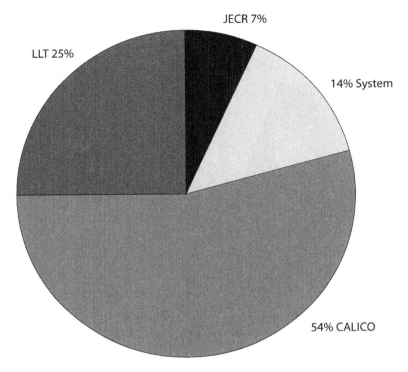

Figure 4.3. Distribution of Articles in Technology Journals

tative sample of journals that may publish studies in technology and second language learning and education.

Selection of Studies

1. Having selected these five journals, the researcher read the abstracts of all articles published in the journals since 1997 to identify possible studies to include in this review. After identifying the possible articles, the researcher read all identified articles to select the ones suitable for a meta-analysis. The following criteria were used for the selection: The article had to report results of an empirical study or multiple studies on the effectiveness or effects of a technological application aimed at improving language learning. Informational articles describing the process of technological applications or products and opinion articles presenting theories or review the literature were included as part of the review but not for the meta-analysis of effects.

2. Technology was more broadly conceived than just computers because the convergence of media is an emerging trend in language education technology. Thus, studies about the application of video, audio, computer-assisted instruction programs, the web, computer-mediated communication, simulation, speech technologies, word processing, e-books, and grammar checkers were all included.
3. The studies included for the final meta-analysis had to have measures of improvement of language proficiency. Self-assessment of improvement or attitudinal surveys were not acceptable.

A total of nine articles were found to meet the above criteria for inclusion in the meta-analysis although many more articles published in these journals dealt with technological applications in language learning. While the meta-analysis was conducted on only the nine studies, the review here draws upon discussions and findings from the other articles as well as a number of books published around the same period of time.

Results

This section is organized into three parts. Part one presents an overview of the literature on technology applications in language education. Part two summarizes how technology has been used to support language learning and the effectiveness of these uses. Part three reports the results from the meta-analysis study intended to assess the overall effectiveness of technology-supported language learning.

Overview of the Literature

The review of recent research on technology-supported language learning reveals a number of interesting points regarding existing research in this area. First, the total number of well designed experimental studies on the effectiveness of technological applications in language learning is very limited. For instance, the four issues in Volume 16 of the *CALICO Journal*, which were published in 1998 and 1999, contain 10 feature articles. Only two of the 10 met the selection criteria to be included in the meta-analysis. Of all the 51 feature articles published in *Language Learning & Technology*, one met the criteria. The majority of the articles are either description of cases – uses of technology in language education and processes of software development – or theoretical discussions of principles of technological applications. Some of the limited empirical studies did not measure learning gains, relied solely on learner self-reports as measures of effectiveness, or were not well designed.

Second, the studies were limited to college level language learners. None of the nine studies was conducted in K-12 settings. Only two of the nine studies were not about college students – their participants were military linguists, also adults.

Third, the target languages under consideration in the studies were also limited. French and Spanish were the most studied (10 out 16 or 63%). Other more commonly studied languages were English as a second language (ESL), German, and Arabic.

Fourth, most of the studies were about the application of a single application instead of systemic large-scale integration of technology. Only two of the 16 studies were about long-term technology integration in the language learning environment. Thus the treatment reported was also short term, lasting from a few hours to a few weeks.

Lastly, the applications of technology to enhance language learning have been wide ranging, both in terms of the types of technology used and the issues language education needs to address. The studies investigated the uses of most available technologies including video, audio, multimedia, communication, network, and speech technologies. These technologies have been applied to support the teaching of various aspects of language learning including vocabulary, grammar, reading, writing, speaking, listening, and culture.

Uses and Effectiveness of Technologies in Language Education

The following paragraphs present detailed discussions of the specific applications that have been studied over the past few years. The discussion is categorized into four groups: access to materials, communication opportunities, feedback, and learner motivation.

Providing Access to Linguistic and Cultural Materials

Access and exposure to engaging, authentic, and comprehensible yet demanding materials in the target language is essential for successful language learning. However for many language learners, whether in classes or self-study settings, such access is often limited. Thus language educators have long looked at information and communication technologies (ICT) as possible solutions to this problem (Egbert, Chao, & Hanson-Smith, 1999; Hanson-Smith, 1999; Salaberry, 2001). The uses of ICT to provide better access and exposure to linguistic and cultural materials fall into the following three areas.

Enhancing access efficiency through digital multimedia technologies. Digital multimedia technologies were used to make access to learning materials more efficient than print media or audio recorders because multimedia (visual, audio, and text) presentations can create stronger memory links than a single medium alone and digital technology allows instant and accurate playbacks, which helps the learner to access specific segments much more easily without spending time to locate them – a tedious and time consuming process (Hanson-Smith, 1999; Thorton & Dudley, 1996). Shea (2000) compared the time students needed to complete their language learning tasks using captioned video versus interactive videodisc (IVD) and found that the students using IVD completed the tasks significantly faster ($p < 0.05$). Labrie (2000) found that although students spent more time learning a set of French words on paper than those who studied on computer (where they could hear a word pronounced and see a picture about the word), they did not learn more words. In another study, Nutta (1998) examined the learning of students who spent the same amount of time (one hour per day for seven days) learning verb tenses in English in two conditions: attending a regular class and receiving instruction from the teacher versus using a multimedia computer program (audio, video, recording capabilities, etc.). Nutta found that the ESL students using the computer program performed as well or significantly better (on three out of six measures, $p < 0.10$) than their counterparts attending the class.

Enhancing authenticity using video and the Internet. Video materials can bring natural and context-rich linguistic and cultural materials to the learner, while the Internet enables the learner to access authentic news and literature in the target language, which can reflect current cultural changes more effectively than printed sources (Bacon & Finnemann, 1990; Hanson-Smith, 1999; Herron, Cole, Corrie, & Dubreil, 1999; Herron, Dubreil, Cole, & Corrie, 2000; Kitajima & Lyman-Hager, 1998; Lafford & Lafford, 1997; Lee, 1998; Weyers, 1999). Weyers (1999) studied the effectiveness of authentic video on college Spanish students. He had one class of students watch a Mexican television show as part of a second semester Spanish class that met 60 minutes daily for a total of eight weeks, while the other class followed the regular curriculum without the video. He found that the video group's performance on both listening comprehension and oral production to be significantly better than the regular group ($p < 0.01$). The video group also outperformed their counterparts on other measures of communicative competence. Herron (2000) found that video also helped their first-year college French learners develop significantly better understanding of the target culture. In another study, Green and Youngs (2000) substituted regular classroom instruction with web activities one class period per week for beginning college French and German students. After a semester, they found that

> the substitution of one class day for directed, pedagogically sound Web activities seems to have allowed the treatment groups to continue to progress toward their personal and professional goals and allowed them to learn language at a rate similar to that of their peers in the control groups. It also appears, in general, that the students had a positive experience using the web. (p. 108)

Enhancing comprehensibility through learner control and multimedia annotations.

Comprehensible input is necessary for language learning, but useful learning materials must also contain enough unfamiliar materials (Krashen, 1985). For language learners, especially beginning and intermediate ones, authentic materials are often beyond their language proficiency and may become incomprehensible without help. To enhance comprehensibility of spoken materials, full caption, keyword caption, or slowing down the speech rate have been found to be effective (Shea, 2000; Zhao, 1997). Zhao (1997) found that the ESL students who were able to flexibly slow down or speed up the rate of speech had significantly better listening comprehension than those who did not ($p < 0.05$). For reading materials, glossing or multimedia annotations have been effective means to enhance comprehension (Al-Seghayer, 2001; Chun & Plass, 1997; Johnson, 1999; Lyman-Hager, 2000). Al-Seghayer (2001) compared ESL students' vocabulary learning in different annotation conditions and found that

> a video clip in combination with a text definition is more effective in teaching unknown vocabulary than a picture in combination with a text definition... The variety of modality cues can reinforce each other and are linked together in meaningful ways to provide an in-depth experience ($p < 0.001$). (p. 225)

Providing Opportunities for Communication

Engaging in authentic communication in the target language is another essential condition for successful language learning yet such opportunities do not exist for most learners. ICT has again been used in many different ways to create opportunities for language learners to communicate in the target language (Hanson-Smith, 1999; Kelm, 1998; Muyskens, 1998; Warschauer & Kern, 2000). Efforts in this area can be summarized into two groups: interaction with the computer and interaction through the computer with remote audiences.

Interactions with the computer. Communicative interactions can occur in either written or spoken language or a combination of both. At the simplest level, a computer program can generate utterances either orally or in writing that require the learner to respond by selecting an answer with a mouse click or providing simple writing responses (Hanson-Smith, 1999). With the advancement of speech synthesis and recognition technologies (Ehsani & Knodt, 1998), the learner can also carry on near natural conversations with a computer program around preselected and programmed topics (Bernstein, Najmi, & Ehsani, 1999; Egan, 1999; Harless, Zier, & Duncan, 1999; LaRocca, Morgan, & Bellinger, 1999; Wachowicz & Scott, 1999). The learner can also give either written or spoken commands to a computer program in a simulation and game environment. The computer program would then perform the command (Holland, Kaplan, & Sabol, 1999; LaRocca et al., 1999). Harless et al. (1999), for example, tested the effectiveness of a virtual conversation program in Arabic at the Defense Language Institute. The program enabled the students to interview virtual native-speaking characters orally with speech recognition technology. After interacting with these virtual characters for at least eight hours per day for four days, the participants' reading and speaking skills increased significantly ($p < 0.05$) while their listening skill increased 'convincingly.' In another study, Holland (1999) and her colleagues found that a speech-enabled interactive micro-world program which allowed the learners of Arabic to construct objects by speaking to the computer improved student motivation and oral output.

Interactions with remote audiences through the computer. Computer-mediated communication (CMC) and teleconferencing technologies have been used to create authentic communication opportunities for language learners since the 1980s (Beauvois, 1997; Pennington, 1996). The uses of CMC technologies, such as electronic mail, bulletin boards, and chatrooms have been found to have many benefits for language learners (Beauvois, 1997; Cahill & Catanzaro, 1997; Kelm, 1998; Salaberry, 2001; Warschauer, 1998). CMC brings the much needed audience to the language learner (Johnson, 1999). It also promotes more equal and better participation, leading to more output in the target language (Beauvois, 1997; Gonzalez-Bueno, 1998). It fosters negotiation and form-focused learning (Pellettieri, 2000). CMC was also found to enhance the writing process and improve student writing (Schultz, 2000). Although CMC communication is, in most cases, conducted in writing, it has been found to improve oral proficiency as well. For instance, Beauvois (1997) found that second-year French learners who held their discussions online achieved better oral proficiency than those who discussed the texts orally in the traditional classroom setting ($p < 0.05$).

Providing Feedback

The capacity for computers to provide instant and individualized feedback has long been recognized by educators, including foreign language educators (Chao, 1999; Salaberry, 2001). While early applications tended to follow the behaviorist tradition by simply assessing the learner's performance and providing simplistic feedback in a correct-or-incorrect fashion, more recent applications are much more contextualized and pedagogically sound (Salaberry, 2001).

Computer-based grammar checkers and spell checkers. Computer-based grammar checkers and spell checkers represent potentially powerful ways to provide feedback to students' written output (Jacobs & Rodgers, 1999). Although the feedback provided by current grammar checkers is not always accurate – albeit immediate – due to its inability to perform semantic analysis and process deep level structures, Burston (2001) found that advanced students of French benefited tremendously from a French grammar checker. In this study, the students in the treatment group used a French grammar checker while writing their essays, whereas the control group did not. The results suggest that 'the effectiveness of the use of Antidote in improving morphosyntatic accuracy in assigned compositions were overwhelmingly positive.' (p. 507). The treatment group's first essay scored on average 70%, compared to 20% of the control group. The second essay showed similar results: 85% for the treatment group and 54% for the control.

Automatic speech recognition technology. Automatic speech recognition technology holds the potential to provide feedback that would otherwise be impossible. Pronunciation is a fundamental element of language learning, but providing feedback that can be easily accessible and useful is difficult. In traditional instructional settings, feedback and modeling are often provided by an instructor, who may or may not be good at judging the student pronunciation in the first place. Typical ways to provide feedback often include having students repeat the pronunciation or explaining how the sound should be produced in a very abstract fashion. With the advancement of speech recognition technology, the student can receive feedback in more effective ways (Dalby & Kewley-Port, 1999; Ehsani & Knodt, 1998; Eskenazi, 1999; Mostow & Aist, 1999). Mostow and Aist (1999) have suggested visual, template-based, and model-based feedback. First, a computer program can analyze a student utterance and display the features visually, perhaps with a comparison to that of a native speaker. The program can also display the position and movements of the tongue when a student produces an utterance, which can also be displayed in comparison to that of native speakers. Second, computer programs can compare student pronunciation of individual words or sentences to prerecorded templates. For example, good agreement ($r = 0.81$ for high quality speech and $r = 0.76$ for telephone-quality speech) was found between automatic and human grading of the pronunciation of English sentences produced by Japanese English learners (Bernstein, Cohen, Murveit, Rtischev, & Weintraub, 1990). More recent studies have found different levels of correlation between machine and human graders: from 0.44 to 0.85 (Bernstein, 1997; Ehsani & Knodt, 1998). Coniam (1998) also found that such high correlation can be achieved at the discourse level. Third, pronunciation can be evaluated against pronunciation models. In this approach, student pronunciation is not limited to preselected words because the model is a generalization of a template.

Tracking and analyzing student errors and behaviors. Tracking and analyzing student errors and behaviors is another approach language educators have experimented with to provide more helpful feedback. Computer programs can store student responses, which can then be analyzed either by a human instructor (Sinyor, 1997) or the computer (Nagata, 1993). The effectiveness of this approach remains to be determined although Nagata, summarizing her research findings, suggests 'traditional feedback may be as good as the intelligent feedback for helping learners to correct word-level errors (e.g., vocabulary and conjugation errors), while the intelligent feedback may be more helpful for understanding and correcting sentence level errors (e.g., particle errors)' (p. 337).

Integrating Technology in the Language Classroom
As mentioned before most of the empirical studies were about a single application used in a few days. We were fortunate to have found two articles that evaluated the effectiveness of more comprehensive uses of technology over a longer period of time (Adair-Hauk, Willingham-McLain, & Youngs, 2000; Green & Youngs, 2001). These efforts were all carried out at Carnegie Mellon University. The first study (Adair-Hauk et al., 2000) was conducted in 1996, and the second study took place in Fall 1998 and Spring 1999 (Green & Youngs, 2001). Participants of the first study were second-semester French students and those of the second study were first-semester French students and first- and second-semester German students. Both studies followed the same format: the treatment group participated in technology-enhanced language learning activities, while the control group attended a regular class for one of the class periods each week. The technological applications included computerized multimedia grammar and vocabulary exercises, instructional video, online spell checker, French-

English glossary, and the web. Measures of listening, reading, writing, cultural knowledge, and student attitudes were taken during the course of both studies. Speaking was assessed in the first study. The findings are summarized below.

1. For study 1, when change over time was considered, there was no significant difference between the treatment group and the control group in cultural knowledge, speaking or listening. For study 2, there was no significant difference in any of the skills measured (cultural knowledge, listening, reading, and writing) ($p < 0.05$).

2. However, the difference in writing was significant in study 1. The control group's homework writing scores decreased, while the treatment group's increased. Writing test scores also indicate a significant difference between the two groups favoring the treatment group ($p < 0.001$). The treatment group also scored significantly better than the control group in reading ($p < 0.001$).

3. Both studies found that students in the treatment group spent about the same amount of time completing the tasks as their peers in the control group.

Both studies concluded that technology-supported independent language learning is as effective as classroom instruction, if not more.

In order to gain a better sense of the overall effectiveness of technology applications in language learning, a meta-analysis was conducted of the studies that included enough data for such an analysis. Meta-analysis is the analysis of analyses – a statistical technique for aggregating the results of multiple experimental studies (Glass, 1976, 1977; Hedges & Olkin, 1985; Lyons, 1995a). The result of each identified study is converted into a measure called effect size. An effect size is obtained by transforming the findings from each study into a standard deviation unit. The effect size indicates the extent to which experimental and control groups differ in the means of a dependent variable at the end of a treatment phase. An effect size (d) is calculated as the difference between the means of the treatment group and the control group divided by the pooled standard deviation.

For the meta-analysis presented here, more than one effect sizes was calculated for several studies because they had more than one measure (e.g., listening, reading, and writing). But in order to satisfy the independence assumption of meta-analysis (Hedges & Olkin, 1985), only one effect size per study was entered into the study. When two or more effect sizes were calculated, they were averaged. The effect sizes used in this analysis are weighted ds, which corrected sample size biases (Hedges & Olkin, 1985).

The calculation was performed using Meta-analysis Calculator (Lyons, 1995b), a computer program designed for meta-analyses. Table 4.1 summarizes the results of the meta-analysis study.

Table 4.1. Overall Effect of Technology Applications in Language Learning

Analysis	K	N	Mean Weighted d	Standard Dviation	95% Confidence level for d
Averaged	9	419	+1.12	0.78	0.61 to 1.63
All	29	1045	+0.81	0.72	0.55 to 1.07

Notes: Averaged shows the result when only one averaged effect size was included per study, while All shows the result when all effect sizes are included. K = number of effect sizes. N = number of subjects. The number of subjects was repeatedly counted for each effect size for studies that used multiple measures.

As Table 4.1 shows, the mean effect size of the nine studies is quite large, indicating an overwhelmingly positive effect of technology applications on language learning. The confidence interval at the 0.05 level further confirms this finding. Thus judging from this analysis, it is reasonable to conclude that technology has been shown by the published empirical studies to be very effective in improving student language learning. What is worth mentioning is that this analysis put all technologies and their various applications in language learning together. It did not differentiate among the areas of improvement in the target language either. In other words, this is a summary of the empirical findings of the effects of a variety of technological applications on virtually all aspects of language learning (e.g., vocabulary, grammar, reading, listening, writing, speaking, and cultural understanding.). Table 4.2 summarizes the technological applications and measures under investigation in the nine studies comprising the meta-analysis sample.

Table 4.2. Summary of Technology and Content of Studies

Study	Technology	Content	D	Target Language
Adair-Hauck et al. (2000)	web, video	listening, reading, writing, speaking, culture	0.28	German
Al-Seghayer (2001)	computer, video, image	vocabulary	1.11	ESL

Cahill & Catanzaro (1997)	online/phone/chat	writing	1.13	Spanish
Harless et al. (1999)	speech recognition, video	listening, speaking, reading	1.44	Arabic
Herron et al. (1999)	video	culture	2.82	French
Herron et al. (1999)	video	culture	1.61	French
Labrie (2000)	web tutor	vocabulary	0.38	French
Nutta (1998)	computer-assisted instruction	grammar	0.56	ESL
Wevers (1999)	video	listening, speaking	+0.76	Spanish

Discussion and Conclusions

This review study was conducted to achieve three goals: (a) to assess the over-all effectiveness of uses of technology in language education through meta-analysis, (b) to explore patterns of recent efforts in using technology to improve language learning, and (c) to identify effective ways to use technology in language education. In this final section, the findings of the study are summarized and their implications are discussed for future research and development efforts in technology supported language education.

In terms of overall effectiveness of technology on language learning, there is evidence suggesting that technology-based language instruction can be as effective as teacher-delivered instruction. Although the number of available experimental studies is limited, a consistent pattern of positive effects is found across the studies. However, this finding should be interpreted with extreme caution for a number of reasons, in addition to the limited number of studies. First, there may be a tendency for journals to publish studies that report significant positive gains. In other words, studies that found less significant or even negative effect of technology may not have been published. While there is no simple way to verify this assumption, it is to some extent supported by a recent meta-analysis study about the effects of social contexts on computer uses in learning, which found that published studies have a bigger effect size than unpublished studies (Lou et al., 2001). Second, most of the studies had fairly small sample sizes and rarely employed random sampling. Third, the fact that all studies were conducted on college students and adult learners raises questions about the generalizability of the finding to other language learners who may differ in motivation, language background, learning style and ability, and instructional context. For instance, it is very likely that college students are generally more motivated and better learners than K-12 students as a whole. Lastly, in most cases, the researchers of these studies were also the instructors who designed, implemented, and evaluated the technology uses. It is conceivable that the classical 'Pygmalion effect' (Rosenthal, 1973) could affect the results. It is also the case that most of the instruments were designed by the researchers, who were also the instructors, instead of independent standardized instruments. It is possible that these measures might have a bias in favor of conditions where technology was applied.

This review found that recent efforts in applying technology in language education share three interesting characteristics. First, many of these efforts were carried out by individual instructors or small groups of individual instructors with limited resources. Consequently, efforts were of smaller scale. Very often only individual technology was used to affect a very specific part of language education. The review found a very limited number of efforts that attempted comprehensive applications of multiple technologies to the whole process of language education. Second, most efforts involved the development of products which then were used in language teaching. Commercially available language software or tools were rarely used in these studies. As a result, the review found many publications describing the development process, while only few articles reported the effectiveness of these products. In the meantime, the numerous commercial products readily available and widely used in classrooms were not studied. Third, the review found that in general current attempts to use technology in language education were not connected and ignored the language learning at the precollege level. This finding is very surprising, especially viewed in the context of technology applications on other content areas, such as mathematics and science, where a large number of studies of technology applications were conducted at the K-12 level.

What are effective uses of technology in language education? This review shows that the application of technologies can be effective in almost all areas of language education. Modern technology can help enhance the quality of input, authenticity of communication, and provide more relevant and useful feedback. In particular, communication technologies such as the Internet and satellite television have been found to be widely used as a way to bring authentic materials into the classroom, involve learners in more authentic communications with distant audiences, and provide researchers the opportunity to better examine the language learning process. Additionally speech technology, while still not quite ready for full implementation for language education, has already been shown its potential for supporting language learning.

Findings from this review study have significant implications for future work. It is apparent from the literature review that technology, when used properly, can have a positive effect on language learning. It is also apparent that the availability and capacities of information technologies have not been fully taken advantage of by language students or educators. To truly capitalize on modern information and communication technologies to significantly improve language learning, a number of issues must be addressed.

Issue 1: Comprehensive and systematic development of curriculum and content

Technology capacities need to be translated into pedagogical solutions and realized in the forms of curriculum and content for language learners. Current uses of technology, as revealed by the literature review, are fragmented and isolated. There are very few comprehensive technology-based curricula that fully take advantage of the power of available technologies. Thus, in the future, what is needed is the development of full curricula that are supported by available technologies instead of individual tools that are only used infrequently or as a supplement to a primarily print-material-based curriculum.

Issue 2: Basic research to explore effective ways of using technology

The effectiveness of technology on language learning is dependent on how it is used. Certain technologies are more suitable than others for certain learning tasks for certain learners. Therefore research about appropriate ways and contexts of technology use is much needed (Salaberry, 2001).

Issue 3: Technology uses in the classroom

Technology is underutilized in classrooms (Cuban, 2001). The finding that none of the studies found in the major language education and technology journals is about technology use in K-12 classrooms is shocking because studies of technology applications in other subject areas (e.g., mathematics, science, social studies, and language arts) have taken place in mainly K-12 classrooms. The fact that almost all the authors of the reported studies were also the instructors in the experiments suggests a possible explanation: K-12 teachers are not using technology in their teaching and there is a lack of interest among university researchers in studying technology applications in K-12 language classrooms. This finding raises two issues: how to promote technology use in K-12 classrooms and how to encourage more research about technology use in K-12 language classes.

Issue 4: Large scale systematic empirical evaluation of technology uses in schools

There is a clear lack of systematic empirical evaluation efforts to assess the effectiveness of large scale comprehensive uses of technology to support language learning. This, of course, may be accounted for by the lack of large-scale implementation efforts. However, it may also be the result of an overall emphasis on the process rather than result of using technology in language learning. As mentioned earlier in this paper, there was a shift among researchers of language education in the mid-1980s from product-oriented research to more process-oriented research which focuses on understanding how students learn instead of what and how much they learn. For example, many studies on CMC have been about the nature and patterns of student participation in online interactions rather than how much their language skills have improved. While such research is necessary and important, we cannot ignore the practical question of how and in what ways technology uses are effective in improving language learning.

References

Adair-Hauk, B., Willingham-McLain, L., & Youngs, B. E. (2000). Evaluating the integration of technology and second language learning. *CALICO Journal, 17*(2), 269–305.

Al-Seghayer, K. (2001). The effect of multimedia annotation modes on L2 vocabulary acquisition: A comparative study. *Language Learning & Technology, 5*(1), 202–232. Retrieved from http://llt.msu.edu/vol5num1/alseghayer/default.html

Bacon, S., & Finnemann, M. (1990). A study of the attitudes, motives, and strategies of university foreign language students and their disposition to authentic oral and written input. *The Modern Language Journal, 74*, 459–473.

Beauvois, M. H. (1997). Computer-mediated communication (CMC): Technology for improving speaking and writing. In R. M. Terry (Ed.), *Technology enhanced language learning* (pp. 165–184). Lincolnwood, IL: The National Textbook Company.

Bernstein, J. (1997). *Automatic spoken language assessment by telephone* (Tech. Rep. No. 5–97). Menlo Park, CA: Entropic, Inc.

Bernstein, J., Cohen, M., Murveit, H., Rtischev, D., & Weintraub, M. (1990). *Automatic evaluation and training in English pronunciation*. Paper presented at the International Conference on Spoken Language Processing (ICSLP), Kobe, Japan.

Bernstein, J., Najmi, A., & Ehsani, F. (1999). Subarashii: Encounters in Japanese spoken language education. *CALICO Journal, 16*(3), 361–384.

Burston, J. (2001). Exploiting the potential of a computer-based grammar checker in conjunction with self-monitoring strategies with advanced level students of French. *CALICO Journal, 18*(3), 499–515.

Cahill, D., & Catanzaro, D. (1997). Teaching first-year Spanish online. *CALICO Journal, 14*(2–4), 97–114.

Cavanaugh, C. S. (2001). The effectiveness of interactive distance education technologies in K-12 learning: A meta-analysis. *International Journal of Educational Telecommunications, 7*(1), 73–88.

Chao, C.-C. (1999). Theory and research: New emphases of assessment in the language learning classroom. In E. Hanson-Smith (Ed.), *CALL Environments: Research, practice, and critical issues* (pp. 243–256). Alexandria, VA: TESOL.

Chapelle, C. A. (1997). CALL in the year 2000: Still in search of research paradigms. *Language Learning & Technology, 1*(1), 19–43. Retrieved from http://llt.msu.edu/vol1num1/chapelle/default.html

Chapelle, C. A. (2001). *Computer applications in second language acquisition: Foundations for teaching, testing, and research.* Cambridge: Cambridge University Press.

Chun, D. M., & Plass, J. L. (1997). Research on text comprehension in multimedia environments. *Language Learning & Technology, 1*(1), 60–81. Retrieved from http://llt.msu.edu/vol1num1/chun_plass/default.html

Coniam, D. (1998). The use of speech recognition software as an English language oral assessment instrument: An exploratory study. *CALICO Journal, 15*(4), 7–24.

Cuban, L. (2001). *Oversold and underused: Computers in schools 1980–2000.* Cambridge, MA: Harvard University Press.

Dalby, J., & Kewley-Port, D. (1999). Explicit pronunciation training using automatic speech recognition technology. *CALICO Journal, 16*(3), 425–445.

Egan, K. B. (1999). Speaking: A critical skill and a challenge. *CALICO Journal, 16*(3), 277–293.

Egbert, J., Chao, C.-C., & Hanson-Smith, E. (1999). Computer-enhanced language learning environment: An overview. In E. Hanson-Smith (Ed.), *CALL environments: Research, practice and critical issues* (pp. 1–16). Alexandria, VA: TESOL.

Ehsani, F., & Knodt, E. (1998). Speech technology in computer-aided language learning: Strengths and limitations of a new CALL paradigm. *Language Learning & Technology, 2*(1), 45–60. Retrieved from http://llt.msu.edu/vol2num1/article3/index.html

Eskenazi, M. (1999). Using a computer in foreign language pronunciation training: What advantages? *CALICO Journal, 16*(3), 447–469.

Glass, G. (1976). Primary, secondary and meta-analysis of research. *Educational Researcher, 5*, 3–8.

Glass, G. (1977). Integrating findings: The meta-analysis of research. *Review of Research in Education, 5*, 351–379.

Gonzalez-Bueno, M. (1998). The effects of electronic mail on Spanish L2 discourse. *Language Learning & Technology, 1*(2), 55–70. Retrieved from http://llt.msu.edu/vol1num2/article3/default.html

Green, A., & Youngs, B. E. (2001). Using the web in elementary French and German courses: Quantitative and qualitative study results. *CALICO Journal, 19*(1), 89–123.

Hanson-Smith, E. (1999). Classroom practice: Using multimedia for input and interaction in CALL environments. In E. Hanson-Smith (Ed.), *CALL environments: research, practice, and critical issues* (pp. 189–215). Alexandria, VA: TESOL.

Harless, W. G., Zier, M. A., & Duncan, R. C. (1999). Virtual dialogues with native speakers: The evaluation of an interactive multimedia method. *CALICO Journal, 16*(3), 313–337.

Hedges, L. V., & Olkin, I. (1985). *Statistical methods for meta-analysis*. Orlando, FL: Academic Press.

Herron, C., Cole, S. P., Corrie, C., & Dubreil, S. (1999). The effectiveness of a video-based curriculum in teaching culture. *The Modern Language Journal, 83*(4), 518–533.

Herron, C., Dubreil, S., Cole, S. P., & Corrie, C. (2000). Using instructional video to teach culture to beginning foreign language students. *CALICO Journal, 17*(3), 395–430.

Holland, V. M., Kaplan, J. D., & Sabol, M. A. (1999). Preliminary tests of language learning in a speech-interactive graphics microworld. *CALICO Journal, 16*(3), 339–359.

Jacobs, G., & Rodgers, C. (1999). Treacherous allies: Foreign language grammar checkers. *CALICO Journal, 16*(4), 509–529.

Johnson, B. (1999). Theory and research: Audience, language use, and language learning. In E. Hanson-Smith (Ed.), *CALL environments: Research, practice, and critical issues* (pp. 55–64). Alexandria, VA: TESOL.

Kelm, O. R. (1998). The use of electronic mail in foreign language classes. In K. Arens (Ed.), *Language learning online* (pp. 141–154). Austin, TX: The Daedalus Group Inc.

Kitajima, R., & Lyman-Hager, M. A. (1998). Theory-driven use of digital video in foreign language instruction. *CALICO Journal, 16*(1), 37–48.

Krashen, S. (1985). *The input hypothesis: Issues and implications*. London: Longman.

Labrie, G. (2000). A French vocabulary tutor for the web. *CALICO Journal, 17*(3), 475–499.

Lafford, P. A., & Lafford, B. A. (1997). Learning language and culture with the Internet. In R. M. Terry (Ed.), *Technology-enhanced language learning*. Lincolnwood, IL: The National Textbook Company.

LaRocca, S. A., Morgan, J. J., & Bellinger, S. M. (1999). On the path to 2X learning: Exploring the possibilities of advanced speech recognition. *CALICO Journal, 16*(3), 295–309.

Lee, L. (1998). Going beyond classroom learning: Acquiring cultural knowledge via online newspapers and intercultural exchanges via online chatrooms. *CALICO Journal, 16*(2), 101–120.

Levy, M. (1997). *Computer-assisted language learning: Context and conceptualization*. Oxford: Oxford University Press.

Lou, Y., Abrami, P. C., & d'Apollonia, S. (2001). Small group and individual learning with technology: A meta-analysis. *Review of Educational Research, 71*(3), 449–521.

Lyman-Hager, M. A. (2000). Bridging the language-literature gap: Introducing literature electronically to the undergraduate language student. *CALICO Journal, 17*(3), 431–452.

Lyons, L. C. (1995a). *Meta-analysis: Methods of accumulating results across research domains [web]*. Retrieved December 20, 2001, from http://www.mnsinc.com/solomon

Lyons, L. C. (1995b). *The meta-analysis calculator: A SuperCard project for con-*

ducting a meta-analysis based on Hunter, Schmidt, and Jackson (1982) and Hunter and Schmidt (1990) (Version 1.0). Manassas, VA: Author.

Mostow, J., & Aist, G. (1999). Giving help and praise in a reading tutor with imperfect listening – Because automated speech recognition means never being able to say you're certain. *CALICO Journal, 16*(3), 407–424.

Muyskens, J. A. (1998). *New ways of learning and teaching: Focus on technology and foreign language education.* Boston, MA: Heinle & Heinle.

Nagata, N. (1993). Intelligent computer feedback for second language acquisition. *The Modern Language Journal, 77*, 330–339.

Nutta, J. (1998). Is computer-based grammar instruction as effective as teacher-directed grammar instruction for teaching L2 structures? *CALICO Journal, 16*(1), 49–61.

Pellettieri, J. (2000). Negotiation in cyberspace: The role of chatting in the development of grammatical competence. In R. Kern (Ed.), *Network-based language teaching: Concepts and practice* (pp. 59–86). Cambridge: Cambridge University Press.

Pennington, M. C. (1996). The power of the computer in language education. In M. C. Pennington (Ed.), *The power of CALL* (pp. 1–14). Houston, TX: Athelstan.

President's Committee of Advisors on Science and Technology (Panel on Educational Technology). (1997). *Report to the president on the use of technology to strengthen K-12 education in the United States.* Washington, DC: President's Committee of Advisors on Science and Technology.

Rosenthal, R. (1973). The Pygmalion effect lives. *Psychology Today, 7*(4), 56–60.

Salaberry, M. R. (2001). The use of technology for second language learning and teaching: A retrospective. *The Modern Language Journal, 85*(1), 39–56.

Schultz, J. M. (2000). Computers and collaborative writing in the foreign language curriculum. In R. Kern (Ed.), *Network-based language teaching: Concepts and practice* (pp. 121–150). Cambridge: Cambridge University Press.

Shea, P. (2000). Leveling the playing field: A study of captioned interactive video for second language learning. *Journal of Educational Computing Research, 22*(3), 243–263.

Sinyor, R. (1997). An analysis of student behavior and error sources in an Italian CALL context. *CALICO Journal, 14*(2–4), 35–50.

Thorton, P., & Dudley, A. (1996). The CALL environment: An alternative to the language lab. *CAELL Journal, 7*(4), 29–34.

Wachowicz, K. A., & Scott, B. (1999). Software that listens: It's not a question of whether, it's a question of how. *CALICO Journal, 16*(3), 253–276.

Warschauer, M. (1998). Researching technology in TESOL: Determinist, instrumental, and critical approaches. *TESOL Quarterly, 32*(4), 757–761.

Warschauer, M., & Kern, R. (2000). *Network-based language teaching.* Cambridge: Cambridge University Press.

Weyers, J. R. (1999). The effects of authentic video on communicative competence. *The Modern Language Journal, 83*(3), 339–349.

Zhao, Y. (1997). The effects of listener's control of speech rate on second language comprehension. *Applied Linguistics, 18*(1), 49–68.

5   Evolutionary Trajectories, Internet-mediated Expression, and Language Education

Steve L. Thorne* and J. Scott Payne**

Introduction

This article provides a critical review of current trends in the use of technology in second and foreign language (L2) education. It also presents a preview that enumerates a number of nascent or near-future possibilities in this area. To help set the appropriate interpretive frame for readers, we wish to state at the start that this is a kinetic thought piece in which discussion ranges from demography to cognitive neuroscience, from Internet-mediated intercultural communication to podcasting, and from emerging Internet communication tools to evolving and contingent pedagogies. Our aspiration is to provide a synoptic discussion of factors relevant to L2 learning mediated by communication technologies. Our challenge is to balance

* Steve Thorne is the Associate Director of the Center for Language Acquisition, Associate Director of the Center for Advanced Language Proficiency Education and Research (a National Foreign Language Resource Center), and Assistant Professor in Linguistics and Applied Language Studies at The Pennsylvania State University. His research addresses activity theory, additional language learning, and computer-mediated communication.

** J. Scott Payne (Ph.D. Washington State University) is Senior Lecturer in the Department of Linguistics and Applied Language Studies, Assistant Director for Technology and Research at the Center for Language Acquisition, and Co-Director of the Technology Project under the Center for Advanced Language Proficiency Education and Research (CALPER) at The Pennsylvania State University. His research and publications have focused on the intersection between technology and SLA theory and practice with particular attention to the role that individual differences in working memory capacity play in computer-mediated language learning. He is also actively engaged in the development of web applications to support psycholinguistic and corpus-based SLA research and CALL.

significant framing questions and issues with details and concrete examples and, in so doing, to provide an article that stands on its own while also acting as a broad introduction to this special issue of the *CALICO Journal* on computer-mediated communication in the L2 educational arena.

For applied linguists, second and foreign language (L2) researchers, language educators, program administrators, technologists, and perhaps especially for the CALICO readership that includes individuals sharing many of these interests, we have entered an historical period marked by radical transitions in how everyday communicative activity is carried out. These transitions include emerging genres of language use, an increase and diversification in patterns of information consumption, powerful possibilities for producing and disseminating information, and changes in the granularity of information sharing between spatially dispersed coworkers, friends, and family members. In educational contexts, information and communication are transmitted through an abundance of qualitatively distinctive channels to groups that often include an array of copresent as well as distributed participants, and the work students produce in these channels may vary significantly from traditional forms such as essays, paper-and-pencil tests, and term papers. And none of this is particularly noteworthy, at least not to those who directly participate in such practices on a daily basis. Within affluent regions of the world, and for affluent social classes on a global scale, this is how things are done now (for a current and sophisticated discussion of the digital divide, see van Dijk, 2005). Blended courses now include many elements that only a few years ago were only to be found in distance education contexts. Distance education may include a few weekends of face-to-face interaction over the course of a semester. Residential instruction can take the form of self-paced and solitary movement through sequenced materials with occasional interaction with an instructor. With each of these possibilities comes the question of how educational processes and outcomes relate to one another and what kind of role technology might play.

It is also clear that, unlike the CMC L2 research of the 1990s, where the use of the Internet was often treated as a proxy or heuristic to assist with the development of communicative performance within the primary foci of foreign language instruction (i.e., face-to-face communication, aural comprehension, and nondigital epistolary conventions such as letter and essay writing), Internet-mediated communication is now a high-stakes environment in its own right. Business and work activity is conducted via asynchronous and synchronous channels, interviews occur via instant messaging, educational activity is increasingly mediated by course management systems that include email, threaded discussion, and chat, while blogs and wikis, among other technologies, are increasingly incorporated into general education and L2 course activities. Furthermore, with the proliferation of digital multimedia technologies (e.g., digital video cameras and video editing software, web publishing technologies that support audio and video, and cell phones that record still images and video), computer-generated and computer-mediated communication now includes a multiplicity of devices and media that extend far beyond the apparatus conventionally referred to as a computer.

This article explores the evolution of new technologies and the pedagogies that they have engendered and continue to support. We begin, however, with two background sections: the first provides an overview of synchronous computer-mediated communication (SCMC) L2 research, and the second describes increasingly prevalent uses of the Internet to mediate intercultural communication for purposes of L2 learning. We then develop a larger frame of reference for understanding technology-mediated L2 learning and use that brings together historical shifts in technology use, demographics, and what it might mean in the early twenty-first century to be a highly competent communicator. Next we describe and interrogate recently evolved technologies and environments such as blogs, wikis, podcasting, device-agnostic forms of CMC, and advances in intelligent computer-assisted language learning (ICALL). Throughout, we engage in a discussion of praxeological fusions of various media technologies, pedagogical orientations to their use, and the implications of this nexus of practice for the transformation of what it means to teach, learn, and communicate.

A Brief History of Scmc L2 Research

From the early through the mid-1990s, the use of SCMC, commonly referred to as *chat* in foreign language education, was in an exploratory phase. During this period, a flurry of studies in the SLA literature provided an amalgam of anecdotal and empirical evidence suggesting a number of pedagogical benefits for language learning (Kelm, 1992; Beauvois, 1992; Cononelos & Oliva, 1993; Nicholas & Toporski, 1993). The studies of Kern (1995) and Chun (1994) are widely regarded as some of the strongest of the early SCMC studies. Kern (1995) quantitatively assessed the impression that foreign language students communicate more in SCMC environments than they do in large groups in face-to-face classroom settings. Using a quasi-experimental methodology (holding constant students, time period, and topic across SCMC and face-to-face conditions), Kern compiled the following statistics from data from a second-semester French course. From a 50-minute SCMC (using *Daedalus InterChange*) session on the topic of legalizing the French RU 486 abortion pill in the

US, the total number of student messages was 172, teacher messages were zero, and each student averaged 12.3 messages for the period. In comparison, an oral discussion by the same students on the same topic produced 95 student turns at talk and 116 instructor turns, resulting in an average student production of 5.3 turns. In sum, the SCMC treatment produced between two and three times more turns per student and a higher total number of sentences and words compared to the large group oral discussion. Kern states that 'compared to oral discussions, InterChange was found to offer more frequent opportunities for student expression and to lead to more language production' (p 470) (for current research in this area, see Abrams, 2003).

Kern also examined the linguistic quality of the SCMC discussions and concluded that 'students' language output was at an overall greater level of sophistication in terms of the range of its morphosyntactic features and in terms of the variety of discourse functions expressed' (p. 470) (see also Warschauer, 1996; Böhlke, 2003, for similar results). These findings are supported by Chun's (1994) study of fourth-semester German students. Chun concluded that SCMC use promoted increased morphological complexity in non-SCMC written work over the course of the semester (specifically a greater ratio of complex sentences). In agreement with Kern's findings, Chun's students used a wide array of discourse features in their use of SCMC discussions. More recent research has also suggested that SCMC language use is more accurate than that of face-to-face interaction (Salaberry, 2000).

While Kern and Chun's research on L2 uses of large-group SCMC have demonstrable strengths, Ortega (1997) has noted limitations to comparing computer-mediated classroom and whole-class oral discussions. Ortega posited that the variables of group size and communicative task were not accounted for in the early SCMC research (e.g., Beauvois, 1992; Chun, 1994; Kelm, 1992; Kern, 1995). She argued that it is justified to hypothesize that group size and equality of participation are negatively related in traditional oral interactions and positively related in computer-assisted interactions, and that the benefits of electronic over non-electronic interactions will increase with the size of groups ... In other words, the positive equalizing effect of the electronic mode will be accentuated when comparing larger groups, as in the comparisons of teacher-fronted, whole-class discussion with whole-class electronic discussion (p. 86).

While this observation in no way obviates early SCMC research efforts, it calls for closer attention to key pedagogical and group size variables and also sets the stage for future work that examines the possibility of cross-modality transfer between SCMC use and oral language production.

Indeed, one of the enticing characteristics of chat for language teachers and learners has been its seeming resemblance to oral conversational exchange (e.g., Chun, 1994; for an argument against this claim, see Johanyek, 1997; see also Yates, 1996). Since a major goal of foreign language instruction is the development of oral conversational ability, the possible connection between spontaneous L2 language production via text and speech has been a longstanding focus of L2 SCMC research (Beauvois, 1997; Payne & Whitney, 2002; Abrams, 2003; Kost, 2004; Payne & Ross, 2005). Several of these studies have employed quasi-experimental designs to compare the language produced by learners in face-to-face and online settings with respect to the volume of output, frequency of specific linguistic features, and complexity of syntax. These studies specifically asked: Can learners improve their L2 speaking ability through L2 conversation via text? Payne and Whitney (2002) investigated this question by drawing on a psycholinguistic model of language production (Levelt, 1989), together with concepts from working memory theory, to formulate principled hypotheses and predictions about the nature of cross-modality transfer. Their findings showed a significant difference in the oral proficiency gains between experimental (+SCMC) and control (−SCMC) groups. In an extension of this research, emerging CMC tools that support bimodal chat (i.e., a combination of both text and voice chat) may prove promising as an environment for future exploration of these issues (see Blake, this issue, for a report on bimodal chat).

A substantial strand of SCMC research has examined negotiation of meaning from within the interactionist approach to second language acquisition. The interactionist hypothesis is that nonnative speakers may experience (or be given tasks that precipitate) communicative breakdowns that require negotiation to resolve. The negotiation process can include modifications on linguistic and interactional levels, and these modifications are presumed to increase the comprehensibility of the talk at hand (e.g., Long, 1985; Pica, 1987; Varonis & Gass, 1985). This 'comprehensible input' (Krashen, 1982) has been argued to promote the development of a learner's interlanguage. The notion of communicative output, first discussed by Swain (1985), offers a correction to the emphasis on communicative input by claiming that input is decipherable through largely semantic processing while output requires the communicator to syntactically parse and process the target language. These dimensions to communicative output are hypothesized to promote conscious attention to morphological and syntactic form, which, in turn, is argued to foster interlanguage development (e.g., Long, 1996; Schmidt, 1990).

A number of studies have taken the interactionist model, designed for analysis of oral interaction, and applied it to CMC learner data and task configurations. Pellettieri's (2000) research in Spanish (using Unix-based *YTalk*), to take one example, contrasts with the aforementioned research of Kern (1995), Chun (1994), and Beauvois (1992) in a few important respects. Whereas most research on L2 uses of SCMC had examined larger group interaction in relatively open discussions on various topics, Pellettieri focused on dyads engaged in primarily closed tasks (e.g., jigsaw tasks). Pellettieri concluded that dyadic groupings, in opposition to small and large group interaction, promoted an increase in corrective feedback and negotiation at all levels of discourse. This, in turn, prompted learners to produce form-focused modifications to their turns. Additionally, task type, specifically goal-oriented closed tasks, was positively correlated to the quantity and type of negotiations produced. In a similar study from the same period, Blake (2000) assessed the SCMC interactions of 50 intermediate learners of Spanish. Participants were arranged in dyads and asked to carry out three task types: decision making, information gap, and jigsaw. Like Pellettieri, Blake found that jigsaw tasks produced the greatest number of negotiations, but nearly all negotiations were lexical in focus, with very few negotiations addressing problems in syntax or larger units of discourse. Building on this earlier research, Smith (2003, 2004) confirmed that task type affected the extent to which learners engaged in negotiation. Significantly however, Smith also expanded the Varonis and Gass (1985) four-part model of face-to-face negotiated interaction – 1) trigger > 2) indicator > 3) response > 4) optional reaction to response – by explicitly incorporating two additional phases to represent delayed reactions to response turns that are so frequent in SCMC discourse. Smith terms these phases *confirmation* and *reconfirmation*, elements that explicitly conclude a given negotiation routine and which act as discourse markers suggesting the possibility of resuming nonnegotiation interaction (2003). Smith's careful incorporation of prior interactionist studies and development of an expanded model of computer-mediated negotiated interaction, along with other CMC specific adaptations of discourse analysis (Herring, 2001) and conversation analysis (Thorne, 2000), form a foundation for the continued development of analytic tools to support L2 CMC research.

We conclude this overview of CMC L2 research with a discussion of internet-mediated intercultural communication for foreign language learning or 'intercultural foreign language learning' (ICFLL). While such pedagogical efforts are typically and necessarily carried out using well established communication tools, and so are not particularly noteworthy in terms of pushing new technological frontiers, ICFLL presents to the foreign language learning enterprise a dynamic, if also challenging and problematic, paradigm shift.

Internet-mediated Intercultural Communication in Foreign Language Education

The conceptualization of foreign language learning and use as foremost a process of intercultural communication, in both online and offline contexts, has received significant attention in recent years (e.g., Belz, 2002, 2004; Belz & Thorne, 2005; Byram, 1997; Furstenberg, Levet, English, & Maillet, 2001; Kinginger, 1998, 2004; Kramsch & Thorne, 2002; Müller-Hartmann, 2000; O'Dowd, 2003; Tudini, 2003; Thorne, 2003a, 2005). Whether explicitly referenced or implicitly foundational, much (though not all) of this work builds upon prior research in L2 pragmatics (Kasper & Rose, 1999), intercultural communication theory (e.g., Scollon & Scollon, 1995), and/or research that describes language and culture as essentially inseparable and mutually constructive phenomena (e.g., Agar, 1994; Kramsch, 1993, 1998). Internet-mediated intercultural communication used to promote L2 learning has antecedents in earlier traditions such as the educational model developed early in the 20th century by Célestin Freinet (1994). Freinet's pedagogy included presciently modern methods such as cooperative group work, service learning, and inquiry-based learning, most of which were embedded in correspondence activities with other school children in France and around the world (for information on the still vibrant Freinet movement, see http://www.freinet.org/icem/history.htm). In its modern incarnations, the use of Internet technologies to link internationally distributed partner classes, sometimes termed telecollaboration (Warschauer, 1996; Belz, 2001, 2003; Kinginger, 2004) but which we will more descriptively refer to as intercultural communication for foreign language learning (ICFLL), proposes a compelling shift in pedagogical orientation. Rather than focusing on language per se, in relative isolation from its use in interpersonal interaction, ICFLL emphasizes the use of Internet communication tools to support dialogue, debate, collaborative research, and social interaction between internationally dispersed students. The goals are linguistic and pragmatic development and the heightening of cultural awareness of both one's home culture(s) as well as those of the interlocutors. Though ICFLL can produce tension and frustration as often as camaraderie and friendship (e.g., Belz, 2003; Kramsch & Thorne, 2002; Thorne, 2003a), embedding the learning of a foreign language in the larger context of significant relationship development has demonstrated considerable positive effects, especially in the area of pragmatics.

To take one example of pragmalinguistic learning outcomes in ICFLL, in a series of studies, Belz and Kinginger (2002, 2003) described the development of address forms used in French and German (*tu/vous* and *du/Sie*, hereafter T/V).[1] Current sociolinguistic research indicates that T/V usage has become destabilized in the French and German languages (Morford, 1997; Wylie & Brière as cited in Belz & Kinginger, 2003). Additionally, there is sociopragmatic ambiguity around T/V usage in textbooks and within classroom discourse. In this sense, T/V use is not simply rule governed but is instead embedded in a system of meaning potentials that are realized in particular social interactions. Nearly all of the American participants in these interactions exhibited free variation of T/V at the start of the intercultural communication process. Belz and Kinginger tracked usage over time in both email and SCMC sessions and found that after critical moments within exchanges with expert speaker age peers, the American participants began to systemically modify their usage. These critical moments included explicit feedback and rationales for T form usage from German peers. Additionally, the American students had opportunities to observe appropriate pronoun use by native speakers across synchronous and asynchronous CMC modalities. In this way, pragmatic awareness of T/V as an issue (i.e., 'noticing' Schmidt, 1990, 1993) led to the approximation of expert speaker norms in most cases. Belz and Kinginger argued that the American students were motivated to maintain positive face (wanting to be liked; see Brown & Levinson, 1987) with age peers because the relationships students were developing were significant and meaningful, and they focused students' attention on the role of linguistic form in the performance of pragmatically appropriate communication. In further research, the importance of the social relationships built in these transatlantic partnerships have been linked to positive development of other grammatical and morphological features, namely *da*-compounds in German (Belz, 2004) and modal particles in German (Belz & Vyatkina, 2005).

One of the more striking intercultural interventions within foreign language education is that created by Furstenberg and her colleagues (Bauer et al., 2005; Furstenberg et al., 2001; Furstenberg, 2003). Developed in 1997 and continually modified and expanded since, the CULTURA project is based on the premise that L2 students can develop critical perceptions of both their own as well as another's culture through the structured juxtaposition of texts, the creation and interrogation of lexical and semantic networks, and the contestation associated with the sharing of interpretations of these data by participants in intercultural exchanges. What sets CULTURA apart from other intercultural L2 projects is its significant infrastructural development of web-based materials and activities. Students not only utilize CMC for interaction, but also engage one another through web-based questionnaires in which they make word associations (creating semantic networks), sentence completion exercises, and respond to specific situations.

These responses then form the data that each partner class analyzes in an effort to notice similarities and differences and to hypothesize possible reasons for these convergences and divergences. Opinion polls are also made available so that students can discover where their analyses align within the larger context of population-wide national-level trends and beliefs. Increasingly over the semester, students are presented with a diverse set of parallel texts, including films (e.g., French films and their American remakes), French and American newspaper articles on the same topic but which represent divergent cultural positions, and diverse academic and literary texts. The CULTURA project's constructivist approach supports active engagement on the part of students and instructors alike. As anthropologists have noted for decades, most of what matters in culture operates at subtle levels that are difficult to capture or even to recognize. These facets of culture are 'essentially elusive, abstract, and invisible. Our challenge [with CULTURA] was to make them visible, accessible, and understandable' (Furstenberg et al., 2001: 56). The development of multiple heuristics, material artifacts, pedagogically progressive activities, and the use of Internet information and communication technologies makes the CULTURA project particularly noteworthy as a model of institutionalized L2 learning.

Demographics and Stages of Cmc and Internet Adoption

In affluent regions of the world, individual and institutional uses of communication and information technologies have transformed the daily practices of work, school, and interpersonal engagement. For many, Internet mediation has become an omnipresent feature of ordinary communicative and informational activity. Indeed, when talking to high school and college aged students, it is apparent that social as well as academic lives are critically mediated by participation in digital communities such as Facebook (see http://www.thefacebook.com), blog networks, instant messaging, and voice and text messaging over cell phones.

In this section we turn our attention to current and near-future technologies and communicative practices. We begin by providing a demographic overview of Internet adoption and usage as a way to create a unified frame of reference for understanding the complexities of evolving Internet communication tools, changes in everyday communicative and informational activity, and how these forces are rapidly forging both a problematic gap between student populations and conventional educational practices on the one hand and are opening up possibilities for pedagogical innovation on the other. While we present a three-generation cycle representing early CMC use to its widespread adoption (based on data from North America), we wish to state the caveat that these overlapping phases are informed approximations. Our goal is to present a heuristic for historically contextualizing contemporary Internet use and the opportunities and challenges these demographic shifts present to education generally and L2 learning specifically.

The first broad-scale generation of Internet use spanned from the early 1980s to the early 1990s. Internet users at this time were predominantly members of scientific and computer science communities often associated with universities, government, and the defense industry. The primary communication tool was email, though the synchronous tool Unix *TALK* was also commonly used. Most users had a legitimate work-related reason to use the Internet, but, not surprisingly, social uses of the Internet within professional communities became commonplace (Curtis, 1998).

The second phase began in the early 1990s and extended up through 1997–1998. University-supported accounts for faculty, staff, graduate students (and soon undergraduate students) proliferated. To accommodate growing public demand, AOL, Compuserve, and local providers such as the WELL in the San Francisco Bay Area, expanded their capacity while an increasing number of private-sector and business-oriented Internet Service Providers sprang up to serve general population consumers. K-12 institutions were unevenly networked. Primary Internet communication tools included email and *Internet Relay Chat*, while primary information tools were gopher and USENET in the early 1990s, both of which became anachronistic with the development of the World Wide Web in the mid-1990s. MUDs and MOOs, *ICQ, AOL Instant Messenger*, as well as select other tools became popular among more sophisticated users, but email remained the preferred communication tool for everyday social, educational, and professional purposes. It was also during this phase that discussion of digital communication and information began to permeate the media; newspapers created Internet columns and digital-life weekly sections, cybercrimes were reported on television, and the public became increasingly fascinated by phenomena such as online trysts and dating services. This period was marked by generally utopian discourse positing that 'cyberspace' was a democratic, unconstrained, or less constrained, environment that instantiated many of the tenets of postmodernity (Lanham, 1993; Turkle, 1995); critical (Roszak, 1994; Stoll, 1995) and more anthropologically sophisticated perspectives also emerged (Miller & Slater, 2000). An array of Internet related neologisms were created that proved ephemeral (e.g., Crystal, 2001; see also Thorne, 2003b for commentary), but some, such as cyberspace, virtual and e- as modifiers, proved longer lasting. People often interacted anonymously using pseudonyms, but also formed long-term relationships with others. In the case of Slashdot (http://slashdot.org) for computer geek culture and programmers,

MOOs and MUDs for role playing, and USENET groups for theme and topic-focused discussion, virtual community life was taken very seriously by participants (Dibbell, 1993; Baym, 1996).

The third generation, now upon us, includes people born during or after the mid-1980s and who are socialized in the use of the Internet from early ages. These individuals are the first 'digital natives' – users who have literally grown up with digital literacies and communicative practices (Presky, 2001a). For the first time, email is no longer the primary conduit for everyday social, school, and work interaction. Newer tools, particularly instant messaging (Grinter & Palen, 2002), have become dominant for social and age-peer interaction. Additionally, text messaging and voice communication over cell phones abound, as does individual and group engagement with graphically and thematically sophisticated video computer games. Equivalent in importance is the emergence of ubiquitous computing: the expectation of being able to remain in perpetual contact with peers and family members either through instant messaging or cell phones. As Presky (2001b) described it:

> Our children today are being socialized in a way that is vastly different from their parents. The numbers are overwhelming: over 10,000 hours playing videogames, over 200,000 emails and instant messages sent and received; over 10,000 hours talking on digital cell phones; over 20,000 hours watching TV (a high percentage fast speed MTV), over 500,000 commercials seen – all before the kids leave college. And, maybe, *at the very most*, 5,000 hours of book reading. These are today's 'Digital Native' students. (p. 1)

While Presky noted that these numbers, and we concur with his judgment, are approximations that represent relatively affluent US households and hence may vary significantly across populations and social classes, there is compelling demographic information to support these figures. Four years earlier, Tapscott (1997) proposed a similar scenario and described today's 90 million strong school and university age population as the Net Generation (or 'N-Geners'), a demographic force that thinks, performs, learns, and communicates in ways that qualitatively differ from cohorts born prior to the wide adoption of digital communication and information technologies. Through in-depth online interviews conducted with teenagers who were active participants in *Freezone*[2] (see http://www.freezone. com), Tapscott found that N-Geners could be distinguished from previous generational cohorts in a number of ways. Most relevant for the current discussion is their demonstrated proclivity for multitasking, critical consumption of information, and the unique power position in which they find themselves as purveyors of coveted knowledge (i.e., specialized computer skills). We posit that these characteristics stand at odds with the prevailing norms of educational culture and represent a set of opportunities and challenges for language teachers (at least until digital natives occupy the role of teachers): students will process information and learn differently than their teachers, they will be less accepting of traditional definitions of 'classroom' and 'class participation' and the roles assigned to teachers, and they will use technology as a tool for creative expression and as a means of circumventing institutional structures.

[handwritten margin note: Not sure I agree]

Both Presky and Tapscott's ideas align with a materialist understanding of cognitive functioning that links ontogenetic developmental trajectories to the quality, quantity, and frequency of everyday mental activity. In other words, higher order mental functioning – what we become adept at and accustomed to – develops as a consequence of the cognitive demands of habituated activity. Neuroscience research on synaptic plasticity supports this view. Accepting that heritability also plays a role, recent neuroscience research demonstrates that phylogenetically recent cortical areas of the brain (specifically the prefrontal cortex) are hyperadaptive to use and experience. Joseph LeDoux, a leading authority in the field of cognitive neuroscience, described it this way: 'People don't come preassembled, but are glued together by life' (2002: 3). By this, LeDoux was describing synaptogenesis, the process whereby synaptic connections form in adaptation to experiences such as physical activity, visual perception, and emotional response (see also Damasio, 2003; LeDoux, 1996) and in confrontation with cognitive tasks and problems (for a discussion of the relationship between exposure to schooling and measured gains in fluid intelligence, see Blair, Gamson, Thorne, & Baker, 2005).

[handwritten margin note: CALL + neuroscience]

We apply these two empirically supported arguments – that: (a) cognitive engagement through everyday life experience has radically changed since the early 1990s in affluent parts of the world; and (b) everyday cognitive activity has been shown to dramatically influence synaptic development well into adulthood – to the issue of teaching and learning foreign and second languages. We propose that there now exists an amplification of the conventional 'generation gap' between teachers and students, between school-delivered knowledge and performance necessary for high functioning outside of school, and, most germane to our immediate interests, between top-down processes and pedagogies that operate in formal learning environments and bottom-up life experiences of students in secondary and university environments. This gap has been confirmed by recent research by the Pew Internet and American Life Project (2002) based on focus groups (136 students in gender-balanced and racially diverse clusters) and voluntary participation data (200 students who submitted online essays describing their use of the Internet for school). The 2002 Pew report revealed that while nearly all students used the Internet as a regular part of their educational activities, little is known about how the Internet is actually used for schoolwork nor has there been adequate consideration of Internet use as it might substantively inform school policies, practices, and pedagogies.

The above discussion is meant to contextualize the following exploration of newer technologies and adaptive pedagogies that attempt to balance the resources and performance potentials of the digital-native generation with the knowledge bases, analytic traditions, and conceptual-theoretical frameworks that the institution of education can provide. To be clear, we are advocating for a critical syncretism that engenders engagement and relevance through the utilization of students' digital-literacy expertise but that also provides explicit feedback at the level of linguistic form, exposure to and movement toward mastery of a wide range of communication genres, and conscious and guided reflection on foreign language use and intercultural pragmatics (e.g., Boxer, 2002; Kasper & Rose, 2002).

Recent and Evolving Technologies and their Uses in L2 Education

Blogs and Wikis

Blogs and wikis are considered 'second generation' web applications (Godwin-Jones, 2003) and represent relatively modest technological advancements over their static webpage predecessor, essentially eliminating the use of HTML and FTP from the user's end. Blog and wiki technologies contribute to the argument that big innovations in use can come from relatively minor changes in code. Of the two, blogs are more commonly used by individuals, the media, and organizations and have recently come to play a significant role in public discourse, while wiki technologies create the possibility for collaboratively authored and elaborated textual production that has resulted in extraordinary resources such as wikipedia.com (described below).

Blogs

Web logs, blogging, bloggers, the blogosphere (describing the interconnectedness of blogs with one another and other web resources, see Herring, Kouper, Paolillo, Scheidt, Tyworth, Welsch et al., 2005): contemporary nondigital media such as television and newspapers are bursting with these terms.[3] Blog is a term describing a web application that displays serial entries with date and time stamps. Entries are typically presented in reverse chronological order (most recent first). Most blogs include a comments feature that allows visitors to post responses. While blogging's expressive roots tap the one-to-many dynamic of the personal web page and, by some accounts, the USENET discussion lists of the 1990s (Grohol, 2002), blogging has evolved as a set of social and informational phenomena that include mainstream media as well as grassroots and watchdog news reporting, thematic and topic-specific amateur and professional observations, business and commercial information outlets, and, of course, the 'public' journaling of one's 'private' life.[4] In its short history – the first use of the term blog is variably reported to have occurred in either 1996 or 1997 and blogging as a populist movement dates only from the turn of the millennium – the rise of blogging as a form of communicative and informational expression has been mercurial. To take the example of a popular blog provider that makes public its user statistics, LiveJournal (http://livejournal.com) reports over 7 million blogs created, approximately 5 million of which have been updated at least once. Nearly 1 million of its blogs (931,146) have been updated within the past seven days, while 336,005 have updated within the past 24 hours (posted May 25, 2005). LiveJournal reports that female-presenting bloggers outnumber users presenting as males by approximately two to one (67.3% vs. 32.7%, respectively). The ages of LiveJournal users span from 13 (35,856 blogs created by this age group) to 55 (1,229). The 15–20 year age group produces the majority of the blogs on this site, with a rapid taper occurring in the age range of the mid-20s. This demographic profile aligns with the 'digital natives' generation discussion presented earlier, i.e., that the everyday literacy practices of current high school and college students differ significantly from that of older cohorts.

Whereas many CMC technologies are primarily interactive spaces within which certain users might dominate the flow of communication, we have come to think of blogs as 'I, I, me, me, me' environments. By this characterization, we mean to emphasize the individual ownership of blog spaces. While blogs are often richly interlinked with other media, they are controlled by an individual (or a defined community in the case of a group blog) and therefore explicitly reflect an individual's (or group's) point of view. Within L2 contexts, blogging provides an alternative to writing assignments that would normally be presented only to the instructor. The chronological ordering of blog entries creates for each student an archive of their personal work that they can, and do, revisit and reflect upon. In an in-progress research project, Thorne, Weber, and Bensinger (2005a) followed high school level advanced placement Spanish foreign language students who kept weekly blog entries for a full academic year. Their preliminary analysis of the blog entries, survey data ($N = 18$) and interview data ($N = 12$) indicate that the participants had a strong preference for blogging versus traditional journals or weekly essays. All students interviewed reported that they frequently looked back over their own and others' earlier blog postings, and all but one noticed significant progress in their writing over time. Change in language production included using new phrases, improvements in spelling and the use of accent marks, and an expanded repertoire of verbal conjugations. In interviews, students reported the following: 'my writing has become more fluid,' 'my sentences don't stand alone – I write in paragraphs now,' and 'I use more tenses and make an effort to incorporate whatever we're doing in class, subjunctive, conditional, whatever, into my blogs.' Using activity theory (e.g., Thorne, 2003a, 2004, 2005; Thorne et al., 2005a, 2005b) to analyze interrelations between academic and social-personal CMC use, the researchers also found that blog use formed an interstice communicative space where personal expression manifested both academic and non-academic discursive features. Students were writing both to the instructor to fulfill a class requirement while also writing to and for one another. With creative guidance from the instructor and collaboratively chosen topics and tasks, findings indicated that L2 blog use shows the potential to support the performance of multiple linguistically mediated social identities.[5]

In addition to its intraclass use as a journaling tool, blogging is also being used to link together study abroad students and those still at their home universities. One example, billed as a blog-based 'reality show,' is a partnership between Educational Directories Unlimited and the blog provider Mindsay.com that resulted in the launch of http://www.BlogAbroad.com. This service currently highlights the experiences of three study abroad students (on programs in Chile, Italy, and Senegal), each of whom keeps up a blog that is reportedly read by 500–1,000 students a week, who themselves are interested in participating in an international education program. The students abroad act as the on-site investigators, the 'eyes and ears' for pre-study-abroad students. Similar projects are emerging among the Mellon cluster of 37 liberal arts colleges in the northeast of the US. While still in the exploratory phase, early reports indicate that such uses of blogs could serve a number of functions, such as providing predeparture cultural exposure for students still at their home university, helping students currently abroad to synthesize and put into narrative form their cultural and linguistic experiences, and potentially for creating predeparture orientation materials that represent specific student experiences and points of view.

Wiki

Wiki (from the Hawai'ian *wiki wiki* meaning 'quick') describes a web-based environment that supports collaborative writing. The 'WikiWiki concept' was invented by Ward Cunningham in 1995 with a project called the Portland Pattern Repository, a computer programming site.[6] While blogs are highly personal, 'wikis are intensely collaborative. They feature a loosely structured set of pages, linked in multiple ways to each other and to Internet resources and an open-editing system in which anyone can edit any page (by clicking on the "edit this page" button)' (Godwin-Jones, 2003). The radical dimension to wiki use is its problematization of authorship. In the archetypal wiki, there is no distinction between 'author' and 'audience' per se since anyone who reads a wiki page can spontaneously opt to become its author. Individual wiki pages can be password limited to one or a group of users using an access control list, but wiki technology is premised on the idea of universal write/access. This freedom to create, transform, and destroy provides students with power as well as responsibility. However, many wiki engines track each addition, deletion, and modification. In the waka wiki engine, the tracking feature allows users (students) as well as instructors to precisely identify who made changes, how often, and when. Prior versions of a given page are recoverable so regression to earlier drafts is always available. Within the context of group projects, wikis enable students to adopt a 'revise and roll-back' approach to the collaborative production of text and thus obviate the need to meticulously merge individual contributions in order to avoid deleting one another's work. Furthermore, determining the amount of individual participation in a group project for assessment purposes need not rely exclusively on self and peer-assessments by group members or observational hunches by the teacher. Like an archaeological tell, a given wiki's current content is but the top layer of a temporally stratified stack of texts that precisely display the history of the writing process.

Educational projects utilizing wiki technologies are numerous. For example L*Wiki,[7] supported by Penn State's national foreign language resource center – the Center for Advanced Language Proficiency Education and Research (CALPER) – is used by a variety of groups and language courses, including Chinese, German, Russian, Spanish, English composition, and ESL. Primary uses include individual and collaborative student authoring, course project management, and multiparty running commentaries. Perhaps most dramatically, wiki technology supports a number of shared information repositories that are continually expanding, an exemplar of which is Wikipedia (see http://www.wikipedia.org), an online encyclopedia built by contributors from around the world. Currently there are entries in 199 languages. There are more than 100,000 entries each in German, French, and Japanese and more than 579,000 in English. Dutch, Polish, Spanish, and Swedish each contain more than 50,000 entries, and 14 additional languages have 10,000 or more contributions. In application to educational uses of wiki technology, recent research indicates that despite their potential to transform notions of authorship and processes of writing, wiki use does not necessarily promote the production of heterogeneous genres of text. In fact, a contrary case can be made. Based on a corpus analysis of *Wikipedia and Everything2* (another wiki-based encyclopedia), Emigh and Herring (2005) found that structures of postproduction and editorial control resulted in homogeneous, formal, and standardized text types despite the expectation that multiple authors would produce a diversity of text genres. In application to wiki use in L2 contexts, Emigh and Herring's research suggests that instructors would want to clearly describe to students the purposes of the wiki-writing activity and, where appropriate, carefully structure peer and expert-editing protocols to align with desired learning outcomes and final writing products. As with all technologies described in this article, task design and procedural processes are critical for fostering efficient and focused language-learning activity.

iPod + Broadcasting = Podcasting

As the portmanteau suggests, podcasting is an approach for sharing and indexing mp3 audio content on the Internet to be downloaded and listened to locally on a portable mp3 player (e.g., iPod, hence the name) or computer (see also Lafford & Lafford, this issue). Podcasting can be viewed as another avenue for providing language learners with access to diverse authentic materials, building on the text and imagery available on web pages and discussion forums, as well as the audio and video streamed from Internet radio stations and television networks. Making audio available on the Internet is nothing new; however, the combination of real simple syndication (RSS) technology and applications together with portable mp3 players provides an important twist that makes podcasting a highly effective means of distributing audio (video podcasts are possible, though less frequent) and a promising tool for foreign language education. Heralded as open-source radio (Jardin, 2005a), podcasting has the capability of providing language learners with access to a discourse that diverges from the journalistic genre available through Internet radio stations. Examples include the musings of a married couple living in a farmhouse in Wisconsin to the commentary a catholic priest recorded as he was wandering through areas of the Vatican inaccessible to laypersons (Jardin, 2005b).

Submit the query podcasting + 'foreign language' to Google and it becomes readily apparent that the potential benefit of podcasting to foreign language learning is on the minds of the legions of prognosticators inhabiting the blogosphere. Using 'podcatching' software like *iPodder*, students can set a pointer to a podcasting source and configure *iPodder* so that it automatically checks for updates and downloads new content to an iPod and/or computer. While few examples of the integration of podcasting into foreign language instruction are currently documented, the iPod first-year experience at Duke University provides interesting case studies. Duke University students in Lisa Merschel's elementary Spanish courses, for example, have used the university's iTunes site to download listening materials and audio flash cards for improving pronunciation (e.g., a dramatic reading of Don Juan Tenorio by Duke Spanish instructors, oral comprehension exercises for use in class, and songs). These students have also created a diachronic and potentially developmental oral production portfolio by uploading weekly recordings of their own speech (see http://cit.duke. edu/ideas/newprofiles/merschel.do) In Peter McIsaac's course, 'Berlin in the 20th Century,' students downloaded historical recordings of music from Berlin, famous speeches delivered in Berlin, and uploaded interviews they recorded with their iPods of Americans sharing their impressions of pivotal events in the history of Berlin (see http://cit.duke.edu/about/ipod_faculty_ projects.do#berlin). The Duke experiment hints at the potential for podcasting to foster a more seamless integration of in-class and out-of-class activity and materials, in addition to the wealth of authentic foreign language material freely available for download. In German (http://www.podcast.de), for instance, there are well over 100 podcasts currently available on a wide array of topics (e.g., news reports from *Deutsche Welle* read slowly, sports, science, music, and of course, developed pieces). When riding the bus or subway, walking across campus or through a shopping mall, students can create their own mobile immersion environments by opting to listen to foreign language content either assigned as homework or selected based on personal interest. The opportunity presented by podcasting is that it leverages habituated behavior: many students already own portable mp3 players and routinely download content that they listen to during downtime or transition time between activities.

The possibilities for using podcasting as a venue for students to publish original foreign language works are many. For instance, students could produce weekly or biweekly features representing their personal interests that could serve as the impetus for interclass or intercultural exchanges. Or as Ralf Borrmann at Western Reserve Academy has done with his advanced German students (Borrmann, personal communication), the radio play could be revived as a popular genre of expression that may also promote L2 development. Borrmann's students invent the characters, fashion the plot, write the script, and prepare language-learning activities for lower level students in the form of a workbook that accompanies the radio play. The appeal of radio plays in comparison to video projects is that they require less technical skill and hardware. Additionally, guides exist that describe how to compose and choreograph radio plays (see http://www.bbc.co.uk/worldservice/arts/features/howtowrite/radio.shtml).

We find podcasting an interesting addition to the text-based computer-mediated environments we have described thus far. Indeed, one of the principle critiques of textual CMC has been that oral speech and aural comprehension are not explicitly exercised. Podcasting presents a timely intersection between popular uses of iPod technologies among younger and older adults, an integration with blog cultures of one-to-many projection, and, when archived, podcasting broadcasts could be embedded as parts of larger multimodal compositions (voice, text, images, video). Like so many traditional as well as Internet-based expressive technologies, however, L2 uses of podcasting will require that instructors cultivate the delicate balance between minimally constrained creative expression and the channeling of these efforts toward concrete language use that assists students in gaining mastery of particular genres of communication (e.g., dramatic performances, readings of literature, investigative reporting, interviews, talk show formats, and monologues).

Moving toward Device-Agnostic CMC

It could be argued that CMC as a descriptive umbrella term for a genre of network-based communication tools is already anachronistic. It is increasingly the case that one does not need a 'computer' (i.e., desktop or laptop device with keyboard and display) to engage in CMC. Indeed, many electronic devices have computers as an integrated component. Consider personal digital assistants (PDAs) and cell phones: the processing power of these devices currently exceeds the capacity of many desktop computers produced in the early to mid-1990s. This trend towards increasingly compact computing power is fueling the development of new technologies that are laying the groundwork for a new era of device-agnostic CMC. In a world of device-agnostic CMC, users can engage in synchronous communication with one another using different communicative modalities (i.e., text-to-audio or audio-to-text). For instance, one interlocutor could use a cell phone with speech recognition technology, like the *Samsung p207* with *VoiceMode,* which automatically transcribes a caller's speech and sends the message as text to an interlocutor on another cell phone or computer. The keyboard-generated response can be either received as text or converted into speech with text-to-speech technology, a service currently offered by

British Telecom to its mobile phone customers. In this example, the cell phone or computer user could either display the message via synthesized voice or as a text message.[8] The crucial element to this communicative equation is choice – the ability of interlocutors to choose their preferred modality of communication.

This flexibility echoes the set of principles underlying *Universal Design for Learning*, a framework developed by the teachers and researchers at the Center for Applied Special Technology (http://www.cast.org) that leverages technology to support multiple means of representation, expression, and engagement. Initially conceptualized in the interest of assisting learners with disabilities, the basic tenets of this approach are supportive of providing learning environments that maximally accommodate the individual differences among all learners. Within the context of foreign language education, it is now possible to construct learning environments in which students with physical disabilities, especially visually and hearing-impaired students, can seamlessly engage in conversational exchange with peers; basic technological infrastructure will obviate the need for special accommodations. One of the most touted, if also controversial and contested (Janangelo, 1991; Spears & Lea, 1994; Thorne, 2000, 2003a), benefits of text-based CMC is its ability to flatten hierarchy and obscure inherent personal characteristics (e.g., ethnicity, age, and gender) that may cause some people to focus on the messenger and not the message. In a CMC environment where previously incompatible communication devices and communicative modalities are supported in an integrated network, the inability to see or hear will not pose as great an impediment to communication. With appropriate technological mediation, deaf and blind individuals will be able to communicate with each other and everyone else.[9]

From ICALL to ICMC

The inclusion of advanced computational techniques in language learning software, or intelligent computer-assisted language learning (ICALL), has been a focus of research since the early 1990s (see Holland, Kaplan, & Sama, 1995; the special Issue of the *Journal of Artificial Intelligence in Education*, 1994; Gamper & Knapp, 2002 for further discussion). Under the umbrella term of artificial intelligence, this work has focused on the application of techniques from natural language processing (e.g., parsers, taggers, etc.) and speech recognition to help language learners improve their pronunciation (LaRocca, Morgan, & Bellinger, 1999; Rypa & Price, 1999; Dalby & Kewley-Port, 1999), assist children learning to read (Mostow &

Aist, 1999), diagnose errors and provide corrective feedback to students (see the special issue of the *CALICO Journal*, 2003), model and adapt to learner behavior (e.g., Bull, 1994), and support virtual dialogs or speech-interactive environments (Bernstein, Najmi, & Ehsani, 1999; Holland, Kaplan, & Sabol, 1999; Harless, Zier, & Duncan, 1999).

More recently, research has begun to focus on the development of conversational agents that can interact with language learners via an instant messaging client (Zacharski, 2002, 2003). This work represents a new direction in the use of intelligent agents to support language learning by using standardized CMC tools as opposed to specialized applications to support the interaction. Zacharski has developed conversational agents that function as peers and information resources for language learners as they interact in an adventure game. The plan-based approach employed by Zacharski differs from chatterbots (e.g., Alicebot) by structuring interaction around the sort of dialogs frequently found in basal foreign language textbooks and requiring students to successfully complete a number of collaborative tasks. Learners interact with multiple conversational agents and each other via instant messaging, send and receive email messages, and view web pages in search of information to solve the required tasks (Zacharski, 2003). By customizing and integrating open-source instant messaging (e.g., Jabber), email, and web servers together into a unified framework, the system is able to keep track of what is done, when, and by whom and respond in a manner that promotes productive collaboration on the part of the human participants (Zacharski, 2003).[10]

Discussion

This article has described long-standing CMC tools, early and more recent research on their uses in intraclass and intercultural contexts, and promising new tools and approaches to their use in L2 settings. Throughout, we have attempted to develop a number of converging lines of argumentation. The first is that CMC is evolving, increasing in ubiquity, and no longer just about text. While SCMC and asynchronous writing environments like blogs, wikis, and ICALL have continued connections to conventional computing technologies, users can interact with and through these environments from any wireless device with Internet browser capabilities. Podcasting provides expressive possibilities such as audio compositions and makes available a vast and growing number of authentic audio texts and pedagogical materials. A second issue involves changes in everyday literacies and language use. While immigrant populations to digital communication (those of us over roughly 25 years of age!) are managing quite well, many among the younger generation are growing up with communication and media experiences that differ significantly from the conventional literacies and communicative practices that had formed a relatively unbroken continuity for decades. While the precise cognitive and cultural effects of a digitally mediated life from early childhood are unclear, there is evidence to suggest an amplification of the standard generation gap that separates students from teachers and the goals of institutionalized education.

A third point, more intimated than explicitly stated, is that the process of becoming a competent user of digital information and communication tools, largely a non-school-based process, plays a substantive role in the ways participants carry out such activity in educational settings (see Thorne, 2000, 2003a). The view that Internet communication tools are cultural artifacts is an important one; technologies are not neutral mediators of human activity but, rather, are understood by users to serve specific purposes (and not others). One of the purposes of this article has been to outline uses of emerging communication and information tools that leverage the skills and capacities that young people develop in out-of-school contexts, but also to suggest activities that value and impart the rigorous thinking, content expertise, and communicative ability (in both L1 and L2s) that instructed settings are engineered to foster.

Internet-mediated communication demonstrates an aesthetic that continues to spawn novel and widespread genres of language use. The selective and thoughtful use of SCMC, blogs, wikis, podcasting, device-agnostic CMC, and intelligent online environments holds the potential to transform L2 teaching/learning and the roles engaged in by teachers and students in the collective process of development.

Acknowledgment

We are indebted to Julie Belz for her comments on an earlier draft of this chapter.

Notes

1. This research was supported by a United States Department of Education International Research and Studies Program Grant (CFDA No.: 84.017A). Coprincipal investigators were J. Lantolf, C. Kinginger, and S. Thorne.
2. The individuals interviewed who were part of the *Freezone* community cannot be characterized as typical members of their generational cohort; rather,

they represent early adopters. Due to the potential sampling bias and methodologies employed in Tapscott's research, one should be cautious in making broad generalizations. Nevertheless, it is likely that the habitual behavior exhibited by the kids of *Freezone* will become increasingly typical of the students entering universities and colleges in North America in the years to come.

3. The BBC News reported that the term 'blog' had been the most looked-up word on the Merriam-Webster website in the year 2004 (December 1, 2004); thanks to Dorothee Schütz for alerting the authors to this information.

4. According to www.blogger.com, a blog is: 'A personal diary. A daily pulpit, a collaborative space. A political soapbox. A breaking-news outlet. A collection of links. Your own private thoughts. Memos to the world.'

5. See Gutiérrez, Rymes, & Larson (1995) for a discussion of hybridity and its dynamic benefits within educational practice.

6. Ward Cunningham describes wiki as 'the simplest online database that could possibly work' (see http://wiki.org/wiki.cgi?WhatIsWiki).

7. The particular Wiki CALPER is using is a freeware Wiki called *UniWakka* (which is a fork of the WakkaWiki engine) that has been modified to support Unicode encoding (see http://calper.la.psu.edu/uniwiki/HomePage).

8. This capability has existed for approximately 6 months at the time this article went to press.

9. The inclusiveness of device-agnostic CMC need not only apply to human beings. A further provocative wrinkle is the potential challenge to the contemporary definition of CMC: networked computers mediating communication between humans. The objectives underlying the development of the 'semantic web' have already begun to open the door to the inclusion of computers as genuine conversational partners. Unlike the World Wide Web, where information is generated by humans for humans, the basic principle of the semantic web is that machines should be able to participate in the information space of the Web as 'peers,' with the necessary precondition being the development of languages for expressing information in a machine-processable form (Berners-Lee, 1998).

10. A related and promising line of research that has not yet been harnessed for the purposes of language learning is use of stochastic techniques from information retrieval and unsupervised learning, such as latent semantic analysis (LSA) and clustering, to assist intelligent systems in formulating responses to user input. A noteworthy and extensively researched project is the Autotutor project at the University of Memphis (www.autotutor. org). Autotutor is an animated pedagogical agent that 'serves as a discourse facilitator or collaborative scaffold that assists the student in actively constructing knowledge' (Person et al., 2001: 1) in an introductory computer literacy course.

References

Abrams, Z. I. (2003). The effects of synchronous and asynchronous CMC on oral performance. *The Modern Language Journal, 87*(2), 157–167.

Agar, M. (1994). *Language shock: Understanding the culture of conversation.* New York: William Morrow.

Bauer, B., de Benedette, L., Furstenberg, G., Levet, S., & Waryn, S. (2005). Internet-mediated intercultural foreign language education: The *Cultura* project. In J. A. Belz & S. L. Thorne (Eds.), *Internet-mediated intercultural foreign language education.* Boston, MA: Heinle & Heinle.

Baym, N. (1996). The emergence of community in computer-mediated communication. In S. Jones (Ed.), *Cybersociety: Computer-mediated communication and community.* Thousand Oaks, CA: Sage Publications.

Beauvois, M. H. (1992). Computer assisted classroom discussion in the classroom: Conversation in slow motion. *Foreign Language Annals, 25*(5), 525–534.

Beauvois, M. H. (1997). Computer-mediated communication: Technology for improving speaking and writing. In M. D. Bush & R. M. Terry (Eds.), *Technology-enhanced language learning* (pp. 165–184). Lincolnwood, IL: National Textbook Company.

Belz, J. A. (2001). Institutional and individual dimensions of transatlantic group work in network-based language teaching. *ReCALL, 13*(2), 129–147.

Belz, J. A. (2002). Social dimensions of telecollaborative language study. *Language Learning & Technology, 6*(1), 60–81. Retrieved June 10, 2005 from http://llt.msu/edu/vol6num1/belz

Belz, J. A. (2003). Linguistic perspectives on the development of intercultural competence in telecollaboration. *Language Learning & Technology, 7*(2), 68–117. Retrieved June 11, 2005, from http://llt.msu.edu/vol7num2/belz/default.html

Belz, J. A. (2004). Learner corpus analysis and the development of foreign language proficiency. *System, 32*(4), 577–591.

Belz, J. A., & Kinginger, C. (2002). The cross-linguistics development of address form use in telecollaborative language learning: Two case studies. *Canadian Modern Language Review/Revue canadienne des langues vivant, 59*(2), 189–214.

Belz, J. A., & Kinginger, C. (2003). Discourse options and the development of pragmatic competence by classroom learners of German: The case of address forms. *Language Learning, 53*(4), 591–647.

Belz, J. A., & Thorne, S. L. (Eds.). (2005). *Internet-mediated intercultural foreign language education.* Boston, MA: Heinle & Heinle.

Belz, J. A., & Vyatkina, N. (2005). Computer-mediated learner corpus research and the data-driven teaching of L2 pragmatic competence: The case of German modal particles. *CALPER Working Papers, 4*, 1–28. Retrieved June 10, 2005, from http://calper.la.psu.edu/downloads/download.php?143

Berners-Lee, T. (1998). *What the semantic web isn't but can represent.* Retrieved June 10, 2005, from http://www.w3.org/DesignIssues/RDFnot.htm

Bernstein, J., Najmi, A., & Ehsani, F. (1999). Subarashii: Encounters in Japanese spoken language education. *CALICO Journal, 16*(3), 361–384.

Blake, R. J. (2000). Computer-mediated communication: A window on L2 Spanish interlanguage. *Language Learning & Technology, 4*(1), 120–136. Retrieved June 10, 2005, from http://llt.msu.edu/vol4num1/blake/default.html

Böhlke, O. (2003). A comparison of student participation levels by group size and language stages during chatroom and face-to-face discussions in German. *CALICO Journal, 21*(1), 67–87.

Blair, C., Gamson, D., Thorne, S. L., & Baker, D. (2005). Rising mean IQ: Cognitive demand of mathematics education, population exposure to formal schooling, and the neurobiology of the prefrontal cortex. *Intelligence, 33*, 93–106.

Boxer, D. (2002). Discourse issues in cross-cultural pragmatics. *Annual Review of Applied Linguistics, 22*, 150–167.

Brown, P., & Levinson, S. (1987). *Politeness: Some universals in language usage.* New York: Cambridge University Press.

Bull, S. (1994). Student modeling for second language acquisition. *Computers and Education, 23*(1–2), 13–20.

Byram, M. (1997). *Teaching and assessing intercultural communicative competence.* Clevedon: Multilingual Matters.

Cononelos, T., & Oliva, M. (1993). Using computer networks to enhance foreign language/culture education. *Foreign Language Annals, 26*(4), 527–534.

Chun, D. M. (1994). Using computer networking to facilitate the acquisition of interactive competence. *System, 22*(1), 17–31.

Curtis, P. (1998). Not just a game: How LambdaMOO came to exist and what it did to get me back. In C. Haynes and J. R. Holmevik (Eds.), *High wired: On the design, use, and theory of educational MOOs* (pp. 25–42). Ann Arbor, MI: University of Michigan Press.

Crystal, D. (2001). *Language and the Internet.* Cambridge: Cambridge University Press.

Dalby, J., & Kewley-Port, D. (1999). Explicit pronunciation training using automatic speech recognition. *CALICO Journal, 16*(3), 425–446.

Damasio, A. (2003). *Looking for Spinoza: Joy, sorrow, and the feeling brain.* New York: Harcourt.

Dibbell, J. (1993, December 21). A rape in cyberspace. *The Village Voice*, 36–42.

Emigh, W., & Herring, S. (2005). Collaborative authoring on the web: A genre analysis of online encyclopedias. *Proceedings of the Thirty-eighth Annual Hawaii International Conference on System Sciences (HICSS-38).* Los Alamitos, IEEE Press.

Freinet, C. (1994). *Oeuvres pédagogiques.* Paris: Editions du Seuil.

Furstenberg, G. (2003). Reading between the cultural lines. In P. Patrikis (Ed.), *Reading between the lines: Perspectives on foreign language literacy* (pp. 74–98). New Haven, CT: Yale University Press.

Furstenberg, G., Levet, S., English, K., & Maillet, K. (2001). Giving a virtual voice to the silent language of culture: The CULTURA project. *Language Learning & Technology, 5*(1), 55–102. Retrieved June 14, 2005, from http://llt.msu.edu/vol5num1/furstenberg

Gamper, J., & Knapp, J. (2002). A review of intelligent CALL systems. *Computer Assisted Language Learning, 15*(4), 329–342.

Godwin-Jones, R. (2003). Blogs and wikis: Environments for online collaboration. *Language Learning & Technology, 7*(2), 12–16. Retrieved June 14, 2005, from http://llt.msu.edu/vol7num2/emerging

Grinter, R., & Palen, L. (2002). Instant messaging in teen life. *Proceedings from computer supported cooperative work 2002* (pp. 21–30). ACM.

Grohol, J. M. (2002). *Psychology of weblogs: Everything old is new again.* Retrieved June 1, 2005, from http://psychcentral.com/blogs/blog_new.htm

Gutiérrez, K., Rymes, B., & Larson, J. (1995). Script, counterscript, and underlife in the classroom: James Brown versus Brown v. Board of Education. *Harvard Educational Review, 65*(3), 445–471.

Harless, W., Zier, M., & Duncan, R. (1999). Virtual dialogues with native speakers: The evaluation of an interactive multimedia method. *CALICO Journal, 16*(3), 313–338.

Herring, S. (2001). Computer-mediated discourse analysis. In D. Schiffrin, D. Tannen, & H. Hamilton (Eds.), *The handbook of discourse analysis* (pp. 612–634). Oxford: Blackwell Publishers.

Herring, S. C., Kouper, I., Paolillo, J. C., Scheidt, L. A., Tyworth, M., Welsch, P., Wright, E., & Yu, N. (2005). Conversations in the blogosphere: An analysis 'from the bottom up.' *Proceedings of the Thirty-Eighth Hawai'i International Conference on System Sciences (HICSS-38).* Los Alamitos: IEEE Press.

Holland, M. V., Kaplan, J. D., & Sama, M. R. (Eds.). (1995). *Intelligent language tutors: Theory shaping technology.* Mahwah, NJ: Lawrence Erlbaum Associates, Inc.

Holland, M., Kaplan, J. D., & Sabol, M. A. (1999). Preliminary tests of language learning in a speech-interactive graphics microworld. *CALICO Journal, 16*(3), 339–360.

Janangelo, J. (1991). Technopower and technosuppression: Some abuses of power and control in computer-assisted writing environments. *Computers & Composition, 9*(1), 47–64.

Jardin, X. (2005a, April 27). Podcasting killed the radio star. *Wired Magazine.* Retrieved June 10, from http://wiredvig.wired.com/news/digiwood/0,1412,67344,00.html?tw=wn_story_top5

Jardin, X. (2005b, May 14). Audience with the podfather. *Wired Magazine.* Retrieved June 10, from http://www.wired.com/news/culture/0,1284,67525,00.html?tw=newsletter_topstories_html

Johanyak, M. (1997). Analyzing the amalgamated electronic text: Bringing cognitive, social, and contextual factors of individual language users into CMC research. *Computer and Composition, 14*, 91–110.

Kasper, G., & Rose, K. (1999). Pragmatics and SLA. *Annual Review of Applied Linguistics, 19*, 91–104.

Kasper, G., & Rose, K. (2002). *Pragmatic development in a second language.* Oxford: Blackwell Publishers.

Kelm, O. (1992). The use of synchronous computer networks in second language instruction: A preliminary report. *Foreign Language Annals, 25*(5), 441–454.

Kern, R. G. (1995). Restructuring classroom interaction with networked computers: Effects on quantity and characteristics of language production. *The Modern Language Journal, 79*(4), 457–476.

Kinginger, C. (1998). Videoconferencing as access to spoken French. *The Modern Language Journal, 82*(4), 502–513.

Kinginger, C. (2004). Communicative foreign language teaching through telecollaboration. In K. van Esch & O. St. John (Eds.), *New insights into foreign language learning and teaching* (pp. 101–113). Frankfurt am Main: Peter Lang.

Kost, C. R. (2004). *An investigation of the effects of synchronous computer-mediated communication (CMC) on interlanguage development in beginning learners of German: Accuracy, proficiency, and communication strategies.* Unpublished doctoral dissertation, University of Arizona, Tucson.

Kramsch, C. (1993). *Context and culture in language teaching.* Oxford: Oxford University Press.

Kramsch, C. (1998). *Language and culture.* Oxford: Oxford University Press.

Kramsch, C., & Thorne, S. L. (2002). Foreign language learning as global communicative practice. In D. Block and D. Cameron (Eds.), *Globalization and language teaching* (pp. 83–100). London: Routledge.

Krashen, S. (1982). *Principles and practices in second language acquisition.* New York: Pergamon Press.

Lanham, R. (1993). *The electronic word: Democracy, technology, and the arts.* Chicago: University of Chicago Press.

LaRocca, S., Morgan, J., & Bellinger, S. (1999). On the path to 2X learning: Exploring the possibilities of advanced speech recognition. *CALICO Journal, 16*(3), 295–310.

LeDoux, J. (1996). *The emotional brain.* New York: Touchstone.

LeDoux, J. (2002). *Synaptic self: How our brains become who we are.* New York: Penguin.

Levelt, W. J. M. (1989). *Speaking: From intention to articulation.* Cambridge, MA: The MIT Press.

Long, M. (1985). Input and second language acquisition theory. In S. M. Gass & C. G. Madden (Eds.), *Input in second language acquisition* (pp. 377–393). Rowley, MA: Newbury House.

Long, M. (1996). The role of the linguistic environment in second language acquisition. In W. Ritchie & T. Bhatia (Eds.), *Handbook of second language acquisition* (pp. 413–468). New York: Academic Press.

Miller, D., & Slater, D. (2000). *The Internet: An ethnographic approach.* Oxford: Berg.

Morford, J. (1997). Social indexicality in French pronominal address. *Journal of Linguistic Anthropology 7*(1), 3–37.

Mostow, J., & Aist, G. (1999). Giving help and praise in a reading tutor with imperfect listening – because automated speech recognition means never being able to say you're certain. *CALICO Journal, 16*(3), 407–424.

Müller-Hartmann, A. (2000). The role of tasks in promoting intercultural learning in electronic learning networks. *Language Learning & Technology, 4*(2), 129–147. Retrieved June 10, 2005, from: http://llt.msu.edu/vol4num2/muller

Nicholas, M. A., & Toporski, N. (1993). Developing 'The Critic's Corner': Computer assisted language learning for upper-level Russian students. *Foreign Language Annals, 26*(4), 469–478.

O'Dowd, R. (2003). Understanding the 'other side:' Intercultural learning in a Spanish-English e-mail exchange. *Language Learning & Technology, 7*(2), 118–144. Retrieved June 10, 2005, from: http://llt.msu.edu/vol7num2/odowd

Ortega, L. (1997). Processes and outcomes in networked classroom interaction: Defining the research agenda for L2 computer-assisted classroom discussion. *Journal of Language Learning & Technology, 1*(1), 82-93. Retrieved June 10, 2005, from http://llt.msu.edu/vol1num1/ortega/default.html

Payne, J. S., & Ross, B. (2005). Working memory, synchronous CMC, and L2 oral proficiency development. *Language Learning & Technology 9*(1), 35–54.

Payne, J. S., & Whitney, P. J. (2002). Developing L2 oral proficiency through synchronous CMC: Output, working memory, and interlanguage development. *CALICO Journal, 20*(1), 7–32.

Pellettieri, J. (2000). Negotiation in cyberspace: The role of chatting in the development of grammatical competence. In M. Warschauer & R. Kern (Eds.), *Network-based language teaching: Concepts and practice* (pp. 59–86). New York: Cambridge University Press.

Person, N. K., Graesser, A. C., Bautista, L., Mathews, E. C., & the Tutoring Research Group (2001). Evaluating student learning gains in two versions of AutoTutor. In J. D. Moore, C. L. Redfield, & W. L. Johnson (Eds.), *Artificial intelligence in Anthropology, 7*(1), 3–37. *Education: AI-ED in the wired and wireless future* (pp. 286–293). Amsterdam, IOS Press.

Pew Internet and American Life Project. (2002). *The digital disconnect: The widening gap between Internet-savvy students and their schools.* Retrieved June 10, 2005 from http://www.pewinternet.org/pdfs/PIP_Schools_Internet_Report.pdf

Pica, T. (1987). Interlanguage adjustments as an outcome of NS-NNS negotiation interaction. *Language Learning, 38*(1), 45–73.

Presky, M. (2001a, October). Digital natives, digital immigrants. *On the Horizon.* NCB University Press, *9*(5).

Presky, M. (2001b, December). Digital natives, digital immigrants, Part II: Do they really think differently? *On the Horizon.* NCB University Press, *9*(6).

Roszak, T. (1994). *The cult of information* (2nd edn). Berkeley, CA: University of California Press.

Rypa, M., & Price, P. (1999). VILTS: A tale of two technologies. *CALICO Journal, 16*(3), 385–404.

Salaberry, R. (2000). L2 morphosyntactic development in text-based computer communication. *Computer Assisted Language Learning, 13*(1), 5–27.

Schmidt, R. (1990). The role of consciousness in second language acquisition. *Applied Linguistics, 11*(2), 219–258.

Schmidt, R. (1993). Awareness and second language acquisition. *Annual Review of Applied Linguistics, 13*, 206–226.

Scollon, R., & Scollon, S. (1995). *Intercultural communication.* Cambridge: Blackwell Publishers.

Smith, B. (2003). Computer-mediated negotiated interaction: An expanded model. *The Modern Language Journal, 87*(1), 38–57.

Smith, B. (2004). Computer-mediated negotiated interaction and lexical acquisition. *Studies in Second Language Acquisition, 26*(3), 365–398.

Spears, R., & Lea, M. (1994). Panacea or panopticon? The hidden power in computer-mediated communication. *Communication Research, 21*(4), 427–459.

Sprague, D., & Dede, C. (1999). Constructivism in the classroom: If I teach this way, am I doing my job? *Learning and Leading with Technology, 27*(1), 6–9, 16–17.

Stoll, C. (1995). *Silicon snake oil: Second thoughts on the information highway.* New York: Doubleday.

Swain, M. (1985). Communicative competence: Some roles of comprehensible input and comprehensible output in its development. In S. M. Gass & C. G. Madden (Eds.), *Input in second language acquisition* (pp. 235–253). Rowley, MA: Newbury House.

Tapscott, D. (1997). *Growing up digital: The rise of the net generation.* New York: McGraw-Hill.

Thorne, S. L. (2000). Beyond bounded activity systems: Heterogeneous cultures in instructional uses of persistent conversation. *Proceedings of the Thirty-Third Annual Hawaii International Conference on System Sciences (HICSS-33).* Los Alamitos, IEEE Press.

Thorne, S. L. (2003a). Artifacts and cultures-of-use in intercultural communication. *Language Learning & Technology, 7*(2), 38–67. Retrieved June 10, 2005, from: http://llt.msu.edu/vol7num2/thorne

Thorne, S. L. (2003b). [Review of *Language and the Internet*] The biggest language revolution ever meets applied linguistics in the 21st century. *Language Learning & Technology, 7*(2), 24–27. Retrieved June 10, 2005, from http://llt.msu.edu/vol7num2/review1/default.html

Thorne, S. L. (2004). Cultural historical activity theory and the object of innovation. In O. St. John, K. van Esch, & E. Schalkwijk (Eds.), *New insights into foreign language learning and teaching* (pp. 51–70). Frankfurt: Peter Lang Verlag.

Thorne, S. L. (2005). Epistemology, politics, and ethics in sociocultural theory. *The Modern Language Journal, 89*, 393–409.

Thorne, S. L. (2005). Pedagogical and praxiological lessons from Internet-mediated intercultural foreign language learning research. In J. Belz & S. L. Thorne (Eds.), *Internet-mediated intercultural foreign language education.* Boston, MA: Heinle & Heinle Publishers.

Thorne, S. L., Webber, D., & Bensinger, A. (2005a, May). *Interactivity system analysis, AIM, and pedagogical innovation.* Paper presented at the 2005 CALICO conference, East Lansing, MI.

Thorne, S. L., Webber, D., & Bensinger, A. (2005b). *Mediation and interactivity system analysis in and out of school: Instant messaging and blogging in L2 education.* Manuscript in preparation.

Turkle, S. (1995). *Life on the screen: Identity in the age of the Internet.* New York: Simon & Schuster.

Tudini, V. (2003). Using native speakers in chat. *Language Learning & Technology, 7*(3), 141–159. Retrieved June 10, 2005, from: http://llt.msu.edu/vol7num3/tudini/de fault.html

Van Dijk, J. (2005). *The deepening divide: Inequality in the information society.* London: Sage.

Varonis, E., & Gass, S. (1985). Non-native/non-native conversations: A model for negotiating meaning. *Applied Linguistics, 6*(1), 71–90.

Warschauer, M. (1996). Computer-mediated collaborative learning: Theory and practice. *The Modern Language Journal, 81*(4), 470–481.

Yates, S. (1996). Oral and written aspects of computer conferencing. In Susan Herring (Ed.), *Computer-mediated communication: Linguistic, social and cross-cultural perspectives* (pp. 9–46). Philadelphia, PA: John Benjamins Publishing Company.

Zacharski, (2002). *Conversational agents for language learning.* Unpublished manuscript.

Zacharski, (2003). A discourse system for conversational characters. In A. Gelbukh (Ed.), *Proceedings of the fourth international conference on intelligent text processing and computational linguistics* (pp. 492–495). Heidelberg: Springer Verlag.

6 Interactional Features of Synchronous Computer-Mediated Communication in the Intermediate L2 Class: A Sociocultural Case Study

Mark Darhower*

Introduction

Synchronous CMC in the CALL literature

The explosion of Internet use in recent years has brought about previously unheard of means of human communication. Many Internet users world-wide make use of interactive features of the World Wide Web such as synchronous CMC, which allows persons in remote locations to communicate with each other in real time by typing messages onto their computer screen. Today's foreign language learners are likely to be experienced chatters, even if only in their L1 and concerning topics of personal rather than academic interests. Coinciding with the increasing use of synchronous CMC has been a recent focus of interest in the second language acquisition (SLA) literature on the social interactive factors involved in L2 learning. Whereas much SLA research on social interaction deals with face-to-face conversation, the emergence of synchronous CMC brings forth a whole new set of research and practical issues concerning social interaction within the L2 learning context. Chat rooms are theoretically interesting environments in which to investigate L2 interaction, given that chat room interaction combines the textuality of written communication with the real-time interactivity of face-to-face communication.

*   Mark Darhower received his Ph.D. in Spanish Applied Linguistics from the University of Pittsburgh in 2000. He has published numerous software and textbook reviews and presented his work at CALICO's symposia. Currently, he is Assistant Professor of English and Spanish at the University of Puerto Rico at Humacao.

The use of synchronous CMC in language instruction originated in the mid-1980s in the English Department at Gallaudet University in Washington, DC, where it served as a tool to help deaf people to communicate in English rather than American Sign Language (Beauvois, 1997). The idea of electronic networks for interaction (ENFIs) then extended into English composition classes (Bruce, Kreeft Peyton, & Baston, 1993). At the University of Texas at Austin, a program called **Daedalus Interchange** was designed for L1 writing classes. The **Interchange** program included a synchronous CMC component which students used to discuss their compositions with each other.

As the use of synchronous CMC moved into the L2 learning context, researchers working with various languages uncovered numerous advantages of electronic communication as opposed to face-to-face conversation. Kelm (1992), who used **Daedalus Interchange** with intermediate learners of Portuguese over a thirteen-week period, reported that synchronous CMC: (a) increased participation from all members of a work group; (b) allowed students to speak without interruption; (c) reduced anxiety which is frequently present in oral conversation; (d) rendered honest and candid expression of emotion; (e) provided personalized identification of target language errors; (f) created substantial communication among L2 learners; and (g) demonstrated a significant reduction of certain grammatical errors over time. Similarly, Chun (1994) reported that her first-year learners of German performed a wide range of discourse functions in synchronous CMC: they asked more questions of fellow students and the instructor, they gave feedback to others and requested clarification when they did not understand each other, and they ended conversations with appropriate leave-taking utterances. In a study of two groups of French learners, Kern (1995) reported increased language production, a greater level of morphosyntactic complexity, a wider variety of discourse functions, and reduction of anxiety over communicating in the L2, as compared to face-to-face discussion of the same topics. In a study of ESL students, Warschauer (1996) encountered equalization of participation among learners, as well as more formal and complex language in both lexical and morphosyntactic levels. Warschauer (1999) also referred to the ability of synchronous CMC to help overcome the contradiction between focus on form and meaning. In synchronous CMC learners have more opportunity than they do in oral conversation to notice structure, which is believed to be critical for language acquisition (Schmidt, 1993). Also, learners can consult previous text, dictionaries or other language reference materials, or other learners as they type their messages.

In addition to the reported advantages of synchronous CMC, a few researchers have called attention to some potential drawbacks to chatting.

Among these difficulties are problems of limited keyboarding skills, slow speed, less coherence (Bump, 1990); lack of nonverbal communication; and the necessity of learning a new set of turn-taking skills (Salaberry, 1997: 19). Additionally, Kern (1995: 470) cautions that 'Formal accuracy, stylistic improvement, global coherence, consensus, and reinforcement of canonical discourse conventions are goals not well served by Interchange.'

Research findings on advantages and disadvantages of synchronous CMC in L2 learning demonstrate that this medium of communication differs in fundamental ways from that of typical patterns of classroom communication. The study presented here contributes to this growing body of research by employing the sociocultural theoretical framework to illustrate and explain the particular ways that two groups of intermediate Spanish L2 learners utilized chat rooms in their classes. To that end, a brief overview of the tenets of sociocultural theory is in order.

Sociocultural Theory

Evolved from the work of the Russian psychologist and semiotician Lev Vygotsky (1896–1934), sociocultural theory operates on the assumption that human cognitive development is highly dependent upon the social context within which it takes place. (For an overview of the framework, see Lantolf & Appel, 1994.) More specifically, development occurs as the result of meaningful verbal interaction between novices and more knowledgeable interlocutors such as parents, peers, or teachers (Vygotsky, 1962, 1978). Sociocultural theory emphasizes that the locus of learning is not exclusively within the individual's mind but, rather, is a product of social interaction with other individuals. Although Vygotsky's theory embraced all higher mental functions, he was primarily interested in the development of language in relation to thought (Vygotsky, 1962, 1978). Vygotsky distinguished between lower mental functions, such as elementary perception, memory, attention, and will, and the higher, or cultural functions, such as logical memory, voluntary attention, conceptual thought, planning, and problem solving. Vygotsky explained that higher mental functions appear as a result of *transformations* of the lower functions (Vygotsky, 1962, 1978). Fundamental in such transformations are the constructs of *mediation* and use of *tools*.

Mediation and the Use of Tools

In order for transformations from lower to higher mental functions to occur, the individual must make use of psychological tools, such as mnemonic techniques, algebraic symbols, diagrams, schemes, and, per-haps most important, language. These psychological tools function as *mediators*, or instruments that stand between the individual and the goal toward which the individual's action is directed. Vygotsky's claim was that just as individuals employ technical tools to manipulate their environ-ment, they use psychological tools to direct and control their physical and mental behavior. In the L2 learning context, the provision of positive and negative linguistic evidence by more knowledgeable peers and the devel-opment of learning and communication strategies are some of the media-tional means by which the lower linguistic processes develop into higher forms of language use (i.e., discourse competence). Higher mental func-tions, then, must be viewed as *products* of mediated activity, of which lan-guage is one of the principle tools or mediators.

An underlying assumption of the mediation construct is that humans have access to the world only indirectly, or mediately, rather than directly, or immediately (Wertsch, del Rio, & Alvarez, 1995). Mediation is an active process that involves the potential of cultural tools, as well as the unique use of such tools, to shape human action. The introduction of new cultural tools *transforms* the mediation process, rather than simply facilitating forms of action that would otherwise occur (Wertsch et al., 1995). 'By being included in the process of behavior, the psychological tool alters the entire flow and structure of mental functions. It does this by determining the structure of a new instrumental act, just as a technical tool alters the process of a natural adaptation by determining the form of labor operations' (Vygotsky, 1981). The boom of the computer as a cultural/psychological tool in recent years certainly lends support to Vygotsky's thesis.

Donato and McCormick (1994) argue the importance of mediation in L2 learning: 'Initially unfocused learning actions may become adjusted and modified based on how the learning of the language is mediated. Mediation is, thus, the instrument of cognitive change.' They suggest several exam-ples of potential mediators (or tools) in L2 learning, including textbooks, visual material, classroom discourse patterns, opportunities for L2 interac-tion, types of direct instruction, and various kinds of teacher assistance. In today's L2 classrooms, computers would undoubtedly be added to this list. Meskill (1999) considers the computer to be a complex artifact that 'like all contextual artifacts, especially tools used by members of a particular com-munity … bring about major change in the structure and dynamics of dis-course and activity.' Wertsch (1991) suggests that mediational means be viewed in terms of items that make up a *tool kit*, rather than being viewed as a single, undifferentiated whole. The current study explores the implica-tions of including synchronous CMC as an item in the L2 learning tool kit.

Intersubjectivity

Related to the Vygotskian view of cognitive development as a byproduct of collaborative discourse is the concept of *intersubjectivity*. Engaging in collaborative discourse requires a shared communicative context. When interlocutors have similar background knowledge of a topic of conversation, the context may already be shared. If not already present, the shared context must be created (Rommetveit, 1974). Habermas (1998) referred to this concept of shared perspective as *intersubjectivity* in his philosophy of language (see also White, 1995). Rommetveit (1974, 1985) brought the term into the field of psychology, referring to intersubjectivity as the establishment of a shared perspective between an expert and a learner in a problem-solving task. According to Wertsch (1991), reaching intersubjectivity is something that communicants learn to do. The establishment and negotiation of intersubjectivity perpetuates collaborative discourse, which, according to the sociocultural view, is important for language development.

Habermas (1998) developed a speech act theory on the basis of four universal validity claims. Anyone who wants to participate in a process of reaching understanding must adhere to the following principles:

1.   uttering something intelligibly;
2.   giving (the hearer) something to understand;
3.   making herself thereby understandable; and
4.   coming to an understanding with another person.

When at least one of the validity claims is not satisfied, communicative action cannot be continued. In other words, intersubjectivity is lost. When intersubjectivity is lost, interlocutors must achieve a new definition of the situation that all participants can share in order for communication to continue. If the attempt to reestablish intersubjectivity fails, then the communicators are faced with switching to some sort of strategic action (e.g., breaking off communication altogether or recommencing action oriented toward reaching understanding at a different level). Schegloff (1992) studied the process of 'defending' intersubjectivity within a certain number of conversational turns to which he referred as a turn-taking 'repair space'. According to Schegloff, repair of lost understanding generally occurs within three turns of the source of trouble. If the repair attempt is made after three, or sometimes four, turns, then the repair becomes 'next relevant'. The problem with becoming next relevant is that the repair may never again be relevant.

The concept of intersubjectivity has been invoked in recent sociocultural SLA studies. Investigating the sociocognitive functions of the use of the L1 in communicative tasks, Antón and DiCamilla (1998) demonstrated that their dyads of learners used their L1 '...to construct a social space that will facilitate the completion of the task by enabling learners to achieve intersubjectivity, that is, a shared perspective on the task.' They further characterize this state of task intersubjectivity as a 'social and cognitive workplace, in which the students are able to provide each other with help throughout the task'. Antón and DiCamilla also stressed the importance of *maintaining* intersubjectivity throughout a communicative task, implying that maintaining an intersubjective state is conducive to language learning.

The current study seeks to contribute to the body of literature described above by shedding light on the social interaction of a particular group of L2 learners within a chat room context.

The Study

Participants and Context

The participants were 33 learners and the teacher of two intact fourth-semester Spanish classes at the University of Pittsburgh. The classes met for three contact hours per week. Two of the class meetings were held in the classroom, and the third meeting was held in a computer laboratory. The intermediate-level Spanish curriculum at the university employed a content-driven, task-based approach to language teaching. Learners typically spent class time involved in interactive activities with specific communicative goals as defined by VanPatten and Lee (1995). Intermediate Spanish classes at the university delivered integrated-skills language instruction (speaking, listening, reading, and writing), which lent itself easily to an analysis of communication that shares characteristics of both writing and speaking and, ultimately, to the cautious generalization of findings of this research project to other foreign/second language classes that employ an integrated-skills approach.

Method

Prior to beginning the study, learners were asked to select a pseudonym for their chat room discussions. The reasons for the pseudonyms were to promote genuine, uninhibited communication and to afford anonymity in the research findings. The learners in each class were divided into four groups, as the **WebCT** program provided simultaneous access to four separate chat rooms. At the beginning of each chat session, learners were given a handout containing the topic and task. The chat activities were designed by the researcher in coordination with the course instructor in order to meet both the research needs of the study and the instructional needs of the learners. (See the sample activity in the appendix to this article.) Thus, the chat sessions were integrated into the overall course program. All of the chat topics were introduced in prior class sessions and derived from authentic reading passages and/or video segments. During the chat sessions, the instructor sat at her computer at the head of the laboratory, circulating among the four chat rooms and participating for a brief time in each of the discussions. The researcher was present during the chat sessions to assist with technical problems and to observe the research environment.

Research Question

The larger study from which this article originates consisted of five research questions, however only the first of these questions will be treated here: What are some outstanding interactional features in chat among learners and the teacher? The motivation for this question was to complement existing findings regarding L2 discourse in the face-to-face mode with a theoretically framed analysis of L2 discourse in an electronic environment.

Data Analysis

To shed light on the nature of chat room communication, discourse analysis was the principal approach to data analysis in this study. As in most qualitative research, data reduction was necessary and involved systematically selecting from the 300 pages of chat room transcripts examples of discourse features that closely related to the research questions driving the study. The transcripts were organized into episodes corresponding to the week number and the assigned groups. For example, Episode 1A was the chat session of the first group during the first week; Episode 2B referred to the second group in the second week, and so forth. The group members were changed twice throughout the semester to allow learners to communicate with new classmates. In accordance with Miles and Huberman (1994), the search for patterns in the data was driven by the prior preparation of a 'start-up list' of possible interactional features gleaned from the previous synchronous CMC and sociocultural literature. After making multiple passes through the transcript data, specific patterns were identified and indexed. The interactional features were then illustrated in the form of discourse excerpts accompanied by interpretive explanations.

Findings

The interactional features of interest that emerged from the data were intersubjectivity; off-task discussion; social cohesiveness, including greetings and leave takings, use of humor, and sarcasm/insults; exploration of alternate identities and role plays; and the use of the L1 (English). The following discourse excerpts and accompanying explanations will illuminate the occurrences of each of these interactional features throughout the nine weeks of chat sessions in the study.

Intersubjectivity

As mentioned previously, intersubjectivity is defined as a shared orientation or perspective on a communicative task. Put in other terms, communicators who have established intersubjectivity are 'on the same wavelength,' that is, they are able to penetrate each other's subjective reality of the world by means of collaborative discourse. In the overall study, three full weeks (weeks one, four, and eight) of the chat transcripts were analyzed to determine the extent to which intersubjectivity seemed to occur in each episode and to describe the resulting states of intersubjectivity. The current article focuses on two illustrative examples selected from the data. In Segment A, intersubjectivity appeared to be established and maintained throughout the discussion.[1] In Segment B, intersubjectivity was established but subsequently lost.

Prior to the beginning of this segment, gangster movies. In lines 1–29, there were versation – the movie 'The Burbs' and psychological aspects of movies (a subtopic of the assigned activity). Juanita (J) and Eduardo (E) were focused on 'The Burbs,' while Lourdes (L) was focused on the psychological aspects of movies. Benito (B) moved in and out of both topics for a short time and then focused exclusively on the context that Lourdes had established. After the shared perspective between Juanita and Eduardo was apparently diverted, Juanita attempted to join in on the discussion topic created by Lourdes and Benito. For some reason Eduardo dropped out of the conversation after line 19 (although he was still present in the room). Benito and Lourdes continued their in-depth discussion of film in society with Juanita contributing from time to time. The group maintained what appears to be an intersubjective state until the end of the chat session.

In most of the groups this week, the chatters appeared to have established an intersubjective state centered on the assigned topic of movies. In many of those groups, however, the shared perspective on the topic of conversation

SEGMENT A: Movies

		Spanish	English
	J:	algien personas ha visto la pelicula "the burbs"?	have someone persons seen the movie "the burbs"?
	B:	no, no conozco esta pelicula	no, I don't know this movie
	E:	"The Burbs" con Tom Hanks?	"The Burbs" with Tom Hanks?
5	B:	de que se trata?	What is it about?
	L:	Creo que los aspectos psicologicos de las peliculas son muy crucial a sociedad. La pelicula de "gangsters" es no tiene morales buenos a ninos.	I think the psychological aspects of movies are crucial to society. Gangster movies is not have good morals for kids.
10	J:	pero es interasante	but it's interesting
	J:	si the burbs con tom hanks	yes the burbs with tom hanks
	B:	yo creo que es importante para los padres defender sus ninos de ver peliculas con morales malas cuando los ninos son pequenos	I think it is important that parents defend their kids from seeing movies with bad morals when the kids are little
15			
	L:	Hay los individuos en sociedad que viven sus vidas en base de que ellos ven y oyen.	There individuals in society that live their lives based on what they see and hear
	E:	creo que the burbs fue una pelicula muy terrible	I think the burbs was a very terrible movie
20			
	J:	no es comico	it's not funny
	B:	de que se trata "the burbs"?	what is "the burbs" about?
	J:	el tema de the burbs es sobre un neighbor hood donde tom hanks live y todos las personas en el nieghborhhod piensan sus neighbors nuevas son matarlos	the theme of the burbs is about a neighbor hood where tom hanks live and everyone in the neighborhood thinks their new neighbors are kill them
25			
	B:	a, gracias	a, thank you
	B:	yo voy a ver esta pelicula, creo	I'm going to see that movie, I think
30	J:	corey feldman es en the burbs	corey feldman is in the burbs
	L:	Si el cine no existera el mundo seria mejor. algunas peliculas danan las mentes de sociedad	If movies didn't exist the world would be better. Some movies damage the minds of society
	L:	Hay muchas otras formas de diversiones.	There are other forms of fun.
35			
	B:	no se si estoy de acuerdo. croe que el cine puede ser buena cosa. depende del tipo de peliculas. pero entiendo porque dices esto	I don't know if I agree. I think that movies could be a good thing. It depends on the type of movies. But I understand why you say this
40	B:	y quizas tienes razon	and perhaps you're right
	L:	como, el leer, el jugar deportes …jugar instrumentos …el ensenar sobre historia es el mas importante	like reading, playing sports …playing instruments …teaching about history is more important
	B:	si, hay muchissimos cosas que son mas o igualmente importantes.	yes, there are very many things that are more or equally important
45			
	J:	yo peinso que es importante ver las peliculas para divertido, on para seriosos	I think it is important to see movies for fun, on for serious
	J:	no para seriosos	no for serious
50	B:	es necessario hacer otras cosas que ver peliculas. no es bueno pasar demasiado tiempo haciendo una sola actividad	it's necessary to do other things than see movies. It's not good to spend too much time doing one activity
	L:	Si ensenamos sus hijos de la historia ellos ententeran el mundo mejor. ellos ni la repitaran o la cambiaran	If we teach our kids about history they will understand the world better. They will neither repeat it nor change it
55			
	B:	si, tines razon. es necesario conocer mejor la historia.	yes, you're right. It's necessary to know history better
	B:	ustedes creen que hay un razon otra que el dinero que se filman las peliculs	do you think there is a reason other than money that they film movies?
60	B:	por ejempelo para dar un mensaje a la sociedad?	for example to give a message to society?

	J:	hay razon es entertainment	J:	*there is reason is entertainment*
	B:	solo etertainment? no hay otra motivacion a veces?	B:	*only entertainment? Isn' t there another motivation sometimes?*
65	J:	hasta la vista amigos, tu tienes un buen fin de semana	J:	*see you later friends, you have a good weekend*
	B:	gracias!	B:	*thank you!*
	B:	tu tambien	B:	*you too*
	B:	adios lourdes!	B:	*bye lourdes!*
70	L:	Mi opinion de el cine es que es no importante en sociedad. El cine proyecta los vistas negativos. La mayoria de los mensajes son negataivos.	L:	*My opinion about movies is that they are not important en society. Movies project negative views. The majority of the messages are negative.*
75		Estoy de acuerda que es solamente entertainmento. Mi preferencia personal es : No la mira		*I agree that it is only entertainment. My personal preference is:* *Don' t watch it.*
	L:	adios	L:	*bye*

seemed to consist merely of the mention of movie titles and one- or two-sentence commentaries on each title. Unlike the other groups, the group in Segment A went far beyond the mere mention of movie titles, discussing all subtopics of their assigned task and maintaining a level of intersubjectivity that allowed them to examine in considerable depth the issue of films in society. Another notable aspect of this segment is that the learners agreed with each other at some times but did not agree at other times, which demonstrates that they immersed themselves into each other's subjective reality enough to accept or reject each other's perspectives and to explain their positions. Wells (1998, 1999) points out that it is precisely the ability to disagree and trace the disagreement back to the original context of the discussion that illustrates that a true intersubjective the group had been discussing two concurrent strands of constate has been established. Segment B, taken from week one of the study, illustrates the establishment and subsequent breakdown of intersubjectivity.

Pablo (P) (who was actually a female) established a context for the conversation, that is, a potential starting point for intersubjectivity. After greeting his fellow chatters, Javier (J), who presented himself as a Cuban, put forth his perspective on freedom by stating that US citizens enjoy a great deal of freedom, as compared to Cuba. Mía (M) reiterated the word *libertad* 'freedom,' followed by ellipses, presumably to indicate that she was thinking about the proposed topic. It appears that the three of them established a shared context and were attempting to maintain discussion of it. But in line 12, the shared context was redirected by Pablo's statement about youth in Spain, which did not seem to follow the established topic (or if it did, it was not clear *how* it did). Alicia and Mía continued to talk about freedom, but both Alicia and the instructor were drawn to determining how Pablo's statement contributed

SEGMENT B: Freedom

	P:	Debemos hablar sobre la libertad	P:	*We should talk about freedom*	
	J:	Epa pablo como estas	J:	*Hey Pablo how are you*	
	P:	bien estoy cansada	P:	*good I'm tired*	
	P:	y usted?	P:	*And you?*	
5	P:	Mia	P:	*Mia*	
	J:	La libertad? bueno chamo ustedes tienen mucha libertad en los estados unidos	J:	*Freedom? Well man you have a lot of freedom in the united states*	
	A:	La libertad ...	A:	*Freedom ...*	
10	P:	si	P:	*Yes*	
	J:	En cuba no tenemos la libertad como ustedes	J:	*In Cuba we don't have freedom like you*	
	P:	pero creo que la cultura espanola es mejor para jovenes	P:	*but I think Spanish culture is better for young people*	
15	A:	Para mi, la libertad es el derecho a votar y ser un induvidual	A:	*For me, freedom is the right to vote and to be an individual*	
	A:	Pablo ...porque?	A:	*Pablo ...why?*	
	P:	puedes estar con la familia y no necesitas estar desconcierto	P:	*You can be with your family and you don' t need to be [disconcerted]*	
20	M:	Creo que libertad es el derecho para ser que quieres?	M:	*I think freedom is the right to be what you want?*	
	M:	!	M:	*!*	
	I:	Pablo, Que quieres decir con desconcierto?	I:	*Pablo, What do you mean by desconcierto?*	
25	J:	Mia estoy de acuerdo	J:	*Mia I agree*	
	P:	que quieres mia	P:	*What do you want mia*	
	P:	embaressado	P:	*[embarassed]*	
	M:	Quiero mucho, gracias Pablo	M:	*I [want/love] a lot, thanks Pablo.*	
	P:	oue en particular	P:	*What in particular*	
30	I:	Estas embarazado? Pregnant???	I:	*Are you pregnant? Pregnant???*	
	J:	Mia quieres mucho a Pablo?	J:	*Mia do you love Pablo a lot?*	
	P:	nooooooooooo	P:	*nooooooooooo*	
	M:	No	M:	*No*	
	M:	NO	M:	*NO*	
35	P:	la libertad	P:	*Freedom*	
	I:	Entonces, que quieres decir?, como se dice en espanol?	I:	*Then, what do you mean?, how do you say it in Spanish?*	
	P:	quiero hablar sobre la cultura americana	P:	*I want to talk about American culture*	

to the established context. In line 25, Javier agreed with Alicia's last statement about freedom. Between lines 26 and 34, though, the previously shared understanding of the communicative context was again redirected. The communicators apparently did not understand each other, and they made a joke of it (talking about loving each other and being pregnant). In lines 35–36, there was an attempt to regain intersubjectivity with relation to the original topic (freedom). Pablo uttered the word *libertad*, and the instructor pushed Pablo to explain what she meant by her earlier comments. Pablo then indicated that she would rather talk about American culture. This might have been her way of reestablishing an intersubjective state by transforming the topic to something she could relate to more easily.

In this segment, the communicators seem to have achieved intersubjectivity at the beginning, and then to have lost it for a period of time, only to regain it later for very short periods of time. Pablo initiated new contexts several times throughout the segment, and the other communicators attempted to connect with her and share the newly initiated contexts. It can be seen that intersubjectivity broke down whenever at least one of Habermas' validity claims was broken. For example, in lines 18, 27, and 28, the intelligibility requirement was broken when the communicators put forth unintelligible utterances. When the other communicators pursued the intended meanings of these unintelligible utterances all at once, intersubjectivity was lost for a period of time. According to Larsen-Freeman (1980), what people do in discourse sets a task for the other communicators. For example, if one interlocutor stops communicating, then the others are automatically given the task of discourse maintenance. Also, initiating a topic requires one interlocutor to solicit discussion of that topic that the other interlocutors then either accept or reject. In this segment, all four communicators attempted to initiate a conversational context at the beginning, but the solicitations of two of the communicators (Alicia, line 15, and Mía, line 20) were not incorporated into the conversation. It appears that these solicitations were rejected in favor of those of Pablo and Javier. It can also be observed that some of the communicators were silent for significant periods of time (Alicia and Mía), which automatically assigned Pablo and Javier the task of discourse maintenance. As seen in Segment B, due to the dynamics of discourse initiation and maintenance in the chat rooms, intersubjectivity is both fluid and fragile.

According to Schegloff's theory of defending intersubjectivity, repair of lost understanding must generally occur within three turns of the source of trouble. If such repair is not made within the three (or sometimes four) turns, then such repair as is attempted becomes 'next relevant.' The problem with becoming next relevant is that the repair may never again be relevant. Segment B corroborates Schegloff's findings in the chat room context as well. The breakdown in intersubjectivity which occurred in line 23 was still not recovered by line 37, rendering the shared communicative context beyond repair.

This brief exploration of intersubjectivity allowed the researcher to examine and classify the various chat room discussions in this study according to the extent to which it appeared that the learners were able to establish and maintain collaborative discourse within a social space characterized by mutual understanding. When such a social space was maintained, the learners achieved coherent, often substantive, communication. When the shared perspective broke down, it was either subsequently reestablished by means of communicative strategies referred to by Schegloff as 'defense of intersubjectivity,' or, in some cases, never regained. A favorable condition for the development of linguistic competence or fluency, especially at the intermediate level of L2 study, is that learners move beyond 'simple' communication about the immediate context (Givon, 1979). It is when learners move into less immediately obvious contexts that they must work harder to establish a shared framework of understanding. In many of the chat sessions in this study (e.g., Segment A above), learners expanded their 'here-and-now' intersubjectivity (Rommetveit, 1974) to include discussion of concepts and ideas that were beyond the tangible, everyday aspects of their lives, creating this favorable condition for linguistic competence.

The establishment of intersubjective communication is particularly challenging in the chat room environment. First, there is no nonverbal communication in chat rooms since interlocutors do not see each other while they are chatting. Also, the turn-taking system is profoundly modified since there is no systematic control over when communicators enter utterances into the conversation. The challenge becomes to merge several strands of conversation that often occur simultaneously. The above discourse analyses revealed that learners in these intermediate Spanish classes successfully overcame these communicative challenges in order to achieve and maintain shared states of understanding with each other in their L2 throughout 45-minute weekly sessions.

Off-Task Discussion

In several of the chat room discussions, the learners decided to abandon the assigned topic for a topic of their choosing. Off-task discussion, then, became one of the salient features of chat room interaction in the study. Off-task utterances occurred in every episode. Off-task discussion was operationalized as more than five consecutive utterances unrelated to the assigned task. Table 6.1 summarizes the topics of off-task discussion in each of the nine episodes.

Table 6.1. Topics of Off-task Discussions

Episode	Assigned Topic	Off-task Topic	% of Episode
1C	freedom	weekend; England/Ireland	30%
2G	censorship	small talk	34
3C	sexism	music	25
4A	movies	small talk	15
4C	mpvies	study abroad; TV	15
5C	music	Halloween party	39

5D	music	study abroad	27
5E	music	movies	25
6C	marriage	majors; residence; travel	38
6F	marriage	small talk	15
7A	family problems	small talk	14
8A	animals	Thanksgiving; classes	43
8C	animals	Thanksgiving; food	26
8G	animals	Thanksgiving	48
9C	the future	small talk	24
9D	the future	parties	29

Note: Percentages were calculated based on the number of off-task utterances divided by the total number of utterances in the episode.

As can be seen in Table 6.1, about one fourth of the chat episodes included a significant amount of off-task discussion, ranging from 15% to 48% of the entire chat episode. At least three patterns are prevalent in the off-task discussion data. First, the chosen topics of off-task discussion seem to be what learners found interesting and of immediate relevance to their lives. For example, in week eight – the week before Thanksgiving vacation, three of the four off-task discussions were about Thanksgiving. Five of the off-task discussions centered around small talk, characterized as conversations which flowed from topic to topic without converging on any particular topic. The second pattern of interest is that it was very often the same learners who engaged in off-task discussion. While some of the learners never strayed from the assigned topic, others did so in all or nearly all of the chat sessions. For example, one learner with the pseudonym Beatriz initiated and participated in off-task discussion in every chat session that she attended (Episodes 1C, 3C, 4C, 5C, 6C, and 8C in Table 6.1). A third finding regarding off-task discussion is that it always occurred when the instructor was not in the room. Learners often stayed on task for as long as the instructor was in their room, only to go off task immediately after the instructor left.

While it only takes the initiation of an off-task topic on the part of one learner to establish off-task discussion, learners often negotiated whether or not to go off task and what off-task topic to talk about. Segment C demonstrates this negotiation.

As usual, off-task discussion was suggested as soon as the instructor left the room. Carlos (C) asked what his fellow chatters would like to talk about (line 6). Enitza (E) also stated her desire to abandon the assigned topic. Rosario (R) put forth an on-task statement which she probably had begun to type before the topic change was suggested. In lines 13–15, all chatters were in agreement to change the topic. Rosario suggested talking about

SEGMENT C: Animals

	I:	Bueno chicos. Me bvoy para otro cuarto. Hasta luego.		I:	*Well guys. I'm going to another room. See you later.*
	C:	adios.		C:	*Bye.*
	R:	hasta luego		R:	*see you later*
5	C:	bien.		C:	*Good.*
	C:	que quieres hablar sobre?		C:	*what do you want to talk about?*
	E:	no animales. esta aburrido		E:	*not animals. It's boring.*
	R:	Que te parecen como nosotros gastamos mas en comida para las mascotas que en comida para los bebes		R:	*What do you think how we spend more on food for pets than on baby food?*
10					
	C:	si, si, si.		C:	*yeah, yeah, yeah*
	R:	si esta tema es muy aburrida cambiamos al otro		R:	*yes this topic is very boring let's change to another*
15	C:	si,		C:	*yes*
	C:	que tema?		C:	*what topic?*
	R:	cualquiera		R:	*whatever*
	E:	escuela?		E:	*school?*
	C:	como se dice thanksgiving?		C:	*how do you say thanksgiving?*
20	R:	dia de gracias		R:	*"dia de gracias"*
	C:	A mi me gusta el dia se gracias.		C:	*I like thanksgiving*

SEGMENT D: Freedom

	C:	Pienso que necitamos que hablamos sobre de clase		C:	*I think we need to talk about class*
	B:	NO!		B:	*NO!*
	G:	la libertad para mi es dinero		G:	*Freedom for me is money*
5	C:	La profesora da malas notas		C:	*The professor will give us a bad grade*
	B:	bueno, ahora, hablamos sobre otras cosas mas interesante		B:	*well, now, let's talk about other more interesting things*
	C:	Por que dinero? Explicame.		C:	*Why money? Explain to me.*
	B:	no, yo explico mas temprano		B:	*no, I'll explain it earlier [later]*
	B:	no explico solament para ti		B:	*I'm not explaining it just for you*
	C:	Pero no entiendo		C:	*But I don't understand*
	>>	Instructor connected at 11:25		>>	Instructor connected at 11:25
	G:	Yo no quiero pagar para la libertad.		G:	*I don't want to pay for freedom.*
	B:	dinero = la libertad		B:	*money = freedom*
	B:	es facil		B:	*It's easy*
	>>	Instructor disconnected at 11:29		>>	Instructor disconnected at 11:29
	B:	yo quiero viajar a otros paises		B:	*I want to travel to other countries*
	C:	Que paises?		C:	*What countries?*
	B:	y cuidar para mis hijos		B:	*and take care of my kids*
	B:	ingleterra		B:	*england*
	C:	Me gusta ingleterra		C:	*I like england*
	B:	ireland, no se como se dice		B:	*ireland, I don't know how you say it*
	B:	si, yo tambien		B:	*yeah, me too*
	G:	Me gusta bandas de iglaterra		G:	*I like bands from egland*

school, while Carlos suggested talking about Thanksgiving – the topic which they eventually settled on after the episode ended. What is interesting about this exchange is that all of the learners recognized that it was difficult for them to discuss the given topic, and they collectively negotiated a topic that would work for them.

Sometimes when learners negotiated whether or not to go or stay off task, conflicts emerged. In Segment D, a conflict was produced during an off-task discussion of weekend plans, when one learner decided that it was time to get back on task.

When Carmen (C) suggested returning to the assigned task, Beatriz (B) responded with an emphatic NO! Beatriz then summarized in one sentence all she had to say about the assigned topic and indicated her desire to talk about something more interesting to her. Carmen tried two tactics to get back on task. First, she expressed her concern that their participation grade would be lowered for being off task. Then she pushed Beatriz to explain her statement that money equals freedom. When Beatriz refused to accept the solicited topic of discussion, Carmen implored Beatriz one more time (line 11), stating that she did not understand Beatriz's previous statement. The instructor then reentered the room, and Beatriz held on to the assigned topic, if only temporarily. As soon as the instructor left, however, the conversation reverted to off-task mode again.

Although Guajira (G) wished to remain on task, she was not able to do so because the other two interlocutors entered into discussion of another topic. So Guajira conceded and joined the off-task discussion. On another occasion, however, Beatriz's attempt to initiate off-task discussion was overcome by the other two communicators, and the assigned topic was kept. Segment E (from Episode 2G) shows this exchange.

SEGMENT E

	B:	quiero salir para mi casa	B:	*I want to leave for home*
	B:	hoy es VIERNES!!!	B:	*today is FRIDAY!!!*
	G:	podemos ir a paso 2?	G:	*can we go to paso 2?*
	C:	si, pienso	C:	*yes, I think so*
5	B:	esoy de acuerdo	B:	*I agree*

From the above segments, it can be seen that the discussion was triggered when the instructor was not present and when one or more communicators decided to abandon the assigned topic for another, more interesting one. As Larsen-Freeman (1980) pointed out, discursive behavior of one interlocutor assigns certain communicative roles to the other interlocutors. Therefore, when one person solicits an off-task discussion, the off-task discussion occurs only if the interlocutors follow the lead of the solicitor. This situation leads to one of three results. First, the interlocutors can follow the lead of the solicitor and move into an off-task discussion. Alternatively, the interlocutors can remain on task, obligating the off-task solicitor to remain on task as well. Finally, a disagreement can take place about whether to remain on task or go off task. Eventually the disagreement has to resolve itself in favor of either off- or on-task discussion.

Social Cohesiveness

The chatters in this study engaged in extensive (on-task and off-task) electronic discourse which required them to collaborate with each other a great deal in order to establish and maintain coherent discussion. In addition to this type of collaboration, the learners also engaged in communicative behaviors that served the purpose of social cohesiveness.

Chun (1994) reported that her learners performed a wide range of interactional speech acts in chat rooms, including everyday social encounters such as greetings, leave takings, and the use of polite formulas. In the current study, similar language functions occurred very frequently. These discourse functions, which Chun referred to as demonstration of 'minimal sociolinguistic competence,' became an important part of the chat discussions in that they allowed learners to share their feelings with each other and to demonstrate a sense of sociability. Such measures of social cohesiveness enabled learners to construct what Meskill (1999) refers to as a *community of learners*, and what Wenger (1998) calls a *community of practice*. In Wenger's view, learning is largely a function of social participation in communities of practice. 'Participation here refers not just to local events of engagement in certain activities with certain people, but to a more encompassing process of being active participants in the *practices* of social communities and constructing *identities* in relation to these communities.' The following excerpts illustrate learner communicative behaviors which led to the construction of an online discourse community of Spanish learners.

Greeting and Leave-taking

In many of the episodes, the learners (and the teacher when she was present) spent a significant amount of time greeting each other and talking about their current state of being or activities of importance to them before beginning their assigned task. Such conversation was not labeled by the researcher as off-task discussion since the tasks had not officially begun and since this type of discussion appeared to serve a social purpose rather than avoiding the assigned task. Segment F shows an example of greeting talk.

SEGMENT F

		Spanish	English
	A:	Hola Mario, como estas hoy?	*Hi Mario, how are you today?*
	M:	Hola Amparo. Estoy muy bien. Y tu??	*Hi Amparo. I' m fine. And you??*
	A:	mmm ...estoy asi asi	*mmm ..I' m OK*
	M:	Que paso en tu vida? Cualquier	*What happened in your life?*
5		interesante?	*Whichever interesting?*
	A:	es viernes, pero no puedo salir este noche, porque tengo demasiado mucho tarea	*it' s Friday, but I can' t go out tonight, because I have too much much homework*
	A:	:-(	*:-(*
10	I:	Hola como estan? que hay de nuevo?	*Hi how are you? What' s new?*
	A:	fui a ver Dracula anoche	*i went to see Dracula last night*
	I:	Amparo estas contenta?	*Amparo are you happy?*
	A:	Estoy asi asi	*I' m OK*
	M:	Lo siento Amparo ...Como fue la	*I' m sorry Amparo ...How was the*
15		ballet?	*ballet?*
	A:	Fue bueno	*It was good*
	A:	Me gusta mucho a Renfield	*I like Renfield a lot*
	I:	Ampero, A que ballet fuiste?	*Ampero, What ballet did you go to?*
	M:	Me gusta la ballet, pero a veces The	*I like ballet, but sometimes The*
20		Pittsburgh Ballet no baila bien!	*Pittsburgh Ballet doesn' t dance well!*
	A:	Fui a Dracula	*I went to Dracula*
	A:	si! es la verdad	*yes! It' s the truth*
	I:	Te gusto?	*Did you like it?*
	A:	Si, me gusta	*Yes, I like it*
25	M:	Recuerdaste quien bailo la primeras partes?	*Did you remember who danced the first parts?*
	I:	A mi tambien me gusta EL ballet, pero prefiero la danza moderna ...	*I like ballet too, but I prefer modern dance ...*
	A:	ummm ...recuerdo caras pero no	*ummm ...I remember faces but not*
30		nombres ..lo siento	*names ..I' m sorry*
	A:	tengo la programa en mi casa	*i have a program at my house*
	I:	Tienes El programa de Dracula?	*Do you have the program of Dracula?*
	A:	si, en mi casa	*yes, at my house*
	M:	Ahhhh ...Cree que fue el ballet aqui en	*Ahhh ...[?] think it was the ballet here*
35		Pittsburgh ...Tienen sus libros?	*in Pittsburgh ...Do you have your books?*
	I:	Mario, ?recuerdaste?	*Mario, you remembered?*
	A:	?	*?*
	I:	Como se dice " recordar" en preterito?	*How do you say "to remember" in the*
40			*preterit?*
	M:	Si, recorde(?) mi libro.	*yes, I remembered (?) my book.*
	I:	Se dice " recordaste". Bueno, empecemos con los pasos ...	*You say "you remembered." Well, let' s start the steps ...*

Many of the episodes in the study began with this sort of lengthy greeting and small talk before learners dove into their assigned tasks. In very few episodes did the learners begin the tasks immediately without taking time to greet each other. It appears, then, that getting sufficiently acquainted with each other each week was an important part of building their online discourse community. In some of the episodes, the leave takings were rather elaborate as well. Segment G shows one of these.

The chatters bid each other farewell in a more elaborate way than simply saying *adiós* 'good bye.' Isabel (Is) initiated the leave taking, Javier (J) and the instructor (I) both wished the others a nice weekend, and Adia (A) expressed her enjoyment of having chatted with everybody. Employing

SEGMENT G

	J:	tienen un buen dia …		J:	*have a good day*
	J:	chao		J:	*bye*
	Is:	pienso que es todo para hoy		Is:	*I think that is all for today*
	J:	si		J:	*yes*
5	Is:	adios …		Is:	*bye …*
	P:	si, hasta luego		P:	*yes, see you later*
	I:	Que tengan buen fin de semana		I:	*Have a good weekend.*
	A:	Me gusta hablar con Uds. Adio		A:	*I like talking to you. Bye.*
	Is:	si y ud tambien		Is:	*You too*
10	Is:	yo tambien		Is:	*Me too.*

their developing L2 sociolinguistic competence in this way, they exited the conversation maintaining the type of social cohesion that they established and maintained throughout the entire chat session.

Use of Humor

In addition to greetings and leave takings, social cohesiveness was evident in other parts of the chat room conversations. In some of the episodes the learners and the instructor engaged in various forms of humor such as teasing and joking with each other. Sometimes the jokes were one-liners (e.g., in a conversation about animals in week eight, one learner said *Tengo un gato y un novio.* 'I have a cat and a boyfriend.'). At other times the joking occurred over several turns of conversation and involved most or all of the group as shown in Segment H.

SEGMENT H: Sexism

	P:	Las chicas son buenas para tres cosas …		P:	*Girls are good for three things...*
	Y:	cuales son?		Y:	*What are they?*
	P:	cocinar, limpiar, y hacer bebes		P:	*Cooking, cleaning and making babies*
	E:	el sexismo va a existar siempre		E:	*sexism is always going to exist*
5	Y:	estas serio, pico?		Y:	*are you serious Pico?*
	E:	tipical		E:	*typical*
	N:	Pico, eres uno de dos hombres en este clase, no es dificil saber cual eres		N:	*Pico, you are one of two men in this class, it's not difficult to know which one you are*
10	Y:	jeje		Y:	*hehe*
	E:	pico, eres en un cuarto con tres chicaa! tenga cuidad		E:	*pico, you're in a room with three girls! be careful*
	P:	no me importa		P:	*I don't care*
	Y:	si, ten mucho cuidado		Y:	*yeah, be very careful*
15	P:	que van hacer?		P:	*what are you going to do?*

In the midst of a conversation about sexism, Pico (P), the only male in the group, put forth a sexist remark. It is, of course, possible that what he expressed in this segment represented his true opinions, but, judging from the entire episode from which the segment came and the researcher's observations of laughter during the chat session, it seems that Pico was in a playful mood during this chat session. It appears that he was taking advantage of his being the only male in the room to be playful with his female interlocutors.

The use of humor and teasing has a potential to develop strong positive and negative feelings. The humor that occurred in the above two segments contributed to the social cohesiveness of the chat room environment and thereby nourished the online discourse community. It is also noteworthy that the language play occurred almost entirely in Spanish, with very little recourse to English. Thus, when learners engage in speech events such as teasing and joking, they have an opportunity to expand their sociolinguistic competence in their L2.

Identity/Role Play

If joking and teasing contributed to the social environment of the chat rooms, role playing and experimenting with new identities were two other noted interactional features that seemed to fulfill similar purposes. Two of the female learners adopted masculine names for their chat pseudonyms (Mario and Pablo). While Pablo never assumed a masculine role in the conversations, Mario did. In the first episode, for example, Pablo stated that she was tired (*Estoy cansada*) using the feminine form of the adjective which immediately revealed her female identity. In another episode, when the topic was sexism, she took on a very pro-female stance. Mario, however, acted the opposite. In the first episodes, whenever she described herself with adjectives in Spanish, she used the masculine form (*Estoy cansado*). She even went as far as to correct another learner who asked her *Por que estas cansada?* and used the feminine ending. In the sexism discussion, Mario took on a very neutral stance without revealing her female identity. She maintained her male identity throughout the chat sessions. Mario's maintenance of a male identity not only had social but also linguistic ramifications. It forced her to pay close attention to Spanish morphology (especially nouns and adjectives), which she did consistently throughout the study.

Beyond the adoption of particular pseudonyms, some learners also engaged in role plays throughout their chat sessions. Segment I illustrates one of these role plays.

The interlocutors initiated the role play situation for Selena (S), which is also the name of a famous Mexican American singer whose murder had made international news. Selena followed the role play with her comment about

SEGMENT I

	B:	selena viva!!
	G:	yay selena!
	S:	Calmadas porfavor, Orita estoy trabajando en un nuevo cancion.
5	B:	haha
	B:	bueno
	M	bidi bidi bam bam
	C:	Mi padre ama Selena
	M	ahh, bueno
10	B:	me gusta su cancion antes de muertes
	M	Este conversacion es muy interesante]
	B:	si
	S:	Tambien tengo una nueva linea de ropa.
15	B:	haha, me gusta ropa
	B:	pero, me gusta ropa que cubrir mi cuerpo
	M	Selena, nos tenemos lo mismo apeido
	S:	QUe bien, te voy ayudia con un vestido

B:	*selena alive!!*
G:	*yeah selena!*
S:	*Calm please, Right now I' m working on a new song.*
B:	*ha ha*
B:	*good*
M	*bidi bidi bam bam*
C:	*My father loves Selena*
M	*ahh, good*
B:	*I like her song before deaths*
M	*This conversation is very interesting]*
B:	*yes*
S:	*I also have a new line of clothing.*
B:	*haha, I like clothing*
B:	*but, I like clothing that covers my body*
M	*Selena, we have the same last name*
S:	*Great, I' m going help you with a dress*

working on a new song. María (M) typed the words to one of Selena's favorite songs, and Carlos (C) added that his father really likes Selena. When Selena referred to her new line of clothing, Beatriz (B) added that she likes clothing that covers her body, a comment that apparently refers to the attire of the singer. After this segment, the learners returned to serious conversation of the assigned topic. The role play gave learners the chance to talk about a famous Spanish-speaking person as well as to enjoy themselves in their chat session.

Sarcasm/Insults

Similar to joking and teasing, the transcripts of the chat sessions in the study show many instances of use of sarcasm and insults. Segment J contains one of these instances.

The learners had been instructed to each look up the constitution of a Spanish-speaking country and to comment on the liberties granted therein. When Mía and Pablo both wished to discuss the constitution of Mexico, Pablo began to get difficult with Mía. She limited her disagreement to saying 'no' (lines 5–7). By lines 14–15, however, she became aggressive with Mía, stating that there is no rule that says they could not both work with the Mexican constitution. Sarcastically, she asked Mía if she was happy and told her not to cry. Javier was caught in the middle and seemed to be confused, perhaps thinking that they all needed to decide on one constitution. In Segment K, Pablo made a cyber attack on another learner, but this learner decided to return the insult.

SEGMENT J

	I:	Bueno, Que paises quieren leer?		I:	OK. What countries do you want to read?
	M:	Quiero leer Mexico		M:	I want to read Mexico.
	P:	estoy leeyendo sobre mexico		P:	I'm reading Mexico
	J:	Venezuela		J:	Venezuela
5	P:	no		P:	no
	P:	no		P:	no
	P:	no		P:	no
	M:	si si		M:	yes yes
	J:	Okay CUBA		J:	Okay Cuba
10	I:	No que? Pablo o Si que Mia?		I:	NO what? Pablo or Yes what Mia?
	M:	no tengo mexico		M:	I don't have Mexico
	M:	Pablo no tiene		M:	Pablo doesn't have
	P:	nosotros las dos pueden tener mexico ... no hay una regala		P:	we both can have mexico ...There's no rule
15	P:	bien?		P:	OK
	P:	estas contenta		P:	are you happy
	M:	contenta como te dices?		M:	happy how do you say to yourself?
	P:	no lloras		P:	you don't cry
	J:	lo siento		J:	I'm sorry
20	P:	lo siento		P:	I'm sorry.

SEGMENT K

	P:	me gusta tori amos y los indigo girls		P:	I like tori amos and the india girls
	PL:	bah		PL:	bah
	P:	jodate		P:	fuck you
	N:	no, no deseo		N:	no, I don't want
	J:	ninos por favor no usan malas palabras		J:	kids please don't use bad words
5	P:	me gusta tu mama		P:	I like your mama
	PL:	esta bien		PL:	that's OK
	P:	tu eres muy extrano Pico		P:	you're very strange Pico
	PL:	me come		PL:	you eat me

Pico (PL) indicated his disagreement with Pablo's choice of good music groups. Although his comment (*bah*) was rather mild, Pablo (P) responded with an expletive. Natalia (N) and Javier (J) interjected mitigating comments, but Pablo continued to insult Pico. Unlike Javier in the previous episode, however, Pico decided to return the verbal attack with a comment that temporarily ended the incident. A short while later, however, another round of insults emanated from Pablo (see Segment L).

Segments J–L illustrate what is commonly referred to as *flaming* in Internet terminology, electronic discourse characterized by inappropriate or excessive emotionalism, bluntness, or hostility (Sproull & Kiesler, 1991). It is believed that flaming is a very frequent Internet phenomenon, and that aggression in general is higher online than off (Wallace, 1999). It is likely that anonymity and not being face-to-face contribute to this high amount of flaming. In other words, people may feel more comfortable insulting others

SEGMENT L

	P:	vi bob Dylan y paul simon, tom petty, yes (tres veces), allman brothers durante el verano pasado y roger waters de pink floyd y rusted root		P:	*I saw bob dylan and paul simon, tom petty, yes (three times), allman brothers last summer and roger waters of pink floyd and rusted root*
5	J:	Pablo mentirosa		J:	*Pablo liar*
	P:	Quieres preguntar a mi madre		P:	*you want to ask my mother*
	J:	Si		J:	*Yes*
	J:	donde estas tu mama		J:	*where are you your mom*
	P:	no me gusta los barenakedladies		P:	*I don't like barenakedladies*
10	PL:	el grupos o mujeres desnudos		PL:	*the groups or naked women*
	P:	puedo darte su numero de telefono puta		P:	*I can give you her phone number bitch*
	P:	tu no me sabes. cierra la boca mentiroso		P:	*you don't know me. Shut your mouth liar*
15	J:	AH Okay por favor ninos obstena de usar palabras malas. Cuanto vezes tengo que decirlo		J:	*AH Okay please kids abstain from using bad words. How many times do I have to say it?*

while hidden behind their computers than in a face-to-face situation. Learners in this study sometimes spouted off insults which were interspersed with more serious interaction, at some points taking over the serious interaction completely. One researcher working with college English composition students noted a great deal of cursing among the students which he called a 'tidal wave of obscenity and puerility' (DiMatteo, 1990). In this study, it appears that flaming, at least to some extent, is a form of humor among learners. It does not appear that the learners truly meant to insult each other but rather to have fun with each other in Spanish in their learner-centered chat room discourse community. It is likely that they picked up these expressions from native speakers of Spanish and decided to practice using them with their classmates in the chat rooms. The use of profane language in this study, then, indicates another way in which these learners developed their sociolinguistic competence in Spanish. After all, knowing how, when, and whom to insult must be learned in an L2 as well as in an L1. It was notable in this study, for example, that none of the learners ever insulted the instructor as they did each other. In this way, the chat room context provided a communicative forum for the development of a type of sociolinguistic competence which, as would be expected, is not promoted in the typical L2 classroom but is, nevertheless, part of native speakers' use of the L2 that these chatters are learning.

Use of English

A final interactional feature of interest in the study was the minimal use of the learners' L1 (English). Both learners and instructor maintained Spanish as the language of communication throughout the nine chat sessions with few exceptions. When English was invoked, it was almost always to express an unknown lexical item in Spanish. Learners usually stated the entire sentence in Spanish and placed the unknown word in parentheses in English (e.g., *es una* (guess), ... *mirar a un* (website ...), and ... *las programas son* (fake)). English was also used to clarify a word or expression in Spanish when the meaning was less than clear. Some examples include '*que es 'violada'*? rapist or victim?' '*que significa 'amenazar'*? Threatened?' Finally, English was occasionally used to give instructions for the task at hand, for example, 'ok go to file and click on "choose new window"' and '*la instructor dice* "you should stick to the lesson plan"'.

It appears that when English was used, it was for the purpose of efficiently maintaining conversation in Spanish. For example, many of the English lexical items that were used in the chat sessions contained less common concepts that the learners probably had not been exposed to in the L2. Words used in this study such as 'overblown,' 'kinky,' 'yuck,' and 'old boy network' represent concepts that may not be part of common, everyday speech that formed the basis of the learners' L2 experience. In order to express the meanings of these words, the learners could either attempt to circumlocute in Spanish or to use the word in English and continue the conversation. In some cases the latter, more efficient option was chosen.

The use of the L1 in L2 classes remains a debated issue in foreign language methodology. Many advocates of communicative language teaching would not condone any L1 use in the L2 class, believing that L2 learners need as much exposure and practice as possible within a solely L2 context. The L1 could also be viewed, however, as a semiotic tool to be strategically employed in maintaining communication in the L2 when the interlocutors all share the same L1. It is much easier to say a word in English and to continue the conversation in Spanish than to spend a long time trying to explain a concept in Spanish and still not getting the exact meaning across. Use of the L1 – an essential part of the learners' linguistic repertoire – as a mediational tool is consonant with a sociocultural view of L2 learning. With only minimal, strategic use of English, these learners were able to maintain 50 minutes of electronic conversation almost exclusively in Spanish.

Conclusion

The purpose of this study was to examine the interactive features of synchronous CMC that emerged throughout nine weeks of in-class chat sessions. Discourse analyses revealed the unique ways in which learners took ownership of the chat room environment and constructed a dynamic, learner-centered discourse community characterized by discussion of topics of mutual interest, social cohesiveness and group belonging, joking, teasing, experimenting with identities, role plays, and even playfully insulting each other. In other words, the learners in this study used their L2 in the chat rooms for solidarity and enjoyment while, at the same time, developing their sociolinguistic competence.

The sociocultural theoretical framework, with its emphasis on social aspects of language learning, is a robust paradigm in which to frame this study of chat room communication as mediator of language learning. The social, cognitive, and affective functions of interaction illustrated in this study are consonant with the sociocultural view of discursively constructed L2 learning. The study also lends support to Vygotsky's claim that the employment of cultural tools, such as the computer in this case, not only facilitate the achievement of a given task but can also alter the entire process and outcome of task performance. As SLA researchers and practitioners, it would benefit us to acquire as full an understanding as possible of the nature of computer mediation in the L2 learning process. It is hoped the empirical account provided by this study will fuel the ongoing investigation of that endeavor.

Note

1.   In this and all subsequent transcripts, the researcher attempted to render in English the same grammatical and lexical inaccuracies as in the original Spanish.

References

Anton, M., & DiCamilla, F. (1998). Socio-cognitive functions of L1 in collaborative interaction in the L2 classroom. *Canadian Modern Language Review, 54*(3), 314–342.

Beauvois, M. (1997). Computer-mediated communication (CMC): Technology for improving speaking and writing. In M. Bush & R. Terry (Eds.), *Technology-enhanced language learning* (pp. 165–184). Lincolnwood, IL: National Textbook Company.

Bruce, B., Kreeft Peyton, J., & Batson, T. (Eds.). (1993). *Network-based classrooms: promises and realities*. New York: Cambridge University Press.

Bump, J. (1990). Radical changes in class discussion using networked computers. *Computers and the Humanities, 24*(1), 49–65.

Chun, D. (1994). Using computer networking to facilitate the acquisition of interactive competence. *System, 22*(1), 17–31.

DiMatteo, A. (1990). Under erasure: A theory for interactive writing in real time. *Computers and Composition* [Special Issue], *7*, 71–84.

Donato, R., & McCormick, D. (1994). A sociocultural perspective on language learning strategies: The role of mediation. *Modern Language Journal, 78*(4), 453–464.

Givon, T. (1979). *On understanding grammar.* New York: Academic Press.

Habermas, J. (1998). *On the pragmatics of communication.* Cambridge, MA: Cambridge University Press.

Johnson, K. (1995). *Understanding communication in second language classrooms.* Cambridge: Cambridge University Press.

Kelm, O. (1992). The use of synchronous computer networks in second language instruction: A preliminary report. *Foreign Language Annals, 25*(5), 441–454.

Kern, R. (1995). Restructuring classroom interaction with networked computers: Effects on quantity and characteristics of language production. *The Modern Language Journal, 79*(4), 457–476.

Lantolf, J., & Appel, G. (1994). Theoretical framework: An introduction to Vygotskian perspectives on second language research. In J. Lantolf & G. Appel (Eds.), *Vygotskian approaches to second language research.* Norwood, NJ: Ablex.

Larsen-Freeman, D. (1980). *Discourse analysis in second language research.* Rowley, MA: Newbury House.

Larsen-Freeman, D., & Long, M. (1991). *An introduction to second language acquisition research.* London: Longman.

Meskill, C. (1999). Computers as tools for sociocollaborative language learning. In K. Cameron (Ed.), *Computer-assisted language learning (CALL): Media, design and applications* (pp. 144–152). Exton, PA: Swets and Zeitlinger Publishers.

Miles, M. B., & Huberman, A. M. (1994). *An expanded sourcebook: Qualitative data analysis* (2nd edn). Thousand Oaks, CA: Sage Publications.

Rommetveit, R. (1974). *On message structure: A framework for the study of language and communication.* New York: John Wiley and Sons.

Rommetveit, R. (1985). Language acquisition as increasing linguistic restructuring of experience and symbolic behavior control. In J. V. Wertsch (Ed.), *Culture, communication and cognition* (pp. 57–68). Cambridge: Cambridge University Press.

Salaberry, R. (1997). A theoretical foundation for the development of pedagogical tasks in computer-mediated communication. *CALICO Journal, 14*(1), 15–33.

Schegloff, E. (1992). Repair after next turn: The last structurally provided defense of intersubjectivity in conversation. *American Journal of Sociology, 97*(5), 1295–1347.

Schmidt, R. (1993). Awareness and second language acquisition. *Annual Review of Applied Linguistics, 13*, 206–226.

Sproull, L., & Kiesler, S. (1991). *Connections: New ways of working in the networked organization.* Cambridge: MIT Press.

VanPatten, B., & Lee, J. (1995). *Making communicative language teaching happen.* New York: McGraw Hill.

Vygotsky, L. S. (1962). *Thought and language.* Cambridge, MA: MIT Press.

Vygotksy, L. S. (1978). *Mind in society*. Cambridge, MA: Harvard University Press.

Vygotsky, L. S. (1981). The instrumental method in psychology. In J. Wertsch (Ed.), *The concept of activity in Soviet psychology* (pp. 143–184). Armonk, NY: M. E. Sharpe.

Wallace, P. (1999). *The psychology of the Internet*. New York: Cambridge University Press.

Warschauer, M. (1996). Comparing face-to-face and electronic discussion in the second language classroom. *CALICO Journal, 13*(2), 7–25.

Warschauer, M. (1999). *Electronic literacies: Language, culture and power in online education*. Mahwah, NJ: Lawrence Erlbaum Associates.

Wells, G. (1998). Using L1 to master L2: A response to Antón and DiCamilla's 'sociocognitive functions of L1 collaborative interaction in the L2 classroom.' *Canadian Modern Language Review, 54*(3), 343–353.

Wells, G. (1999). *Dialogic inquiry: Towards a sociocultural practice and theory of education*. New York: Cambridge University Press.

Wenger, E. (1998). *Communities of practice: Learning, meaning, and identity*. New York: Cambridge University Press.

Wertsch, J., del Rio, P., & Alvarez, A. (Eds.). (1995). *Sociocultural studies of mind*. Cambridge: Cambridge University Press.

Wertsch, J. V. (1991). *Voices of the mind*. Cambridge, MA: Harvard University Press.

White, S. (Ed.). (1995). *The Cambridge companion to Habermas*. New York: Cambridge University Press.

Appendix

Sample Chat Room Task (Week 4: 'Movies')

Step 1: After seeing some information about movies in 'Yahoo' in Spanish, think about a movie that you have seen recently (it can be a movie that you read about in Yahoo or any other movie). Mention the movies in the chat room. Have you seen a movie in Spanish?

Step 2: Everyone should describe a movie that the others have not seen. Speak briefly about the characters and what happened in the movie. The others should ask questions for clarification and additional information. Be careful with the use of the preterite and the imperfect when you describe what happened in the movie. [*El protagonista era una persona muy amable (imperfecto). Se enamoró de una persona antipática (pretérito).*] If someone has seen a movie in Spanish, they should comment on the differences between this movie and Hollywood movies.

Step 3: After everyone has described a movie, mention if you liked the movie you saw or not, and explain why.

Step 4: Discuss the role that movies have in contemporary society. Why are movies filmed? Why do people go to the movies or rent movies on video? What are some positive and negative aspects of movies in society? You can mention, for example, psychological, social and economic aspects.

Step 5: Give your opinion about what society would be like if movies did not exist. Be careful with the use of the conditional and the imperfect subjunctive. [*Si el cine no existiera (imperfecto del subjuntivo), la sociedad sería (condicional) muy aburrida.*] Mention both positive and negative aspects. Do you agree with your classmates?

Step 6: Everyone should summarize their general opinion about movies in society. Have you changed your ideas as a result of today's conversation?

7   A Theoretical Foundation for the Development of Pedagogical Tasks in Computer Mediated Communication

M. Rafael Salaberry*

Introduction

The use of instructional media in the second language classroom has been a common practice for a long time. For instance, Price (1987) reports that teachers used pictures to teach Latin in the seventeenth century. In modern times the use of computer technology has captivated the attention of the teaching community. However, technological innovations have not always been conducive to higher achievement in language learning. Nelson (1995) argues that some of the innovations in language teaching tend to suffer from the extravagant claims made by their proponents. The introduction of the tape recorder or the VCR, for example, have presented teachers with incredible breakthroughs in technology which have not been paralleled with equal advances in learning outcomes. In fact, in some cases these advances have

*   M. Rafael Salaberry (PhD, Cornell University 1997) is Professor of Spanish Linguistics and SLA at Rice University. He is also the Director of the Center for Languages and Intercultural Communication (CLIC). Prof. Salaberry graduated from Cornell University in 1997 and has held positions at University of Minnesota, Penn State University, and University of Texas-Austin. He has extensive experience doing research in second language development, bilingualism, second language teaching, educational applications of technology, and linguistics. Prof. Salaberry has published eight books with John Benjamins (2000, 2002, 2005), Georgetown University Press (2003, 2006), Continuum Press (2008), Multilingual Matters (2009), and Mouton de Gruyter (2014). He has also published his work in peer-reviewed journals such as *Applied Linguistics, Bilingualism, The Canadian Modern Language Review, Hispania, Language Learning, Language Learning and Technology, Language Testing, The Modern Language Journal,* and *System.*

helped create the wrong teaching paradigm (e.g., the language learning lab in conjunction with the strictly behavioristic audio lingual method). The recent 'explosion' of the internet has presented second language teachers with yet another promise of a technological innovation which will create 'a paradigmatic shift' in teaching and learning second languages. However, some researchers have already offered their verdict on that prediction. For example, Bates (1995) cautions against the overly optimistic reliance on the emergence of new paradigms in learning as a consequence of improved telecommunication systems. He predicts that computers will become 'as significant to the learner as the electricity that carries the power to the refrigerator: essential for its operation, but *independent of the function that the refrigerator performs*' (p. 227, italics added). More important, Muns (1995) contends that the Internet has not created any 'radically new conceptual means of communicating' (p. 152).

The pedagogical benefits of Computer Mediated Communication (CMC) in L2 (Second Language) learning is rapidly becoming one of the most discussed topics in foreign language teaching. In this article I will address the pedagogical merits of this new medium of communication in relation to current research 'in Anthropology, Cognitive Psychology, Communication Theory, Linguistics, and Second Language Acquisition (SLA). The outline of the paper is as follows. Section 2 analyzes the use of computer technology in SLA: a review of the uses of CALL applications, Intelligent CALL programs, and ALS (Advanced Language Systems). Section 3 presents a principled approach to the uses of CALL-based systems according to their inherent limitations. Section 4 outlines the proposed theoretical foundation that supports the design of pedagogical applications for CMC environments. Section 5 describes the types of pedagogical uses of computer based telecommunications according to the theory developed in the previous part. Finally, section 6 presents the conclusion and suggestions for further research.

The Use of Technology in Education

Many inventions have shown the promise of starting a revolution in the transfer of information among humans. The following are prominent examples of such predicted revolutions: the first appearance of writing systems, the invention of the printing press by Gutenberg, the invention of the telephone by Bell, the mass production of audio and video tape recorders, the invention of the photocopy machine by Xerox, and the widely extended use of 'microcomputers'. The appearance of the Internet has been hailed as the latest technological for sharing information. An article in *Newsweek* magazine (Levy 1995) praises the Internet as the new frontier in the transfer of information: 'You talk about a revolution? For once, the shoe fits ... It really is about opening communication to the masses. And 1995 was the year that the masses started coming' (p. 27). In fact, the Worldwide Web (WWW) has been doubling every 53 days in a sort of factorial growth. Language teaching professionals wonder whether the emergence of a system which opens up a myriad of communication channels will have lasting effects on pedagogical practices. The relevant question is: does the pervasive nature of an information transfer system such as Internet create a paradigmatic shift on the teaching of foreign languages (or education in general)? Some researchers have argued forcefully in favor of such a paradigm shift (e.g., Harasim, 1990; Dede, 1993; Berge & Collins, 1995). For instance, Berge and Collins argue that CMC generates a shift from instructor-centered to student-centered learning (p. 2). However, is this shift a direct consequence of the emergence of computer based telecommunications?, or is it a result of the pedagogical approach of the teaching practices that rely on that medium? It is true that, perhaps, the advent of a new communication system reveals hitherto unnoticed features of a successful learning environment. In fact, Berge and Collins acknowledge that CMC is changing instructional methodology in two ways: generating improved technological tools to use a full range of interactive methodologies, and – more important – by focusing teachers' perspectives on the appropriate learner-centered design of instruction (p. 2), This is no minor feat. However, many L2 teachers would not be impressed by such an discovery. After all, foreign language teachers have been promoting a learner-centered approach for quite some time (see Canale & Swain, 1980; Savignon, 1983; Rivers, 1987; Kenning & Kenning, 1990 *inter alia*).

The potential pedagogical effect of the technological tools used in L2 instruction (e.g., VCRs, audio tape recorders, satellite TV, etc.) is inherently dependent on the particular theoretical or methodological approach that guides its application. In fact, in some cases, the emergence of technological breakthroughs has been wrongfully guided by inaccurate theoretical assumptions: the use of the language learning lab in conjunction with the audiolingual method (ALM). That is why Price (1987) notices that *different methodological approaches* favor the use of one medium over another. In other words, it is not the medium itself that determines the pedagogical outcome, but the specific focus of the theoretical approach on the language learning phenomena. On the other hand, instruction which is well designed and rightfully targeted can be extremely successful even if the nature of the technology itself is not in accordance with the major tenets of the prevalent methodological approach. Hence, TV programs such as *Sesame Street* and *Mr. Rogers* are successful for delivering instruction to large groups of children in spite of the passive nature of TV viewing (Ahern & Repman, 1994). These examples of the use of technological tools (the language learning lab and children's TV programs) reveal that educators should be knowledgeable in two areas: educational theory and practice, and the process of instructional design and use of different technologies (Bates, p. 246). Without a strong foundation in those two bodies of knowledge L2 teachers will not be able to make principle-guided decisions in their pedagogical use of technological tools. A case in point has been the relative failure of Computer Assisted Instruction (CAI) in the creation of significant instructional changes in the L2 classroom.

A review of CALL applications in L2 teaching

A critical analysis of the pedagogical uses of CALL applications may be presented from three different perspectives: the theoretical foundation that guides CALL design, the empirical research that measures the pedagogical effectiveness of CALL, and the technological capabilities of computers. First, a minimal theoretical framework in CALL applications should recognize that the 'effective use of any medium in language teaching depends on *the role* the message in that medium plays in the language-learning situation, *the content* of the materials, and the *ways these two interact within each student's language-learning experience*' (Price, 1987: 156; italics added). However, the majority of CALL applications have not relied on any type of theoretical rationale except for the theoretical framework already built into basic CALL exercises: the computer is the ideal environment for the implementation of the type of Programmed Learning from the behavioristic tradition (the 'wrong-try-again' approach: Underwood, 1984: 45). Nevertheless, there are several examples of principle-based applications of technology in the L2 literature which reflect the basic tenets of a learner-centered curriculum (Künzel, 1995). For instance, Higgins (1988) developed a theoretical foundation for the design of CALL programs based on the notion of the computer as a magister or a pedagogue.[1] Another example is Communicative CALL (Underwood, 1984) which reflects a true paradigmatic shift in teaching: a change in pedagogical theory but not necessarily due to a change in technology. The computer formerly used for grammatical drill practice was no longer seen as a teacher or as a tool, but rather as a helper or facilitator.[2] The theoretical rationale of Underwood was based on the ideas of Chomsky (language 'grows' in a normally rich linguistic environment) and Krashen (comprehensible input). Even in the absence of consensus on these theoretical foundations in particular, it is important to underline that Communicative CALL reflects a well-informed pedagogical practice due to its strong theoretical base. In fact, Underwood lists a set of criteria that should guide the development of 'Communicative CALL': communication is the goal, grammar is taught implicitly, only the target language is used, the program is flexible (more than one single response allowed), it allows exploration of content, it provides on and off-screen tasks, it does not attempt to incorporate tasks which are better implemented in other media, and, most important, it is fun!

On the other hand, a principled approach to the use of technology in the classroom may also lead to the reassessment of dismissed technological options. For example, the demise of the language learning laboratory came about as a consequence of the fall of the behavioristic tradition that informed the audiolingual method (Chomsky, 1959). However, a proper assessment of the pedagogical value of the language lab within a principled approach of SLA has led Underwood to conclude that the value of the dismissed language learning laboratory of the 1960s and 1970s should be reassessed: 'the solution ... is to use the lab as a true audio-visual or multimedia center' (p. 37). In sum, the most recent CALL programs have assigned a great deal of importance to a principle-based approach to developing computer based instruction. On the other hand, it is quite noticeable that the majority of theoretical arguments favoring the latest development of CALL applications are based on the hypotheses developed by Krashen and colleagues (e.g., Underwood, 1984; Higgins, 1988; Kenning & Kenning, 1990; Nelson, 1995).[3] This particular theoretical approach does not invalidate the pedagogical value of those CALL programs. However, it does raise some concerns about the validity of embracing such a monolithic approach in a field of inquiry with so many theoretical perspectives. More specifically, the history of support of Krashen's perspective is not comforting considering the fact that many researchers have argued forcefully against Krashen's hypotheses.[4]

A second drawback of archetypal CALL programs has been the lack of appropriate empirical studies that assess the benefits of such programs. Alternatively, these studies may generate useful research hypotheses which can properly frame the potential use of CALL programs within a variety of pedagogical approaches. Several investigators have reported various deficiencies in the few empirical studies addressing the pedagogical benefits of CAI on learning (e.g., Reeves, 1993; Schmitt, 1991). Schmitt has noted the following four major research design flaws: small sample sizes, lack of criteria for what constitutes appropriate software, faulty statistical analysis, and inadequate length of treatment to measure educational outcomes. Reeves mentions the lack of a theoretical framework, the infrequency and brevity of the experimental treatments, the small sample sizes, and the large attrition in number of participating subjects. Reeves claims that research on computer based instruction has traversed three distinct stages: research on the effect of computer literacy (do computers help learning?), research specific types of applications, and finally, research on the analysis of learner control variables (how learners selections of rate, content, and nature of feedback affect learning). From a theoretical perspective, the final stage is the most valuable: interactive instruction gives the learner the chance to choose the learning path. It is also the most relevant because it underlies most of the research efforts of the recent multimedia environments. However, the contradictory results of most empirical studies addressing the issue of learner control variables reveal fundamental research design problems. Another major methodological problem of some of these empirical studies includes the lack of use of a control group to measure increased learning as an outcome of the use of CALL applications (e.g., Chapelle & Jamieson, 1986; Liu and Reed 1995).[5] The study of Chapelle and Jamieson serves to exemplify yet another difficult issue in the design of empirical studies analyzing CALL: the Hawthorne effect (positive effect of exposure to something new: Künzel, 1995). The solution offered by Reeves to solve these problems is to conduct extensive, in-depth studies to 'observe human behavior in our field and relate the observations to meaningful learning theory that may be later susceptible to quantitative theory' (p. 44). This is a necessary step considering the fact that very few working hypotheses are available to explain the phenomena under study. Qualitative descriptive studies can generate a number of specific hypotheses which can be tested later. However, the use of qualitative studies should not rule out the design of quantitative studies that present a clear theoretical rationale and a sound research design.

A critical review of previous CALL studies is important because the newly arrived studies on the effect of computer based telecommunications on learning show similar defects. For example, the study conducted by Veasey (1991) on the use of e-mail as a pedagogical tool shows some of the above mentioned problems. First, Veasey does not present a theoretical framework: the intent was to examine the benefits and uses of e-mail as an instructional support tool in the classroom environment without an explanation of why those benefits were expected. Second, the research design was poorly controlled: the dependent variable was the gain score from a pre-test to a post-test even though these tests were clearly different (a written exam and a course project). Third, the scoring of the tests was not done by independent judges, but by the researcher who was also the instructor of the course. Finally, the frequency and brevity of the e-mail contacts was clearly insufficient to measure any significant effects: a weekly e-mail message per student during a period of three months: roughly 12 messages total![6] However, it is important to mention that the procedure of data collection of this study included a student journal and a follow-up open-ended informal interview. These two additional features of the research design provided some valuable analysis in the discussion section of that study.

Finally, the major drawback of using CALL applications to enhance L2 learning is the fact that computers are not good at conversations (Nelson, 1995: 2). That is precisely why Underwood claims that communicative drills are an obstacle for CALL design (p. 62). In spite of their inherent limitations, some researchers have attempted to recreate the normal sociocultural nature of human interaction in computer-human exchanges. Weizenbaum's Eliza (1976) is a notorious example. However, Eliza could only deceive a human for a certain period of time, because the machine could not 'interact' with humans; it could only create the illusion (Kossuth 1984). Should we expect that future developments in AI (Artificial Intelligence) will improve the quality of human-machine interactions? We should now turn to the analysis of what has been labeled Intelligent CALL: ICALL.

Is ICALL a viable alternative to the shortcomings of CALL?

The most recent research on artificial intelligence has centered on the development of expert systems (programs that try to match human expertise in some domain). This line of research is an elaboration of the notion of multiple intelligences developed by Gardner (1983): intelligent behavior in any domain requires a lot of knowledge in that specific area. Anderson (1990) argues that viable attempts to elaborate expert systems should be concerned with the teaching of specialized levels of expertise (e.g., complex problem-solving skills). Anderson analyzed the effect of a machine tutor that helped computer science students learn the production rules that underlie the use of a computer programming language (LISP). The students' success revealed that what underlies the acquisition of a complex skill such as computer programming is the finite system of 500 production rules encoded in the LISP tutor. However, it is doubtful that the success obtained in the above mentioned problem-solving domain (algorithmic nature) could be reproduced in a second language learning situation. Intelligent machine tutors that teach language require the following base components: a representation of the subject knowledge, a model of the learner, a language understanding system, and a means of self-adjustment, i.e., learning from experience (Higgins, 1988: 19). Except for the representation of subject matter (and only to a certain extent) machines fail in the representation of the other three components.[7] This is not surprising. After all, as in any systemic approach to computer assisted instruction (Steinberg 1991), the real 'magister' is not the machine but the person who writes the program. To develop an algorithmic representation of all the subject matter of linguistics, cognitive psychology (model of the learner), and even a procedure to learn from experience is a hopeless endeavor. We have not yet been able to represent these bodies of knowledge explicitly.[8] Hence, Higgins argues that the attempt to create 'intelligent tutoring systems' is a fallacy.

AI architecture is still a long way from being able to create anything close to mirror the complex system of communication instantiated in any human language and is, hence, unable to introduce any qualitative leap in the design of CALL programs. In fact, none other should be the case according to Weizenbaum (1976) because language 'involves the histories of those using it, hence the history of society, indeed of all humanity generally.' In essence, linguistics has not been able to encode the complexity of natural language in a finite number of discrete rules (e.g., Pinker, 1979; Chomsky, 1980, 1988).[9] That problem has been acknowledged by several of the most adamant proponents of Intelligent CALL.

Holland (1995) lists the reasons that have prevented ICALL from becoming an alternative answer to CALL. The most important reason for this failure is that NLP (Natural Language Processing) programs – which underlie the development of ICALL – cannot account for the full complexity of natural human languages (p. viii). As a consequence, ICALL programs present the following shortcomings: NLP-based programs are still at an experimental stage, most NLP applications require the use of large and expensive computers, and consequently, little attention is given to interface design.[10] The valuable contribution of ICALL programs lies on the provision of form-focused instruction – a more humble goal. In this respect, Garrett (1995) argues that ICALL programs may offer a challenge to two major assumptions which underlie the development of Communicative CALL: the use of individual learning strategies/styles, and the learner-centered approach of communicative teaching.[11]

As far as the type of language teaching that machine tutors can provide, one readily thinks of the type of grammar instruction which may be synchronized with the particular stages of development of the students' normative grammar. The machine tutor can become a high tech version of a combination of reference grammar, dictionary, thesaurus, etc.: an on-line reference database. But, most important, the vast majority of studies in cognitive psychology recognize that machine tutors cannot gauge appropriately the needs of the students: lack of self-adjustment and learning from experience (e.g., Weizenbaum, 1976; Anderson, 1990). Anderson states that 'private human tutors appear to be quite tuned to the needs of students' compared to machine tutors (p. 267). That is to say, the feedback provided by machine tutors does not respond appropriately to the needs of the students because machines cannot adapt efficiently or effectively to the constraints of the learning situation for each individual case. Bloom (1984) has shown that the vast majority of students (approximately 98%) do better when they receive private tutoring instead of classroom instruction. This shows that students learn better when they receive the type of instruction that responds to their individual needs (individual abilities, expertise level, increased motivation, etc.). Ironically, the advantage of machine tutoring systems resides on the fact that they constitute a particular type of individualized instruction which is cost-effective even if not as pedagogically effective as the human counterpart. In sum, machine tutors cannot achieve the same level of responsiveness to the learning situations as humans (Higgins' *pedagogue*), but they do constitute a better alternative than most types of mass instruction (Higgins' *magister*). In any case, it is important to underline that current pedagogical practices in the L2 classroom rely mostly on interactive teaching and learning and not lecturing (e.g., Crookes and Gass 1993; Nunan 1992; Rivers 1987).

Summarizing the previous discussion, it is clear that developers of ICALL should be responsive to the needs of the L2 student when developing language learning programs. In that respect, I wonder why we should rely on programs based on AI to carry out a pedagogical task that can be implemented more effectively and efficiently in various other ways (e.g., direct human contact, e-mail exchanges, telephone conversations, etc.). Furthermore, it seems irrelevant to argue that we can increase the communicative value of AI-based exercises by exchanging information in class, since that feature of the activity is not a prerogative of AI-based exercises. If 'Intelligent' machine tutors cannot provide a cogent and practical pedagogical alternative to CALL, can we, instead, rely on the capacity of computers to store information and combine different media to improve language learning? This alternative proposition is perhaps less sophisticated than ICALL, even though it does not lack supporters who have labeled it as the 'true revolution' of CALL (Dede, 1993; Gayeski, 1993; Jacobson & Spiro, 1995; Liu & Reed, 1995; Murray, 1991; *inter alia*).

Advanced Language Systems: on the cutting edge?

Multimedia 'is a class of *computer-driven interactive communication* systems which create, store, transmit, and retrieve textual, graphic, and auditory networks of information' (Gayeski 1995: 4, italics added). Without further analysis, notice that in this definition interactions are 'driven' by the computer (as opposed to human-driven interactions). In other words, the machine takes control of the learning process: the *Magister* in Higgins' terms. This word of caution finds an echo in exaggerated claims made by some of the proponents of multimedia with respect to the pedagogical value of the (interactive) use of various media (e.g., Fredericksen, Donin, & Décary, 1995; Jonassen & Wang, 1993; Jacobson & Spiro, 1995).

For example, Murray (1991) claims that 'we are beginning to see the possibility of inventing methods that promise to be different in kind rather than degree' (p. 1).[12] Murray distinguishes various levels within an ALS: natural language processing, knowledge representation, discourse structure and narrative structure (p. 3). It is possible to cluster these four groups into just two if we take into account the operational distinction between AI and interactive Multimedia features of such a system.[13] The first two levels defined by Murray can be associated with the AI architecture of the program: a language parser which would be able to approach the human's language capacity in order to create 'real life exchanges' with the computer (see above discussion on drawbacks of NLP parsers). On the other hand, the design of the interactive multimedia section should be more concerned with discourse and narrative structure: the level at which we encounter the functional use of language (the sociocultural 'parser' of language). With respect to this second level (i.e., hypertext and multimedia environments), the author makes a good argument in regards to the potential pedagogical value of using such a new medium. For instance, she isolates the two basic elements of narratives – character and plot – in order to show how their manipulation in a hypermedia environment can add different degrees of 'texture' to the narrative 'text.'[14] This factor becomes a crucial one for dealing with different discourse modes/cultural perceptions as is particularly the case in SLA: '(t)he experience of the narrative may be an experience of this variation of visions of the same event rather than a succession of events' (p. 11).

Murray states that ALS systems 'would be the natural extension of classroom simulation games and role playing, enriched by interactive video materials that capture authentic situations and language' (p. 12). In other words, with ALS, computers are still assisting language learning by means of their amazing capacity to store information, not by introducing a new, hidden dimension in the social development of a second language. Granted, it is true that the advent of interactive multimedia introduced a new perspective on the concept of storage of information. However, we have not yet devised any new approach to take advantage of that amazing power except for what is already an inherent trait of the new technological medium (Jacobson & Spiro, 1995). In fact, Murray does not address the issue of the psycholinguistic validity for the use of such a medium in order to aid the language acquisition process. In other words, hypermedia in general appears to be a promising tool for achieving pedagogical purposes, even though there is yet no theoretical foundation for the design of psycholinguistically sound and valid programs in hypermedia. In essence, the design of ALS must be able to go beyond making use of the inherent technological capabilities of the hypermedia environment, and develop the kind of rationale based on what SLA theories can inform us about the process of acquiring a second language.

A more radical perspective on the use of multimedia is based on the hope that these systems will foster a new model of teaching 'based on learners' navigation and creation of knowledge webs' (Dede 1993: 114), This radical perspective is formally defined as hypermedia technology.[15] Hypermedia is the 'computerized way of representing the semantic network in human memory through its nodes and links' (Liu and Reed, 159).[16] Hypermedia systems are assumed to foster higher order thinking skills representing a paradigmatic shift in pedagogical practices brought about by a revolutionary technology. However, the arguments displayed by these researchers are not convincing. In some cases, the arguments are unfounded: knowledge representation can evolve into knowledge construction (Dede 1993: 119), users will develop metacognition: thinking about thinking (Dede 1993: 119), etc. In other cases, the authors do not offer any rationale that explains why these proposed qualitative changes in cognitive processing will occur due to the *use and interaction with multimedia systems*. The failure of ALS is the attempt to emulate on the computer all relevant aspects of the language learning situation. A more modest – but more feasible objective – is to regard the computer as a mere storage of large multimedia databases. In this way researchers and designers can approach the task of creating software applications from a more realistic perspective.

Towards a Rationale for the Appropriate use of CALL and Multimedia Applications

The previous analysis of CALL and multimedia applications has shown that the so-called paradigmatic shift in the learning process might be more of a novelty rather than a true revolution in the use of an emerging technology. However, it is not accurate to say that the advent of the microcomputer has not brought about some fundamental changes in the educational process. These innovations can be classified into four major types: (a) innovative research technologies; (b) new procedures for the assessment of students' learning profiles; (c) a new rationalization for the preparation and management of teaching resources; and (d) an extended resource/reference database for the students.

a.   Computers are powerful processors of data. As such, they constitute an appropriate tool to collect, store and analyze information from notoriously rich and complex processes such as language learning. This is especially true considering the fact that the lack of a precise theory of SLA does not allow researchers to obviate any minor aspect of the data collection procedure. Doughty (1992) argues that more than using them as teachers, computers are better exploited for collecting data and testing second language acquisition.

b.   In the same vein, computers can be used to model the developmental path of the learner, or the interaction of the learner with the input data. For instance, learner computer tracking systems 'record meticulously the number of keystrokes, content items seen by the user, navigation strategies, and paths constructed through the program' (Gay & Mazur, 1993: 46). Gay and Mazur report that their tracking system allowed them to investigate the interpretation and use of an interactive multimedia fiction program: *El Avión Hispano*.[17] The tracking data was created in **HyperCard**, and later converted into an Excel spreadsheet form. The analysis of the students' construction of the story space allowed designers and researchers to investigate the styles of use of the fiction program, the effect of the interface (e.g., use of cinematic techniques in the design), the use of linguistic resources (e.g., low use of the thesaurus), etc. Similarly, Garrett (1995) argues that machines are probably much better than humans at recording, tabulating, and organizing the data that can inform teachers of the learning history of each learner.

c.   Computers have helped teachers manage educational resources and carry out administrative tasks in an efficient way. When computers are regarded as data storage devices of the same nature of audio tapes, video tapes, notebooks, etc., teachers realize that pedagogical tasks can only be designed by humans and not by machines (there is no risk of machines taking the place of teachers). The recent appearance of some relatively unsophisticated authoring programs (**HyperCard**-based) such as **CALM** (Computer Assisted Language Multimedia) represents an example of the type of resources that give teachers the chance to create an enormous amount of academic activities tailored to the needs of the students in little or no time.[18] Kenning and Kenning (1990) argue that if L2 teachers let the computer manage the learning process, pedagogical activities may well turn out to be second rate applications. As a consequence, teachers should 'treat the computer in the same way as any other resource … the teacher must identify the learning experiences that should be provided, and then consider whether the computer is able to provide them more effectively than other means' (p. 78). The design of successful CALL applications should incorporate the following components: the selection of suitable materials (content), the selection of an adequate methodology to achieve the pedagogical goal, the proper analysis of the type of interface required by the teaching objective (e.g., computer based instruction versus computer assisted instruction), *and the careful planning and management of the teaching resources* (Kenning & Kenning, 1990: 81).

d. The large data storage of computers brings about the powerful nature of multimedia systems: providers of target language input in sufficient quantities (e.g., Kenning & Kenning, 1990; Stevens, 1992). From this standpoint, the true interactivity of multimedia – the associative nonlinear interaction of video, audio, text, and graphics – becomes the central asset of the system. There is no need to pose any breakthrough for the cognitive processing of multimedia environments (e.g., Dede, 1993; Murray, 1991) to recognize the value of a more extended database of information. It is true that the extended availability of resources enhances the learning activity. However, the real cause of improved performance is the nature of the learning process in such environments: learner-centered instruction. From a learner-centered approach, the interaction with extensive multimedia databases is prompted by the learner's curiosity, problem-solving needs (i.e., hypothesis testing), learning style/strategy, etc. This is a very positive outcome of the use of multimedia systems. However, it is essential to recognize that we are still far from identifying any qualitative changes in the cognitive processing of an information database which integrates various media.[19] A principle-based approach to language teaching-learning should be able to account for the 'real engine of change' (causative mechanisms) in the development of the target language: the involvement of the learner in the learning process. In this respect it is reasonable to assume that CMC may foster extended interaction in the L2. For instance, Berge and Collins (1995) claim that 'if designed well, CMC applications can be used effectively to facilitate collaboration among students' (p. 4). Does computer mediated interaction constitute a more revolutionary change in the development of language learning technologies?

Computer Mediated Communication

Is there a revolution yet?

Several authors have stated that the major goal that we are pursuing in the development of CALL or multimedia programs is the 'general discourse competence that includes the ability to express, interpret, and negotiate meanings within the social context of interpersonal interactions' (Murray 1991: 2). That being the case, we can actually devise much more effective and efficient exercises than the ones proposed by advocates of ALSs if we do not let the nature of the medium govern the design of the activity to achieve the final objective. For instance, with only e-mail we can accomplish the same goals of various ALS programs like 'No Recuerdo,' 'A la Recherche de Philipe,' etc. in a very effective and efficient way. With only two computer terminals at two different sites (i.e., two countries which represent the target languages) we can devise problem-solving activities, simulations, cooperative tasks, etc. to create meaningful interaction through e-mail. The options for the design of pedagogical activities are endless, and only determined by the technological limitations of e-mail communication, not by the lack of creative options for setting up a task of this sort.[20]

Santoro (1995) defines CMC as the 'use of computer systems and networks for the transfer, storage, and retrieval of information among humans' (p. 11). This definition can be interpreted in its broadest term comprising three different categories: Computer Assisted Instruction (CAI), Information (internet resources in general), and Conferencing Services (electronic mail, bulletin boards, listservs, etc.). These three categories reflect a continuum of the role of computer mediation in normal human interaction. The maximal use of computer mediation occurs in CAI/CALL applications where the computer is the sole 'interlocutor.' Hence, CALL, ICALL, and ALS are all dependent on a large database of information that allows the computer to create the illusion of true interaction (humanlike). The minimal use of computer mediation occurs in Conferencing Services. For the purposes of this analysis I will only consider Information and Conferencing Services as the representatives of computer based interactions. Based on the work of Bates (1995), Berge and Collins (1995), Steinberg (1992) and the previous discussion, I will present a list of the major characteristics of CMC which should guide the design of pedagogical activities implemented in that medium:

1.   the learner addresses a specific audience for purposes other than demonstrating a skill
2.   expansion of the network of peers (sharing the work with fellow students)

3. increased access to cross-cultural information (sharing information with other communities)
4. increased access to experts' advice/guidance (expert-novice interaction, native speaker-nonnative speaker contacts, etc.)
5. freedom from time and location constraints (e.g., non-accessible regions or conflicting schedules)
6. emergence of new discursive environments: absence of nonverbal cues (e.g., more spontaneous participation in group work, increased participation of minorities)
7. emotional involvement (increased motivation)
8. unparalleled access to information databases and help on-line
9. emergence and expansion of a new asynchronous mode of communication (e.g., e-mail)
10. safer environment in which learners may try to communicate with more advanced speakers without 'losing face'[21]

These various features have been previously analyzed by several researchers, even though it is possible that not all investigators agree on one single list of characteristics of CMC environments. However, I believe that this list is particularly useful for the analysis of interaction among L2 learners. I will underline the three most important traits of the above mentioned features of CMC environments as they appear to be especially relevant ones for the design of pedagogical environments in the L2 classroom: interaction for purposes other than strictly academic skills, the new discursive nature of electronic communication, and the asynchronous nature of computer based telecommunications. One of the most important features of CMC is the fact that students contextualize their learning when they interact with other users (usually outside their academic environment). These out-of-classroom users are more interested in hearing about the content of the students' activities rather than in assigning the students a grade, As a consequence, learners direct their own learning because they are in charge of their own actions. In other words, the students go about the process of constructing knowledge from problem to solution (contextualized) instead of going from solution to problem (decontextualized academic environment). From this perspective, the notion of problem is necessarily tied to its social nature as explained in Lave and Wenger (1991), or Schön (1983). For example, the traditional grammatical syllabus in L2 teaching gives learners the means to achieve a goal that is not existent yet in the students' representation of the problem space. The appropriate and real contextualization of the activity, through – for example – tandem e-mail projects, simulations, Usenet discussions, etc. gives students the chance of engaging in the socially, mediated construction of knowledge through CMC.

Another influential feature of CMC environments is the emergence of a new discursive world. As such, the discourse properties of CMC environments are the product of a new cultural context. For example, users of e-mail have become quite adept at communicating certain emotions by means of using a combination of keyboard symbols that present a pictorial representation of emotional states: smileys such as :o) or ;-). This shows the discourse of e-mail to be qualitatively different from traditional written or oral communication. Some of the features of this new medium are the following: lack of nonverbal communication (neither paralinguistic nor nonlinguistic cues), a new set of turn taking skills, and finally the cohesion of CMC discourse. CMC discourse is more disconnected at the level of adjacent contributions 'in favor of a more complex cohesion pattern that extends over a long discourse domain' (Graddol 1991: 335). Of these features, the absence of nonverbal communication seems to have the most consequences. For example, the two following effects have been reported in the literature on CMC: minority interests are better represented (Graddol, 1991: 336), and students are more spontaneous to share ideas (Ahern, 1994: 236; Rheingold, 1994: 62–64). It is clear that these are not minor consequences of the use of CMC. For some users such as people with physical disabilities they constitute the most important feature of this new medium (Kinner & Coomb, 1995). For others, the type of nonverbal communication of CMC environments can generate more interesting discussions on-line (as opposed to classroom interaction).

The asynchronous nature of interaction (except for cases in which real-time interaction is purposefully used such as Inter Relay Chat: IRC) implies first, the flexibility of asynchronous communication which eliminates all the constraints and difficulties of time schedules; second, a time lag between transmission and reception of messages which gives the user more time to reflect on the answer; and third, an array of choices which this time lag offers to different groups as they structure information (Ahern and Repman 1994).[22] The defining features of CMC environments reviewed above generate interesting questions about the nature of human interaction and the possible impact of various pedagogical uses of the Internet. However, why should we assume that collaboration helps learners develop their linguistic system? To answer this questions one must define the notions of collaboration and interaction as they pertain to CINIC.

Situated cognition: Interaction around the computer

Several researchers have explicitly argued for a clear distinction between 'on-screen' and 'off-screen' learning environments in the context of CALL.

Boyd-Barrett and Scanlon (1991) state that 'the educational significance of computing to significance, not in the machines, but in the ways in which teachers and learners interact with them, and in doing so, the ways in which teachers and learners interact among themselves' (p. vii). The analysis of the *interaction with the machine* has prompted many researchers to investigate the effects of learning in multimedia environments (see above for strengths and weaknesses). On the other hand, the analysis of *interaction around the computer* has induced researchers to investigate the nature of the social setting of learning.[23] For example, Crook (1991) argues that intelligence is normally exercised in social contexts, and Hymes (1972) states that language acquisition does not occur in a vacuum: language use is what determines language. Even neo-Cartesian perspectives on language (the notions of competence and performance in the Chomskyan paradigm) give a special status to the effect of the social setting on language: the notion of 'pragmatic competence' (Chomsky, 1980).

However, some researchers have argued for an even more pervasive and deeper effect of normal social interaction on cognitive development (e.g., Crook, 1991; Gay & Grosz-Ngate, 1994; Graddol, 1991; Steinberg, 1991). For example, Crook states that 'cognitive development involves a necessary coordination of our thinking with that of others' (p. 158), Steinberg argues that current research in cognitive psychology shows that students 'construct understanding rather than reproduce instruction' (p. 18). And, Gay and Grosz-Ngate argue that working in groups promotes learning as an interactive process; thereby, developing critical thinking, social skills and the acquisition of specific knowledge (p. 420). Most of these positions constitute a development of the work of notable psychologists and philosophers like Vygotsky (cognitive functions are socially mediated or constructed) or Wittgenstein (linguistic knowledge is tied to 'language games'). In general these positions reflect a profound reappraisal of the social nature of language acquisition: situated cognition. For example, according to Vygotsky (1978), the mechanism of thought is the internalization of external behaviors which occur while interacting with others. The most important 'tool' used in social interaction is language; hence, language is assumed to mediate thinking: from interindividual contexts to intraindividual cognition. This is the major component of a theory of situated cognition: it places the emphasis on how knowledge is attuned to the socio-historical environment instead of searching for general structures of knowledge (Resnick, 1994).

More recently, there have been a series of attempts at raising awareness of what constitutes the true nature of the learning process in situated cognition (e.g., Lave & Wenger, 1991; Resnick, 1994; Schön, 1983). Lave and Wenger have claimed that learning can be regarded as the special type of social practice commonly found in apprenticeships: legitimate periph-eral participation. In apprenticeships, participation is legitimate because it gives access to the social organization of the working environment, and it is peripheral because of the gradual process of incorporation to the social structure of the practicing community. The increased access of learners to participatory frameworks entails a great deal more of learning than in typ-ical decontextualized settings such as academic environments. Lave and Wenger have emphasized that the success of many types of apprenticeships reveals the social nature of learning and knowing. They claim that a learn-ing curriculum is 'a field of learning resources in everyday practice *viewed from the perspective of the learner*' (p. 97, italics added). On the other hand, academic curricula constrain and limit the choices of the learner and the structuring of resources, in essence, 'the meaning of what is learned' (p. 97). Lave and Wenger argue that the advantages of apprenticeship over regular schooling are based on the following differences: a broad initial view of the task by taking part in ongoing activities instead of the discrete presentation of the system (grammatical syllabus), the importance of being in a relevant setting for learning (immersion in target language communities), and the existence of strong goals for learning.

The notion of a teaching curriculum as not beneficial for learning finds an echo in the work of Schön (1983) who has developed the concept of the reflective practitioner. The reflective practitioner 'does not keep means and ends separate, but defines them interactively as he frames a problematic sit-uation' (p. 68). In other words, academic work leads students to be skillful at 'selective inattention'. As a consequence, immersion in the uncertainty of the natural social environment overwhelms the person who has learned to manage the situation in a controlled, decontextualized way. For example, native speakers cannot describe the knowledge that underlies their use of language (nor can linguistic theory); however, L2 learners are exposed to a standardized version of the target language in academic instruction which places the emphasis on linguistic structure instead of pragmatic knowledge. Most classroom learners who have had the opportunity to engage in normal linguistic interaction (outside of the classroom) have a hard time under-standing that appropriate interaction in the L2 relies as much on pragmatic as on morphosyntactic knowledge. Resnick has cogently summarized this predicament: 'the special situation of the classroom – calling for private rather than socially shared work and isolating mental activity from engage-ment in the social and physical world – builds skill and knowledge that allow students to function in school, but often fail to transfer to the worlds of work, civic, and personal life' (p. 491).

In sum, there are two major effects of true social interaction on the L2 learning process: an increased awareness of the sociocultural nature of the target language, and the development of situated cognition (from the inter-individual context to intraindividual cognition). There is abundant evidence in the literature of SLA for both effects. For instance, Porter (1986) argues that offering learners the opportunity to interact with native speakers outside of the classroom helps these students acquire adequate sociocultural models of the L2 (e.g., pragmatic features of communication such as prompts and repairs). On the other hand, allowing learners to interact with other fellow students – nonnative speakers – with a similar level of proficiency helps learners engage in more extended interactions that help them refine their nonnative grammatical system (e.g., morphosyntax).[24] Finally, it is important to highlight the fact that situated cognition does not entail doing without some type of instruction. In particular, Lave and Wenger have emphasized the fact that their notion of LPP does not constitute a teaching methodology (p. 40). Hence, the pedagogical design of CMC activities in the L2 classroom will be necessarily dependent on what we know about L2 development (within the constraints of situated cognition).

The research findings of SLA: Immersion settings

I have argued that the type of pedagogical practices based on CMC environments may offer a more 'revolutionary' perspective than the most sophisticated ALSs. I have also claimed that this revolution does not come about because of the nature of the technological medium per se, but because of the type of learning that it promotes: a learner-centered interactive approach. Concomitantly, there exists a wealth of empirical evidence in SLA that justifies the contention that CMC will be beneficial for promoting language development. In fact, the concept of interactive teaching and learning has been part of pedagogical practices of the L2 classroom for quite some time. For example, Rivers (1987) is a collection of papers that highlights the role of interaction in L2 learning. Rivers claims that linguistic interaction is represented by collaborative activity among two interlocutors and the context of the situation: interaction involves expressing one's ideas and comprehending the ideas of others (p. 4). Many pedagogical practices reflect this concern about the nature and function of social interaction in L2 learning. For example, Strevens (1987) suggests 'bypassing the inescapable intermediary' – the language teacher – and search for valuable resources in the nonacademic community (telephone friendships, national cultural agencies, penpals, etc.). In the same vein, Dough and Ryan (1987) show how the case study method used in the classroom can generate the careful listening to others and the effective expression of one's own ideas so necessary for social interaction (see also Kramsch, 1993).[25]

Accordingly, several L2 researchers have investigated the validity of such pedagogical practices. For example, Doughty and Pica (1986) and Long (1985) have proposed that the role of negotiation of meaning in normal conversation is the key factor in the overall process of SLA. Doughty and Pica argue that group and pair work are essential for increasing the amount of student practice time in classroom teaching (avoidance of teacher fronted classes). Most important, group work generates the type of information exchange in which learners engage in conversational modification (clarification requests, confirmation and comprehension checks). This type of modified interaction is argued to be absolutely essential to make input comprehensible, and eventually to lead to successful acquisition of the target language.[26] Accordingly, we have seen that CMC promotes a great deal of linguistic interaction: notice that L2 learners have increased access to language interaction with the target language community. However, is the environment created by computer based telecommunications appropriate to generate the pedagogical conditions of interactions argued by Doughty and Pica?

In the acquisition literature it has been claimed that natural settings are qualitatively better than pedagogically constrained environments (e.g., classrooms) because they provide positive instead of negative evidence (Pinker, 1979). For example, Schwartz (1993) argues that natural settings constitute the right language learning environment because 'negative data do not figure prominently, if at all ... in the input these L2ers receive' (p. 161). But, this is not true. judging by the vast majority of case studies, it is clear that learners resort to a conscious processing of the L2 (at least for highly literate learners who are the normal subjects of these types of studies). This analytic process occurs when students seek to validate their 'working hypotheses' with native speakers (or any available data at their disposal). For instance, Schmidt and Frota (1986) analyzed the data from the diaries kept by Schmidt while learning Portuguese in Brazil. Even though Schmidt was actually taking formal classes in Portuguese, he was resistant to the formal teaching of grammar in the classroom: he was an avid seeker of communication opportunities to improve his L2 in the context of natural interaction. At the end of the study Schmidt acknowledged that it is extremely difficult to achieve any degree of success in the L2 unless the adult learner resorts to an active conscious processing of the L2 system. Therefore, it is difficult to uphold Schwartz' argument on the non-effect of negative data: negative feedback seems to have been absolutely necessary for Schmidt and many other literate subjects learning the L2 in the natural setting. On the other hand, if Schwartz prefers to rely on the study of 'less literate' subjects, one should remember that there is a wealth of evidence pointing in the direction of less than perfect results even in those circumstances (e.g., Perdue & Klein, 1992; Schmidt, 1983). Hence, are classroom learners at a disadvantage compared with students who learn the L2 in the natural setting?

According to popular wisdom semester-abroad programs are more successful than regular classroom learning (participants appear to be more 'fluent'). However, Huebner (1995) presents some data showing that study abroad students do not seem to be approaching the task of language learning in any way different than they approach regular classroom instruction. Similarly, DeKeyser (1991) argues that such notion of success has been greatly exaggerated: his data show that most students enrolled in programs abroad merely transfer the same learning strategies previously received in classroom instruction. Hence, immersion in the natural language environment (second language versus foreign language learning) is not necessarily the actual determinant of success in L2 attainment. It might be more accurate to say that the natural setting constitutes the environment in which the real causes of success can be better implemented. That is to say, there might be no qualitative differences between classroom-based courses and semester abroad programs. Any differential success could be attributed to different degrees of motivation, amount of exposure to the L2 data, varied settings of language use, heightened communication requirements created by native speakers, interactional exchanges in the target language, etc. Quite clearly, these conditions are normally present in natural settings. But, instead of attributing any 'magical effect' to the students' participation in semester-abroad programs, we should define the actual causing factors of success in the L2 to implement sound pedagogical practices in academic environments as well.

DeKeyser claims that there are two major advantages on the side of naturalistic environments. First, they provide the learner with a sort of natural communicative drill because so many communicative contexts keep reoccurring. Gass and Varonis (1994) argue that the interactive nature of negotiation helps learners to focus their attention on the problematic parts of the learners' discourse ('language' as a whole). The results of this heightened attention to the imperfect nature of their IL system, will show up at a later time. Second, natural settings provide learners with a greater variety of contextual information which, in turn, leads to a better integration of language related events in long-term memory (episodic memory). There is no reason to believe that these conditions could not be implemented in regular on-campus courses.[27] In fact, some universities already provide opportunities for immersion-like environments (e.g., Language House programs, language clubs, etc.).[28] However, these programs are very expensive both in terms of financial costs and in terms of human resources. A more effective and efficient alternative is provided by the type of learning environment brought about by computer based telecommunications where the amount and frequency of interaction among users is only limited by the interest of the students themselves.

Pedagogical uses of Computer Mediated Communication

One of the most important features that define a technological tool is the increase in efficiency to perform a given task. Computer based telecommunications offer language teachers an extremely cost-effective medium to generate different types of interaction among students (both in terms of financial investment and time resources). For example, to program a simulation of human interaction requires a lot of effort in time and money; but, to design a communicative-based pedagogical activity, on the internet requires almost no programming effort. Moreover, the results can be more effective especially regarding the access to audiences outside the academic environment. Nevertheless, pedagogical tasks using computer based telecommunications should be carefully designed. For example, without skillful preparation the interaction can be poor and the students can remain passive: real discussion is unlikely to occur without careful planning and preparation (Bates, 1995: 206). I believe that the implementation of pedagogical tasks in CMC environments should be attentive to two important features of the design process: the nature of interaction among humans (communication paradigm) and the roles of the learner in such interaction (language learning goals).

With respect to the type of communication occurring in CMC environments, I propose that a distinction be made between the concepts of interaction and communication to the effects of providing a better theoretical foundation for the pedagogical uses of internet environments. Reddy (1979) has argued that the concept of communication as the packaging of ideas into language form is a fallacy (the conduit metaphor). Humans do not encode and decode meaning, but they actually construct meaning out of linguistic (and nonlinguistic) interaction (e.g., Frawley & Lantolf, 1985). The technical distinction between interaction (mutual or reciprocal action or influence) and communication (a process by which meanings are exchanged between individuals through a common system of symbols) can help us keep in perspective the pedagogical value of Computer Mediated Interaction (CMI) for L2 learning. Information on how to design activities for the L2 classroom around communication/interaction paradigms is available from multiple sources including online references (Frizzler, 1995). For example, Paulsen

(1995) presents a classification of four types of techniques according to the communication paradigm they represent: information retrieval (one-alone), electronic mail (one-to-one), bulletin boards (one-to-many), and computer conferencing (many-to-many).

Second, to better understand the role of the type of learning associated with CMI it is useful to rely on a framework of reference that defines the various roles of the learner. In L2 learning, Higgins (1988) has identified four learner types (absorber, experiencer, explorer and practitioner) according to a classification of CALL lessons into four types (instructional, revelatory, conjectural, and emancipatory) (p. 39). The Instructional lesson – typical of programmed learning – is based on the metaphor of the learner's mind as an empty vessel that is to be filled with knowledge: student as absorber. The revelatory lesson presents a structured experience (e.g., a simulation) that will presumably guide the learner towards discovery: student as experiencer. The conjectural lesson sets a series of tasks that the learner must complete (task-based): student as explorer. Finally, the emancipatory lesson provides tools (e.g., online resources such as dictionaries, etc.) to facilitate learning: student as practitioner. The first two types of lessons are the least effective towards learning because the computer takes over the instructional process: the learner is not in charge of learning, but s/he is the subject of teaching (see analysis of Lave and Wenger above). The third and fourth types of instruction are more conducive to learning according to the above discussion. More specifically, the third type of lesson is based on the notion of a pedagogue that guides the learner towards acquisition of knowledge (Zone of Proximal Development, master-apprentice, etc.). On the other hand, the fourth type (emancipatory) does not specify the goals of instruction for the students (learning curriculum of Lave and Wenger). CALL applications and Multimedia environments have created lessons of the first three types mentioned by Higgins (instructional, revelatory and conjectural). On the other hand, I believe that we can assume that CMI environments will be conducive to the types of lesson that generate situated learning (types 3 and 4: conjectural and emancipatory).

The actual design of pedagogical activities based on CMI environments will be tied to the particular goals of the teacher and the students. In this respect, several researchers have already developed a series of basic guidelines that should inform teachers the specific design of pedagogical applications on the internet including online references (e.g., Frizzler, 1995; Paulsen, 1995; Warschauer, 1995). Hence, I will refer the reader to such resources for concrete applications as the analysis of particular techniques lies beyond the scope of this paper. In contrast my goal has been to offer a theoretical rationale for the pedagogical use of CM; environments to enhance L2 acquisition.

Conclusion

With the advent of CMI the computer is moving away from the role of sub-stitute teacher to becoming a tool that facilitates the learning process (e.g., Bates, 1995; Higgins, 1988; Kenning & Kenning, 1990; Underwood, 1984). However, CMI represents only the medium where this type of learner-centered instruction (the real engine of pedagogical innovation) is thriving. More important, it is not true that 'the internet mediates human interaction better than any other medium' (Levy, 1995: 27). The fact that a new set of rules of discursive interaction has emerged in the internet does not entail that CMI is more conducive to communication than, for instance, face-to-face interaction.[28] Further research should implement well-designed studies that assess the effectiveness of CMI environments on the development of second languages as specified in the above mentioned theoretical accounts. More important, future empirical investigations should avoid the pitfalls of some of the original studies on the effectiveness of CAI applications. In par-ticular, experimental studies should include a clear theoretical rationale that guides the investigation, an iterative design that promotes a more encom-passing framework of analysis (Gay & Grosz-Ngate, 1994: 419), various mechanisms that report on students' participation (journals, videotaped activities, computer tracking tools, follow-up questionnaires, etc.), and the isolation and analysis of discrete grammatical items instead of relying on global measurements of proficiency.

Acknowledgments

I would like to express my gratitude to Geri Gay, María J. Tort, Mark Warschauer, the CALICO Editors, and three anonymous reviewers for their comments on an earlier version of this paper.

Notes

1. As early as 1988, Higgins stated that 'computers will gradually enter lan-guage classrooms in their most menial roles, as word-processors, as data-base, ... In ten years' time we will look back on this debate and wonder what the fuss was about' (p. 103).
2. Unfortunately, this communicative perspective has not been at the founda-tion of most widely used programs, which seem still to favor a behavioristic approach.
3. In fact, it is not surprising that the same single monolithic foundation guides the programs developed in ICALL (see Oxford 1995).

4.   E.g., McLaughlin, 1990; Gregg, 1984, 1990 *inter alia*. Schwartz constitutes a recent attempt to defend and validate Krashen's view from a formal UG (Universal Grammar) approach (see Gregg, 1984 for a critique and Schwartz, 1988 for a response). An alternative theoretical position on L2 development is presented in the section on The Research Findings of SLA: immersion Settings.

5.   The lack of a control group does not allow the researcher to rule out the effect of simple exposure to the teaching material as the only cause of increased achievement irrespective of treatment method. The use of both a treatment and a control group shows the incremental effect of instruction with the CALL application versus normal improvement with no treatment.

6.   The fact that the researcher found an effect on the dependent variable in favor of the experimental group does not guarantee that such an effect was caused by the treatment considering the low impact that 12 e-mail messages might have on the outcome of a three-month course.

7.   See Steinberg (1991) for an analysis of the deficiencies of systemic approaches to instructional design (especially pp. 51–79).

8.   Furthermore, researchers in artificial intelligence concede that machines cannot learn from experience the same way humans do (e.g., Weizenbaum, 1976).

9.   The whole question is whether 'rules' should be sought in the first place. An alternative approach is based on the representation of knowledge in neural networks (e.g., Rumelhart & McClelland, 1986). However connectionist models may also be open to some serious criticisms (see Baumgartner & Payr, 1995).

10.   By contrast, most multimedia CALL applications do not attempt to use NSP; thereby, avoiding these problems. However, neither Multimedia nor ICALL can create natural communicative environments that truly represent *human interaction*.

11.   Garrett argues that SLA research has not provided any definitive answer on the use of preferred versus no-preferred learning styles/strategies: would learners do better if they were taught to use strategies that do not come naturally? (p. 346). However, O'Malley and Chamot (1990) have presented data that show that learners do not seem to respond favorably to the explicit teaching of non-preferred learning strategies. Second, Garret states that 'it may be premature to assume that a high degree of learner-centeredness necessarily benefits language learning. Again, we do not have the research evidence to support such as assumption' (p. 347). However, I believe that a learner-centered approach to language learning is supported by a strong theoretical foundation and a growing body of empirical research (for theoretical foundation see Lave & Wenger, 1991; Schön, 1983; etc.; for empirical evidence see DeKeyser, 1991; Tarone & Yule, 1989; etc.).

12.   However, it is not clear that such a qualitative change may actually happen due to the introduction of multimedia environments.

13.   In fact, Murray implicitly acknowledges such division when she discusses the nature of one of the programs designed by ALLP: '(i)n our most ambi-

tious design, (the) two techniques – keyboard-based conversations and authentic speakers on videodisc – are combined within one exercise' (p. 2). That is to say, the author is trying to combine AI and interactive multimedia features of CALL programs.

14. In this instance the term text is used with reference to the world of meaning created by the receiver (reader) in interaction with the hypermedia environment.

15. In fact, this idea is not new. The very first goal of the harbinger of the internet in 1950 was to 'automate symbol-handling tasks; and thus help people think faster, better …' (Rheingold, 1994: 65).

16. Propositional networks are associative structures of propositions (semantic) which constitute the foundation of connectionist models (e.g. Rumelhart & McClelland, 1986).

17. *El Avión Hispano* (designed by Zulma Iguina, Cornell University) includes full motion video, a composing space for writing, a fortune teller, an in-flight magazine, a thesaurus, grammar help, etc.

18. The time commitment to learn how to use CALM goes from about four to eight hours.

19. For example, Dede (1993) mentions that the emergence of the cinema introduced a new 'dimension to communication beyond spoken language, written language, and still images' (p. 128). Even though it is true that a new storytelling environment emerged (the narrative style of films is different from written or play narratives) the essence of the story telling process was not altered. In other words, the channel of communication altered the style but not the sociocultural nature of story telling as a human need (Fiske, 1990).

20. Incidentally, research on this type of pedagogically-sound project does not seem to be as attractive as most ALS programs because of the lack of commercial profitability (so far).

21. To produce language in front of a machine may be less threatening than interacting with another human being; however, only the latter type of language production may possibly qualify as language use. Linguistic exchanges with a computer terminal may just represent language practice (for extended discussion of this topic see the section heading Situated Cognition: Interaction Around the Computer).

22. L2 learners may become more proficient in the particular type of discourse determined by the restricted communication channel of electronic interaction. In turn, this type of interaction may not necessarily prepare students for successful face-to-face interaction.

23. The terms in italics have been borrowed from Crook (1991).

24. The concept of the zone of proximal development (ZPD) of Vygotsky appears to be a necessary tool for the analysis of the types of interactions mentioned by Porter. The ZPD is defined as '… the distance between the actual developmental level as determined by independent problem solving and the level of potential development … under adult guidance or in collaboration with more capable peers' (Wertsch, 1985: 273).

25. In the case study method, students analyze cases (professional or nonprofessional) and they present their findings to the classroom group and/or experts.
26. However, Sato (1990) argues that clarification requests did not lead her subjects (Tai and Thanh) to the discovery of morphological markers of tense; only lexical markers were incorporated into their IL. Sato argues that there are three possible reasons that may explain those results: past tense verbal inflections in English are not perceptually salient, native speakers tend to produce phonological reductions, and the subjects' L1 does not present consonant clusters in such high frequency as is common in English past tense inflection (p. 91).
27. There is no need to uphold the acquisition-learning distinction of Krashen and Schwartz (see Gregg, 1984; McLaughlin, 1990) considering that it is based on the unfalsifiable paradigm of so called conscious/unconscious cognitive processes. I claim that it is not the cognitive structure, but rather the participatory framework of language use that helps adult learners acquire the L2: situated and non-situated cognition (see heading Situated Cognition: Interaction Around the Computer).
28. Incidentally, to the best of my knowledge, there are not enough published studies that determine whether the students participating in this type of extra-curricular on-campus activities achieve the same degree of success attained by semester-abroad students.
29. This position has obvious pedagogical as well as administrative consequences.

References

Ahern, T. (1994). The effect of interface on the structure of interaction in computer mediated small group discussion. *Journal of Educational Computing Research 11*(3), 235–250.

Ahern, T., & J. Repman (1994). The effects of technology on online education. *Journal of Research on Computing in Education 26*(4), 537–546.

Anderson, J. (1990). *Cognitive psychology and its implications.* New York, NY: W. Freeman and Co.

Bates, A. W. (1995). *Technology, open learning, and distance education.* London: Routledge.

Baumgartner, P., & S. Payr (Eds.) (1995). *Speaking minds: Interviews with twenty eminent cognitive scientists.* Princeton, NJ: Princeton University Press.

Berge, Z.. & M. Collins (Eds.) (1995). *Computer mediated communication and the online classroom in distance learning.* Cresskill, NJ: Hampton Press.

Bloom, B. (1984). The 2 Sigma Problem: The search for methods of group instruction as effective as one-on-one tutoring. *Educational Researcher 13*(6), 3–16.

Boyd-Barret, O., & E. Scanlon (Eds.) (1991). *Computers and learning.* Wokingham: Addison-Wesley Publishing.

Canale, M., & M. Swain (1980). Theoretical bases of communicative approaches to second language teaching and testing. *Applied Linguistics 1*(1), 1–47.

Chapelle, C., & J. Jamieson (1986). Computer Assisted Language Learning as a predictor of success in acquiring English as a Second Language. *TESOL Quarterly 20*(1), 27–46.

Chompsky, N. (1988). *Language and problems of knowledge: The Managua Lectures.* Cambridge, MA: MIT Press.

Chompsky, N. (1980). *Rules and representations.* New York: Columbia University Press.

Chompsky, N. (1959). A review of B. F. Skinner's 'Verbal Behavior'. *Language 35*(1), 26–58.

Crook, C. (1991). Computers in the classroom. In O. Boyd-Barret & E. Scanlon (Eds.), *Computers and learning.* Wokingham: Addison-Wesley Publishing.

Crookes, G., & S. Gass (Eds.) (1993). *Tasks and language learning: Integrating theory and practice.* Clevedon: Multilingual Matters Ltd.

Dede, C. (1993). The future of multimedia: Bridging to virtual worlds. In D. Gayeski (Ed.), *Multimedia for learning: Development, application, and evaluation.* Englewood Cliffs, NJ: Educational Technology Publications.

DeKeyser, R. (1991). Foreign language development during a semester abroad. In B. Freed (Ed.), *Foreign language acquisition research and the classroom.* Lexington, MA: D. C. Heath.

Dough, A., & J. Ryan (1987). Preparing the language student for professional interaction.' In W. Rivers (Ed.), *Interactive language teaching.* New York: Cambridge University Press.

Doughty, C. (1992). Computer application in Second Language Acquisition Research: Design, description, and discovery. In M. Pennington & V. Stevens (Eds.), *Computers in Applied Linguistics: An international perspective.* Clevedon: Multilingual Matters Ltd.

Doughty, C., & T. Pica (1986). 'Information Gap' tasks: Do they facilitate second language acquisition?' *TESOL Quarterly 20*(2), 305–325.

Everett, D., & T. Ahern (1994). Computer mediated communication as a teaching tool: A case study. *Journal of Research on Computing in Education 26*(3), 336–357.

Fiske, J. (1990). *Introduction to communication studies.* London: Routledge.

Frawley, W., & J. Lantolf (1985). Second Language discourse: A Vygotskyan perspective. *Applied Linguistics 6*(1), 19–44.

Fredericksen, C., J. Donin, & M. Décary (1995). A discourse processing approach to Computer Assisted Language Learning. In V. M. Holland, J. Kaplan & M. Sams (Eds.), *Intelligent language tutors: Theory shaping technology.* Mahwah, NJ: Laurence Erlbaum.

Frizzler, K. (1995). *The Internet as an educational tool in ESOL writing instruction.* Unpublished Master's Thesis, San Francisco State University. WWW document http://thecity.sfsu.edu/~funweb/thesis.htm.

Gardner, H. (1983). *Frames of mind: The theory of multiple intelligences.* New York: Basic Books.

Garrett, N. (1995). ICALL and Second Language acquisition.' In V. M. Holland, J. Kaplan & M. Sams (Eds.), *Intelligent language tutors: Theory shaping technology.* Mahwah, NJ: Laurence Erlbaum.

Gass, S., & E. Marlos Varonis (1994). Input, interaction, and Second Language production. *Studies in Second Language Acquisition 16*(3), 283–302.

Gay, G., & M. Grosz-Ngate (1994). Collaborative design in a networked multimedia environment: Emerging communication patterns. *Journal of Research on Computing in Education 26*(1), 418–432.

Gay, G. & J. Mazur (1993). The utility of computer tracking tools for user centered design. *Education Technology*, April, 45–59.

Gayeski, D. (Ed.) (1993). *Multimedia for learning: Development, application, and evaluation*. Englewood Cliffs, NJ: Educational Technology Publications.

Graddol, D. (1991). Some CMC discourse properties and their educational significance. In O. Boyd-Barret & E. Scanlon (Eds.), *Computers and learning*. Wokingham: Addison-Wesley Publishing.

Gregg, K. (1990). The Variable Competence Model of Second Language Acquisition and why it isn't. *Applied Linguistics 11*(4), 364–383.

Gregg, K. (1984). Krashen's Monitor and Occam's Razor. *Applied Linguistics 5*, 79–100.

Harasim, L. (Ed.) (1990). *Online education: Perspectives on a new environment*. New York: Praeger.

Higgins, J. (1988). *Language, learners, and computers: Human intelligence and artificial unintelligence*. Singapore: Longman.

Huebner, T. (1995). The effects of overseas language programs. In B. Freed (Ed.), *Second Language Acquisition in a study abroad context*. Amsterdam: John Benjamins.

Hymes, D. (1972). On communicative competence. In J. Pride & J. Holmes (Eds.), *Sociolinguistics*. Harmondsworth: Penguin Books.

Jacobson, M., & R. Spiro (1995). Hypertext learning environments, cognitive flexibility, and the transfer of complex knowledge: An empirical investigation. *Journal of Educational Computing Research 12*(4), 301–333.

Jonassen, D., & S. Wang (1993). Acquiring structural knowledge from semantically structured hypertext. *Journal of Computer Based Instruction 20*(1), 1–8.

Kenning, M. M., & M. J. Kenning (1990). *Computers and language learning: Current theory and practice*. Chichester: Ellis Horwood.

Kinner, J., & N. Coombs (1995). Computer access for students with special needs. In Z. Berge & M. Collins (Eds.), *Computer mediated communication and the online classroom in distance learning*. Cresskill, NJ: Hampton Press.

Klein, W., & C. Perdue (1992). *Utterance structure: Developing grammars again*. Amsterdam: Benjamins.

Kossuth, Karen (1984). Suggestions for comprehension-based computer-assisted instruction in German. *Die Unterrichtspraxis 17*(1), 109–115.

Kramsch, C. (1993). *Context and culture in language teaching*. Hong Kong: Oxford University Press.

Künzel, S. (1995). Processors processing: Learning theory and CALL *CALICO Journal 12*(4), 106–113.

Lave, J., & E. Wenger (1991). *Situated learning: Legitimate peripheral participation*. New York: Cambridge University Press.

Levy, S. (1995, 25 December). The year of the Internet. *Newsweek* 21–46.

Liu, M., & W. Reed (1995). The effect of hypermedia assisted instruction on Second Language Learning. *Journal of Educational Computing Research 12*(2), 159–175.

Long, M. (1985). Input and Second Language Acquisition Theory. In S. Gass & C. Madden (Eds.), *Input in Second Language Acquisition*. Rowley, MA: Newbury House.

McLaughlin, B. (1990). 'Conscious' versus 'Unconscious' learning. *TESOL Quarterly 24*(4), 617–634.

Muns, R. (1995). Online scholarly discussion groups. In Z. Berge & M. Collins (Eds.), *Computer Mediated Communication and the Online Classroom in Distance Learning*. Cresskill, NJ: Hampton Press.

Murray, J. (1991). Anatomy of a new medium: Literary and pedagogic uses of advanced linguistic computer structures. *Computers and the Humanities 25*(1), 1–14.

Nelson, J. R. (1995). *Computer Aided Input in Second Language Instruction*. Unpublished Master's Thesis. Arizona State University.

Nunan, D. (1992). *Collaborative language learning and teaching*. Cambridge: Cambridge University Press.

O'Malley, J. M., & A. U. Chamot (1990). *Learning strategies in Second Language Acquisition*. New York: Cambridge University Press.

Oxford, R. (1995). Linking theories of learning with intelligent Computer Assisted Language Learning (ICALL). In V. M. Holland, J. Kaplan, & M. Sams (Eds.), *Intelligent language tutors: Theory shaping technology*. Mahwah, NJ: Lawrence Erlbaum.

Paulsen, M. F. (1995). An overview of CMC and the online classroom in distance education. In Z. Berge & M. Collins (Eds.), *Computer mediated communication and the online classroom in distance learning*. Cresskill, NJ: Hampton Press.

Paulsen, M. F. (1979). Formal models of language learning. *Cognition 7*(3), 217–283.

Porter, P. (1986). How learners talk to each other: Input and interaction in task-centered discussions. In R. Day (Ed.), *Talking to learn*. New York: Newbury House.

Price, K. (1987). The use of technology: Varying the medium in language teaching. In W. Rivers (Ed.), *Interactive Language Teaching*. New York, NY: Cambridge University Press.

Reddy, M. J. (1979). The conduit metaphor. In A. Ortony (Ed.), *Metaphor and thought* (pp. 284–324). New York: Cambridge University Press.

Reeves, T. (1993). Pseudoscience in computer based instruction: The case of learner control research. *Journal of Computer Based Instruction 20*(2), 39–46.

Resnick, L. (1994). Situated rationalism: Biological and social preparation for learning. In L. Hirschfeld & S. Gelman (Eds.), *Mapping the mind: Domain specificity in cognition and culture*. New York: Cambridge University Press.

Rheingold, H. (1994). *The virtual community: Homesteading on the Electronic Frontier*. New York: Harper Perennial.

Rivers, W. (Ed.) (1987). Interaction as the key to teaching language for communication. *Interactive Language Teaching*. New York: Cambridge University Press.

Rumelhart, D., & J. McClelland (Eds.) (1986). *Parallel distributed processing: Explorations in the microstructure of cognition*, 2 Volumes. Cambridge, MA: MIT Press/Bradford Books.

Santoro, G. (1995). What is Computer Mediated Communication? In Z. Berge & M. Collins (Eds.), *Computer mediated communication and the online classroom in distance learning*. Cresskill, NJ: Hampton Press.

Sato, C. (1990). *The syntax of conversation in interlanguage development*. Tübingen: Gunter Narr Verlag.

Savignon, S. (1983). *Communicative competence: Theory and classroom practice*. Reading, MA: Addison-Wesley.

Schmidt, R. (1983). Interaction, acculturation and the acquisition of communicative competence. In N. Wolfson & E. Judd (Eds.), *Sociolinguistics and language acquisition*. Rowley, MA: Newbury House.

Schmidt, R., & S. Frota (1986). Developing basic conversational ability in a second language: A case study of an adult learner of Portuguese. In R. Day (Ed.), *Talking to learn*. New York: Newbury House.

Schmitt, R. (1991). Methodological weaknesses with CAI research. *Journal of Computer Based Instruction 18*(1), 75–76.

Schön, D. (1983). On explicit and negative data effecting and affecting competence and linguistic behavior. *Second Language Research 15*(2), 147–163.

Schön, D. (1988). A reply to Gregg: In defense of theory building. *Second Language Research 4*(2), 157–173.

Schön, D. (1986). The epistemological status of Second Language Acquisition. *Second Language Research 2*(2), 120–159.

Steinberg, E. (1992). The potential of computer based telecommunications for instruction. *Journal of Computer Based Instruction 19*(1), 42–46.

Steinberg, E. (1991). *Computer Assisted Instruction: A synthesis of theory, practice, and technology*. Hillsdale, NJ: Laurence Erlbaum.

Stevens, V. (1992). Humanism and CALL: A coming of age. In M. Pennington and V. Stevens (Eds.), *Computers in Applied Linguistics: An International Perspective*. Clevedon: Multilingual Matters Ltd.

Strevens, P. (1987). Interaction outside the classroom: Using the community. In W. Rivers *Interactive language teaching*. New York: Cambridge University Press.

Tarone, E., & G. Yule (Eds.) (1989). *Focus on the language learner*. Hong Kong: Oxford University Press.

Underwood, J. H. (1984). *Linguistics, computers and the language teacher: A communicative teacher*. Rowley, MA: Newbury House.

Veasey D'Souza, P. (1991). The use of electronic mail as an instructional aid: An exploratory study. *Journal of Computer Based Instruction 18*(1), 106–110.

Vygotsky, L. S. (1978). *Mind in society*. Cambridge, MA: Harvard University Press.

Warschauer, M. (1995). *E-mail for English teaching*. Alexandria, VA: TESOL Publications, Inc.

Weizenbaum, J. (1976). *Computer power and human reason*. New York: W. H. Freeman.

Wertsch, J. (Ed.) (1985). *Culture, communication, and cognition: Vygotskian perspectives*. New York: Cambridge University Press.

8 Web 2.0, Synthetic Immersive Environments, and Mobile Resources for Language Education

Julie M. Sykes*, Ana Oskoz** and Steven I. Thorne***

Introduction

At present, education is entering a particularly critical stage that is marked by an urgent need to examine the role digitally mediated, collaborative tools play, not only as learning tools, but as authentic means of communication and relationship building. Concomitant with burgeoning numbers of internet users (approaching 1.25 billion individuals as of September 30, 2007)[1] comes a parallel growth in quantity and variety of mediated expression, the everyday forms of participation in civic, professional, and social life, and,

* Julie M. Sykes is a doctoral candidate in the Department of Spanish and Portuguese at the University of Minnesota where she specializes in Spanish Applied Linguistics, emerging technologies/CALL, and L2 pragmatic acquisition. She also holds a graduate certificate in School Technology Leadership from the University of Minnesota. Julie's most recent project entails the creation, implementation, and empirical investigation of the first synthetic immersive environment for learning Spanish pragmatics, *Croquelandia*.

** Ana Oskoz is Assistant Professor at the University of Maryland Baltimore County (UMBC). She obtained her Ph.D. from the University of Iowa in Foreign Language Education and currently teaches undergraduate and graduate courses in Spanish language and second language acquisition. Her most recent research focuses on the use of Web 2.0 applications, such as wikis and blogs, in the foreign language classroom. Ana Oskoz has presented extensively nationally and internationally and published on CALL-related topics.

*** Steven L. Thorne is Assistant Professor in the Department of Applied Linguistics and Associate Director of the Center for Language Acquisition at the Pennsylvania State University. He also serves as the Advisor for Mediated Learning at the Center for Advanced Language Proficiency Education and Research (http://calper.la.psu.edu).

perhaps most profoundly, the emergence of entirely new social formations that have surfaced only in, and through, internet mediation (for discussions, see Jenkins, 2006; Thorne, 2008a; Thorne & Black, 2008).

The global internet use statistics presented above, supported by sociological research (e.g., Castells, 2004), suggest that, in many economically developed regions, one would find it difficult to conduct common professional and interpersonal activities without internet information and communication tools.[2] In this sense, internet-mediated communication is no longer a supplement to, or practice arena for, communication in everyday life. Instead, it 'is a high-stakes environment in its own right' (Thorne & Payne, 2005: 372). That is, instead of merely simulating other modes of interaction, technology-mediated communication is, in and of itself, the real thing that operates as a critically important medium for all kinds of human interaction. In addition to the changes technology has precipitated in communicative functioning, there are cognitive implications related to the increased use of digital information and communication tools as well. Namely, recent research indicates both a qualitative and physiological shift in cognitive processes based on the prolific use of these tools in everyday life (e.g., Dror, 2007). Our premise, therefore, is that, in considering the future of computer-assisted language learning (CALL), we should continue to leverage educationally oriented, computer-mediated activity, while also remaining aware of the transformational roles many of these collaborative tools play in meaningful language use, both inside and outside of the classroom. A corollary is that, in some cases, mastery of high-frequency and high-stakes mediated genres of communication should also form the explicit goal of educational practice.

This article reviews current trends in the use of digitally mediated communication and offers a vision for near-future second and foreign language learning (L2) that utilizes emerging media as (a) meaningful contexts for L2 language development and (b) a means for adding real world relevance to in-class uses of internet communication tools. In the following sections, we examine these issues in light of two genres of digital spaces – Web 2.0 technologies and multiuser, immersive virtual spaces. We first explore a sampling of three Web 2.0 technologies (i.e., wikis, blogs, social bookmarking) as related to transforming the practice of collaborative content building, dissemination, and categorization. This discussion will utilize specific examples drawn from projects related to L2 learning in Web 2.0 contexts. In the second half of the article, we consider three types of immersive virtual environments, including open social virtualities (e.g., *Second Life* or *There*), massively multiplayer online games (MMOGs) (the most prominent example of which is *World of Warcraft*), and synthetic immersive environments (SIEs, i.e., visually rendered spaces which combine attributes of open social virtualities with goal-directed gaming models to address specific learning objectives). In particular, we will focus on SIEs as they might be used to foster interlanguage pragmatic development and will briefly report on an existing project in this area. The ultimate goal of this article is to spark future research and pedagogical innovation in these Web 2.0 and SIE-related areas in order to arrive at a greater understanding of the complexities involved in the integration of digital media with language learning in ways that will be most relevant to the communicative contexts of the 21st century.

Web 2.0: Wikis, Blogs, and Social Bookmarking

With the introduction of Web 2.0 technologies, we have seen a noteworthy impact on the manners in which content is created, disseminated, and interpreted in society (Brown & Adler, 2008; Levy & Stone, 2006). Each of the Web 2.0 tools chosen for discussion in this article plays an important role in the understanding of a new conceptualization of social knowledge.

Wikis (i.e., collaborative, editable web spaces) facilitate the creation of content by groups of people, often resulting in the production of more accurate, diverse, and thorough informational texts. For example, one would be hard pressed to find an internet user not familiar with *Wikipedia*[3] (http://www.wikipedia.org, currently reporting 'more than 75,000 active contributors and 9,000,000 entries in more than 250 languages,' *Wikipedia*, November 2007), a site that has been described as 'collaborative writing that leverages collective intelligence for knowledge production in the public domain' (Lankshear & Knobel, 2007: 17). While the value of the information on *Wikipedia* has recently been the focus of much debate (Jaschik, 2007), there is strong evidence that *Wikipedia* and related resources have transformed the ways in which knowledge is documented and shared on a global scale (Jenkins, 2008).

In conjunction with the collaborative content creation often found in wikis, blogs provide a new medium of individualized self-expression. A recent count by Technorati estimates the existence of more than 70 million active blogs with the number growing daily. Furthermore, real-time blogging through, for example, *Twitter* (http://twitter.com), is taking this individualized expression a step further by allowing opinions and commentary to be documented and shared synchronously. With increased access to the production and dissemination of information comes an increasing need to organize and personalize relevant information efficiently (Levy & Stone, 2006). Social bookmarking sites, such as *del.icio.us* (http://del.icio.us), support this process by allowing users to catalogue, characterize, and share indexical resources to information.

While space limitations preclude further discussion, we wish to note the growing prominence of social computing networks (e.g., *Facebook* [http://www.facebook.com] and *My Space* [http://www.myspace.com]) and media self-publishing venues (e.g., *Flickr* [http://www.flickr.com] and *YouTube* [http://www.youtube.com]) that allow users to personally connect, socially interact, and share media and activities with one another at a scale that is staggering.[4] *Facebook*, for example, reports 57 million active users and an average of 250,000 new registered users daily since January 2007.

Web 2.0 and L2 Learning

In relation to the development of plurilingual competence, Web 2.0 tools support collaborative and individual text and multimedia production. Relatedly, they foster attention to aspects of language use that span from appropriate lexical choice to syntactic accuracy and from rhetorical style to textual cohesion and genre specificity. Furthermore, they have the potential to encourage awareness of the use of written language and visual expression as forms of representation that are rooted in, often pluralistic, linguistic and cultural conventions.

The aforementioned characteristics of Web 2.0 technologies help explain why reports on the use of wikis and blogs[5] represent an emerging growth market in the economy of CALL research (e.g., Ducate & Lomicka, 2005; Kost, 2007; Thorne & Payne, 2005). Importantly, wikis and blogs are spaces in which students have the potential to move from the conventional epistemic stance of knowledge consumer to that of knowledge producer, and, in so doing, to shift also from mere participation in an educational community to contributive and co-constitutive roles in that community. We would underscore, however, that L2 and general educational uses of these technologies require critical awareness of media literacies and may provide both new resources as well as precipitate significant challenges to teachers and administrators (for a discussion, see Thorne & Reinhardt, 2008). The remainder of this section reports on work currently underway in the CALL arena related to wikis, blogs, and social bookmarking. Each section further explores the unique role these tools can, and perhaps should, play in future language learning endeavors. Examples from current projects are included where available.

Wikis: Collaborative Content Creation

Originally utilized by computer programmers and system designers, wikis have become popular venues for collaboration and communication in a variety of contexts, including the education arena, at both the K-12 and university levels (Farabaugh, 2007; Farabaugh, Farabaugh & Freeland, 2005; Kost, 2007; Oskoz & Elola, 2008; Wang et al., 2005). In part, educators' interest in the use of wikis likely 'derives from the facility [they] offer [for] talking to others, regardless of the distance, and the opportunity [they] provide to gather information. Using [them], we feel connected, both to the people and to various contexts of our world' (Farabaugh, 2007: 42). Furthermore, wikis are readily accessible and are low or no cost for noncommercial (e.g., educational or nonprofit) use.[6] Increasingly, open source (e.g., *Moodle*) and commercial (e.g., *WebCT/Blackboard*) course management systems (CMSs) now include integrated wiki and blog spaces, making them more readily available to practitioners already using such systems.

Early reports on the use of wikis in the L2 classroom have been primarily descriptive and exploratory in nature (Godwin-Jones, 2003; Thorne & Payne, 2005), but a number of projects currently underway have documented innovative uses of wikis in the L2 classroom. These include the application of wikis to connect methodology classes among universities (Lomicka, Lord, Ducate, & Arnold, 2007), to examine students' content and composition development (Oskoz & Elola, 2008), and to assess learners' language use as part of their experience in writing classes (Kost, 2007). From an examination of these studies, as well as the more general literature on wikis, two attributes of this mediated context emerge as especially applicable to the CALL arena. These include a reconceptualization of authorship as well as changes to approaches to the writing process as a whole.

The blurring of historical notions of authorship that emerge as a function of collaborative writing in a universal write-access wiki space revises the conventional author–reader relationship; witness the lack of explicitly defined authorship on sites such as *Wikipedia* to name the most prominent example (see Thorne, 2008b, for a discussion). Fully utilizing wikis in the L2 classroom requires recognition of the learning that can take place through, and as a result of, the collaborative creation of one final product (Brown & Adler, 2008). This has an impact not only on the notion of individualized scholarship, but also the created product as a whole.

In terms of assessment and insight into the writing process, a useful feature for language educators is the ability to explicitly track all registered user contributions to a wiki document (e.g., additions, deletions, alterations, etc.). This feature makes visible many aspects of the historical evolution of a text as well as the content of individual user contributions. Learners themselves can use document tracking features to examine the evolution of a text, potentially enhancing their ability to objectively monitor and control their learning processes. As stated by Farabaugh, 'the discussion tend[s] to be evolving and democratic ... with each participant in turn taking the opportunity to shape the 'reified' experience' (2007: 45). In essence, knowledge building is not only focused on developing a final product; also highlighted are the turn-by-turn dynamics of scholarly authorship within an 'open source epistemology' (Lankshear & Knobel, 2007: 18).

The collaborative value of wikis is further increased when accompanied by the use of web-based voice applications such as the commercial tools *Skype*, *Skype TM*, or *Voice Direct*. Adding a synchronous voice application to the asynchronous collaboration of wikis provides another layer of complexity and richness to students' work and increases the level of accountability for the participants (Oskoz & Elola, 2008). Collaboration goes beyond the editing of sentences, organization of paragraphs, and addition of content. Given that the final product is a representation of all of those involved, the synchronous voice discussion becomes a negotiation of ideas, more closely mimicking collaborative scenarios that often happen in the non-academic world (e.g., Brown & Adler, 2008; Jenkins, 2006). From a pedagogical point of view, instructors can design activities that engage learners, both synchronously and asynchronously, to enable collaborative engagement on a more complex level. To take an example from one of our institutions, students in advanced writing classes in Spanish participate in research projects in which pairs of students collaborate in the development of content and language learning related tasks via wiki. While students complete most of the work and the revisions in the wiki, they have the opportunity to fine tune and discuss any content or linguistic concerns synchronously by using tools such as *Voice Direct*. Through archival searches of these online discussions, a record of the collaborative process is created that can be easily accessed and reviewed.

From a research point of view, the use of wikis, in conjunction with voice (or written) chat, supplies a large amount of data regarding students' collaboration across drafts, the depth of students' discussions with voice/written chat, and organizational, linguistic and content related differences between first and final drafts (Oskoz & Elola, 2008). This information can provide additional insights into the complex L2 writing process, which, in turn, can inform pedagogical applications in the classroom.

Blogs: Self-expression and (the Potential for) Enhanced Readership

Blogs come in many shapes and sizes and have evolved as a set of 'social and informational phenomena that include mainstream media as well as grassroots and watchdog news reporting, thematic and topic-specific amateur and professional observations, business and commercial information outlets, and, of course, the 'public' journaling of one's 'private' life' (Thorne & Payne, 2005: 382). They are free (e.g., *Blogger.com* [https://www.blogger.com/start]), easy to create (i.e., often a matter of merely entering content and uploading), and customizable (making them attractive to advanced users). In addition, they provide a space in the public domain to which information can be added instantaneously (Richardson, 2006) and made available to a global audience.[7] Thus, blogs are especially useful for encouraging individual (and less frequently, group) authorship that is relevant to a larger, interactive community.

Blogs are receiving increasingly more attention in CALL research and second language instruction (e.g., Bloch, 2007; Ducate & Lomicka, 2005; Elola & Oskoz, 2008; Fidalgo-Eick, 2006) as primarily individual authoring environments. While blogs are often richly interlinked with other interactive digital spaces, blogs tend to be highly personal and have been described as 'I, I, me-me-me' environments due to the fact that they are typically controlled by a single person and explicitly reflect that individual's point of view (Thorne & Payne, 2005: 382). Their potential to enhance L2 writing skills through meaningful tasks and extended readership is often the subject of attention.

Despite the individually oriented perspective often associated with blogging, their use also offers significant opportunities to cultivate interaction. Readers can respond to writers' entries with comments that can result in de facto threaded discussions (Campbell, 2003). Student maintenance of individual journals by participating in blog communities, different from essays written to an unknown or overly narrow audience (e.g., the instructor), provides students with a sense of authorial purpose (Fidalgo-Eick, 2006). Moreover, blogs can be used to enhance students' reading and writing, both in their native language and the target language(s) (Ducate & Lomicka, 2005). Furthermore, students can access entries on different topics by experts and other learners as well as explore links referenced within a blog. Learners can also read blogs written by individuals around the world, supporting the analysis of – and interaction with – cultural information viewed as a form of legitimate cultural eavesdropping.

In addition, blogs can be envisioned as a tool for students to develop intercultural communicative competence, defined as openness to difference and a capacity to contingently and dynamically interact with members of other speech communities and cultures (e.g., Byram, 2000; Belz & Thorne, 2006; Thorne, 2006). In a recent project (Elola & Oskoz, 2008), blogs were used to connect residential foreign language students with international partners. Following discussion of a series of tasks related to family, health, art, and urban living, students, working primarily in pods of four (two students in the US and two students in Spain) presented evidence of intercultural competence. Overall, students found the experience to be successful and both groups perceived that blogging had a positive effect in their intercultural competence development.

Alternative Forms of Blogging

Current blogging practices involve more than the written word. Three popular forms of multimedia blogging – audioblogging, moblogging, and vlogging – include the primary objective of blogging through multimedia (i.e., audiofiles, pictures, and videos) as an addition to, or replacement of, textual postings. Similar to text blog posts, multimedia blogs are organized by the time and date posted. Moblogging, for its part, allows users to upload pictures taken from cell phones, PDAs, and digital cameras, presenting an opportunity for real-time documentation and charting. Finally, vlogs support the addition of video, usually accompanied by text, images, and additional contextual information. Paraphrasing Godwin-Jones (2005), moblogging and vlogs are particularly compelling at a time in which so many cell phones have built in digital cameras and the capacity to create video clips. Given the facility to download MP3 or other audio files and the large number of students who own cell phones, these three variables bring new possibilities and projects to the L2 classroom. For example, in study abroad contexts, without the need to wait for access to a computer, students upload images and text directly from their cell phones, thus sharing more vividly and rapidly their experiences with others, be it family or classmates. These formats have been little explored in L2 education research but are growing in popularity with campus study abroad offices and organizations (a Google search on the query 'study abroad blogs' returned 277,000 hits, the first five pages of which were nearly all relevant).

Social Bookmarking: The Social Organization of Collective Knowledge

With the explosion of shared content available in these emerging digital spaces, the ability to categorize and annotate information that is meaningful and relevant to an individual is important (Levy & Stone, 2006). However, due to the sheer volume of content available in digital spaces today, it is impractical (and likely impossible) to effectively manage the information at a local level (e.g., each individual user). Therefore, while the word 'bookmarking' does not necessarily make us think of collaboration, social bookmarking, in essence, is the collaborative management of digital content. Instead of individually bookmarking each site of collective interest, social bookmarking allows one to annotate in a minimally designed webpage such as in *del.icio.us* URLs to different web pages. Below each URL, the user is able to provide a small description of the webpage content where the user(s) select words as tags.[8]

The benefits of using social bookmarking as a research or instructional tool include: (a) creating an 'outboard memory,' a page that stores links that could otherwise get lost in an array of emails and printouts; (b) connecting with people who share the same interests and who could become potential collaborators; (c) clustering tags which reveal unique combinations of an individual's research themes; (d) creating a multiauthored, bookmarked page that might ultimately benefit the entire team when working on a project; and (e) providing insights into the owner's (owners') research (Alexander, 2006). Social bookmarking creates a space where students can share their personal and professional inquiries. Sites such as *del.icio.us* provide the possibility of creating private networks localizable to students in a class, enabling the creation of a bank of resources to which everybody would have access.[9] The benefits of social bookmarking go beyond the sharing of information among users. As with the aforementioned communication environments described above, its benefits are maximized when used in conjunction with other tools, for example the linking of social bookmarking with blog and wiki projects.[10]

In general, we consider the Web 2.0 tools presented in this article as essential to the transformation from individual to collective content creation, dissemination, and categorization. Future CALL research and L2 pedagogy would benefit from continued exploration of these tools as serious, relevant contexts for the creation and shaping of knowledge in meaningful, real-world contexts.

Online Virtual Worlds: Open Social Spaces, Massively Multiplayer On-Line Games, and Synthentic Immersive Environments

An important area that warrants significant attention in considering the relevance of mediated contexts are the realms of open social spaces (e.g., *Second Life, There,* and *Active Worlds*), massively multiplayer online gaming spaces (MMOGs) (e.g., *World of Warcraft, Everquest,* and *Eve Online*), and synthetic immersive environments (SIEs) (e.g., *Croquelandia* and *ZON*). The commercial endeavors in this context form a billion dollar empire and engage participants from all over the world. Recently, educational researchers have begun to assess these interactional spaces and gaming models as beneficial for learning (e.g., de Freitas, 2006; Gee, 2003,

2005; Jenkins & Squire, 2004; National Summit on Educational Gaming, 2005; Prensky, 2001; Steinkuelher, 2004, 2007), and, more specifically, for achieving communicative and intercultural competence (e.g., Bryant, 2006; García-Carbonell, Montero, Rising, & Watts, 2001; Thorne, 2008c; Thorne & Black, 2007, 2008). Mediated experiences in different online social and gaming worlds allow users to experiment and interact with a wide variety of norms of communication and social interaction (e.g., Steinkuehler, 2006). Thus, each type of visually rendered virtual space presents distinct possibilities for language development based on the affordances, constraints, and unique interactional opportunities of the space itself. In the discussion to follow, we first address considerations of communicative norms within various types of online immersive worlds. We then explore the use of SIEs for L2 learning with specific reference to a project that targets the complex issue of interlanguage pragmatic development.[11]

Communicative Norms in Online Virtual Worlds

In thinking about the complex, collaborative nature of immersive spaces, it is critical to examine not only the features unique to each type of space, but also the communicative norms and practices associated with their use. Examining why and how construction and negotiation of communicative functions occur in intercultural language learning through computer-mediated communication (CMC), Thorne (2003) presents a cultural-historical framework for understanding how internet-based tools mediate communication (see also Lantolf & Thorne, 2006). Based on this framework, Thorne postulates that 'digital communication technologies have made possible substantive aesthetic shifts in human communicative practices' and argues that such practices emerge within distinctive cultures-of-use – that is, the unity of local and contingent aspects of interaction with 'the historically sedimented characteristics that accrue to a [computer-mediated-communication] tool from its everyday use' (2003: 40). The historically developed cultures-of-use of a mediated communication environment, involving norms and expectations of appropriate language use, shape interactional dynamics and, by extension, the forms of language development and literacy engagement taking place in these contexts (see also Thorne, 2000).

Historically, the field of second language acquisition has seen an increasing level of importance placed on communicative norms as part of evolving models of communicative competence (Bachman, 1997; Canale & Swain, 1980; Hymes, 1972; Thorne, 2006[12]). Immersive modalities offer significant opportunities for engaged interaction and language socialization within specific genres and communicative norms. Attention to the relationship between innovative mediated communication technologies and the development of advanced language skills, such as pragmatics, should be considered, not only in terms of how they function as learning tools, but also as relevant interactive contexts in and of themselves. Thus, when considering any mediated environment, it is critical to place value on the inherent norms of the interactive space itself as well as the application of learned skills to other communicative contexts.

Full participation in virtually rendered spaces requires pragmatic control of the communicative norms local to a specific online community as well as mastery of the interface and virtual topography. Users of *Second Life*, for example, must learn a designated set of in-world features before they are permitted to navigate away from 'Orientation Island.' Moreover, to be a highly skilled player in *World of Warcraft*, one must not only be able to complete quests, gain assets, and navigate through three continents of geographic space, but also to interact with others in an appropriate manner utilizing the norms established by expert players of the game. This point will be elaborated shortly.

To add further complexity, participants may take on numerous identities in immersive spaces through careful manipulation of sociopragmatic factors as they carry out and creatively transform roles they visually embody in the virtual space (Gee, 2003, 2005; Prensky, 2001). For example, in *Second Life*, an open social space designed as a simulation of 'life,' users can select the gender of their avatar, design their own clothing, and modify their behavior based on, for example, location or the presence/absence of other participants. Behavior in *Second Life* can be, and should be, tailored to suit a variety of social contexts such as the tropical island bar, classroom, or commercial, high-power board room of a company on virtual Main Street. Moreover, experienced players are quite adept at identifying new users based on the appearance of their avatar (Sadler, 2007).

Players of MMOGs can take this experimentation one step further by selecting a race, class, or profession. In *World of Warcraft*, to take an example from the most widely played MMOG (with over 9,000,000 players worldwide), users begin the game by selecting a race (which influences geographical area, game-suggested personality, and other social features) as well as a class (which influences abilities and the manner in which the game is played). Once this selection has been made, a user's avatar is then constrained by the societal norms of that race in Azeroth (the simulated world in which the characters live). For example, Night Elves are described in the official game documentation as a race having more sophisticated personalities with a tendency to make dry jokes whereas Gnomes are depicted as the 'nerdy' race that is marked with extreme intelligence and mechanical abilities. Each of these constraints is game suggested, yet user selected and enacted (or not, as is frequently the case).

In MMOGs such as *World of Warcraft*, it is common for users to create two or more characters (known as 'alts' or 'toons') in order to experience the game from different perspectives. This seems to indicate that social experimentation is an inherent characteristic of these spaces. In addition to experimenting with roles and personalities, learners can also experiment in terms of gesture, physical context, audio enhancement, and transferring of assets within the various types of immersive spaces. As Gee suggests, '[g]ames are an invitation to play out different sides of our desires, feelings, values, fears, fantasies, and identities' (2005: 70). In relation to language learning, such opportunities for identity play precipitate sociopragmatic considerations that can involve gesture and personal space (e.g., Rosenbloom, 2006), political action (e.g., Sawyer, 2005; *Second Life Herald* 2006, 2007), critique and coconstruction of 'culture' (e.g., Mistral, 2007), caretaking (Kushner, 2006), emotional connection with others and with the game space (e.g., Slater et al., 2006), sexual encounters (e.g., Cheng, 2006), and commerce (e.g., Shamoon, 2006).

Virtual Social Spaces and Massively Multiplayer Online Gaming Spaces

While there is a growing body of research addressing the use of *Second Life* in education, up to this point (see de Freitas, 2006, for a review), relatively little research has specifically addressed the use of MMOGs for L2 language development. In a preliminary analysis of these issues, Thorne (2008c) analyzes intercultural communication occurring in MMOGs as related to other internet-mediated communication modalities. A detailed analysis of an interaction between an expert speaker of English living in the US and an expert speaker of Russian living in the Ukraine indicates evidence of a number of positive assets for language learning (e.g., natural, unscripted interaction, emotional bond with the interlocutor, reciprocal alterations in expert status, explicit other and self-correction, extended repair sequences, and exhibited motivation for language learning). Additionally, the interaction represented in this case study demonstrated numerous complex communicative functions such as solidarity building, greeting and leave taking, apologizing, and requesting (see also Nardi, Ly, & Harris, 2007). Despite the limited work in this area, the inherent characteristics of both open virtual spaces and MMOGs offer numerous potential benefits for the development of complex communicative skills, such as pragmatics, in a second language.[13] The following section describes a project currently underway aimed at leveraging the possibilities of immersive spaces for language learning.

Synthetic Immersive Environments

SIEs represent a unique variety of online immersive space that is carefully designed to function as a social space while, at the same time, incorporating the beneficial attributes of MMOG models. In other words, SIEs are engineered spaces which integrate the many benefits of online gaming to produce explicit, educationally related outcomes in simulated, relevant interactional contexts (Sykes, 2008). SIEs carry significant potential in that they allow creators to target specific skills and educational objectives, while creating a meaningful collaborative space in which learners themselves are at the center of their own learning.

A large-scale research project which entails the creation, implementation, and analysis of the first SIE targeted at attaining advanced L2 skills is currently underway (Sykes, 2008). The *Croquelandia* space[14] is an SIE designed for the learning of Spanish pragmatics in which learners are immersed in a three-dimensional, graphically rich social space that emulates various regions of the 'real' Spanish-speaking world. During their time in *Croquelandia*, learners are engaged in a variety of game-like, goal-directed activities (e.g., quests) designed to provide behavior-based corrective feedback to users through interaction with non-player characters (NPCs), native speakers, and other group members. Learners are able to practice in the SIE in order to improve their pragmatic competence in a low-risk, yet emotionally engaging, immersive space. Interaction with, and within, this SIE carries the ultimate goal of enhancing learners' ability to deal with various pragmatic features of L2 Spanish. Initial learner perception and outcome data indicate a positive effect of the use of SIEs for pragmatic development. The following section explores some of the advantages and disadvantages of the use of SIEs for learning L2 communicative norms, especially considerations relevant to pragmatics.

The Advantages and Disadvantages of Sies for L2 Pragmatic Learning

Advantages

Considering the complexity of the issues inherent in the internet-mediated communicative contexts themselves as well as the numerous pragmalinguistic and sociopragmatic factors influencing pragmatic appropriateness, it might appear impossible to harness this technological tool for L2 pragmatic learning. However, the whole might be less complex than all of its individual components. Research has shown that pragmatics is indeed teachable and should be included in L2 language learning (Cohen, 1996; Kasper, 1997; LoCastro, 2003; Rose & Kasper, 2001; Rose, 2005). Furthermore, internet-mediated tools offer immense potential to overcome some of the inherent difficulties in teaching pragmatics (Sykes, 2005). Some of these difficulties include: (a) individual personality differences and sensitivity to certain contextual factors influencing the interaction (Bardovi-Harlig, 2001; Kasper, 1997); (b) assessment and feedback challenges (Cohen, 2004; Roever, 2004; Salaberry & Cohen, 2006); and (c) immense variation (dialect, social, individual) (Márquez-Reiter & Placencia, 2005).

One of the biggest advantages of using SIEs for learning pragmatics, as well as other complex communicative norms and functions, is their flexibility and built-in complexity. In other words, it is an internet-mediated modality which encourages the use of an integrated set of complex features to learn about complex language functions (i.e., pragmatics) in a realistic amount of time, not something that is merely created for a learning exercise. Gee (2003) describes the mechanism driving games, which is equally applicable to SIEs,

So here we are with something that is long, hard, and challenging. However, you cannot play a game if you cannot learn it... Of course, designers could keep making them shorter and simpler to facilitate learning... But, no, in this case, game designers keep making the games longer and more challenging, and still manage to get them learned (p. 6).

This is much like pragmatics. The more you know, the more difficult it becomes, and the longer it takes to truly master the necessary pragmalinguistic and sociopragmatic skills.[15] SIEs provide a mechanism for making this a possible and realistic endeavor. This complexity also makes SIEs unique from other types of internet-mediated environments.

Simulated Roles and Identities

As noted in the previous discussion regarding online immersive spaces, one of the most positive assets for L2 pragmatic learning is the possibility to take on numerous, simulated identities and participant roles. In doing so, learners are able to experiment and practice pragmatic functions in diverse social contexts and settings. In SIEs, assumed participant roles move a step beyond those found in a synchronous CMC environment. Not only can learners simulate and manipulate the roles they are taking on, they can also embody them in the visually simulated space (Gee, 2003, 2005; Prensky, 2001). Through this experimentation, the goal is that learners begin to understand the impact language has on their level of success (high or low) in specific communicative contexts. Furthermore, the intention is that they will also start to integrate the pragmatic skills acquired in the SIE into their repertoire for use in nonmediated interaction and other digital contexts.

Emotional Connection

Another important advantage of SIEs is the emotional connection users often feel in response to the environment. This is especially beneficial in SIEs because the virtual environment itself can be constructed in ways that are relevant for a specific population of learners. For example, *Croquelandia* utilizes digital models created from photographs taken in geographical locations throughout the Spanish-speaking world (e.g., Otavalo, Ecuador, and Merida, Mexico). Retrospective interviews with the participants indicate that this 'simulated realism' was especially impressive to learners involved in the project because it allowed them to feel like they were 'really there' (Sykes, 2008).

This emotional connection with the content is an important benefit of the SIE space. Research has shown that immersive spaces are highly engaging and produce emotions of 'real' consequence (Prensky, 2001; Slater et al., 2006; Wilcox, Allison, Elfassy, & Grelik, 2006). It allows the opportunity for learners to feel the results of their actions without causing real-world harm to the people around them. de Freitas (2006) notes that 'By creating games as metaphors, children and adults can utilize role play and narrative forms to imagine and empathize with other people, events from history, or with potential scenarios in the future and to experiment and rehearse skills in safe, protected environments' (p. 6). They also can begin to see the world around them reflectively and thoughtfully, making pragmatic features more important to their perceived success. This advantage is similar to that found in the telecollaboration studies using asynchronous CMC and synchronous CMC (Belz, 2003; Furstenberg, Levet, English, & Maillet, 2001; Thorne, 2003) in which learners build emotional bonds (positive or negative) with their collaborative partners. In SIEs, these emotional connections may motivate learners to continue practicing so they can successfully cultivate their relationships with other human beings, either collaboratively in the virtual space or in other contexts within the Spanish-speaking world.

Authentic or Low-Risk Practice

An additionally noteworthy attribute of SIEs is the extensive opportunity to practice. Practice and hypothesizing is an important component of L2 pragmatic learning. First of all, learners have the opportunity to interact with native speakers in a nonthreatening environment where they already share common ground (i.e., the SIE itself). As observed by Thorne (2008c) in an analysis of discourse between a Russian student and an American student, bonds are built fairly quickly and include interaction around the space as well as aspects of the world outside of the SIE. This can lead to a number of practice opportunities by bringing together interlocutors from around the world, especially in large-scale commercial games.

Another advantage is the low-risk practice opportunities provided through interaction with NPCs (de Freitas, 2006; Gee, 2003, 2005; Mistral, 2007). This is an advantage for L2 learning because high-stakes speech acts, such as apologizing, can be performed without offending 'real' interlocutors. Yet, at the same time, learners can feel the impact of their errors based on elements built into the space (e.g., lost assets, fewer invitations, angry NPCs). Thus, different types of practice can provide advantages to L2 pragmatic learning in a number of ways, either through interaction with other human beings or interaction with elements built into the spaces themselves.

Disadvantages

Despite the many potential benefits offered by SIEs for pragmatic learning, it is important to discuss the drawbacks as well. The biggest potential disadvantage in SIEs is the danger of learning the pragmatics of the space and not necessarily skills of the L2 itself. As previously mentioned, online immersive spaces are constrained by, and create, their own communicative norms. Thus, two people who are extremely close and get along very well in an SIE may not necessarily be able to transfer that relationship, and those in-game communication repertoires, to face-to-face communication. Gee (2003) describes the case of a player who had reached a very high level in a MMOG only to have his character killed off. In this particular game, the only way to be resurrected is to be invited back in by another player. The player in question posted numerous requests including his home telephone number, and, eventually, someone helped him get back in. However, it took a great deal of time for this to happen and only a few players were willing to help. In other words, the communicative norms maintained in the MMOG did not carry into communicative contexts outside of the immersive world. In this case, the request was granted, but there was no guarantee outside of the playing space that the same type of solidarity existed in other contexts. A way to overcome this drawback is to continue to focus on skills for L2 pragmatic performance that enable learners to deal with a variety of contextual and mediated (as well as nonmediated) situations.

Another disadvantage of using online immersive worlds for L2 learning, especially applicable in the case of multimillion dollar immersive environments such as *Second Life* and *World of Warcraft,* is the stigma educators might have about embracing the positive aspects of the spaces themselves. Gee (2003, 2005) comments extensively on the perceptions that many have about the representation of violence or gender in the learning spaces. While he does not embrace many of the criticisms, the issues themselves could create difficulties when implementing these learning tools in the educational setting. (For a discussion of the evolving role of gender and gaming, see Cassell & Jenkins, 1998.)

Conclusion

Using Web 2.0 tools and various forms of online immersive worlds suggest a number of profound transformations to traditional approaches for second language education. In each of the contexts described above, students' agency – defined here as the socioculturally mediated capacity to act (based on Ahearn, 2001) – has the potential to evolve beyond the confines of the subject-position associated with the conventional institutional identity of 'student.' Intrepid uses of new media fray the boundaries separating study from play, student from player, and information consumer from knowledge producer. In many of these contexts, from social bookmarking and wiki use to MMOG play, expertise is distributed across participants engaged in multiple systems of activity that relate to the local enterprise at hand. Additionally, when new media is put to wise use, we see tremendous potential for an increase in the ecological relations between the language practices and identity dispositions developed within instructional L2 contexts and the broader plurilingual communicative contexts of life outside of the academy. As mentioned at numerous points in this article, the developmentally successful use of Web 2.0 tools and immersive worlds will not be straightforward and cannot be taken for granted. However, the research and pedagogical reports discussed here strongly suggest a powerful potential of Web 2.0 and online immersive spaces for second language learning.

Notes

1. As measured by internetworldstats.com (http://internetworldstats.com).
2. See Tapscott (2000), McGrath (2004), Warschauer (2003), and Van Dijk (2005) for discussion of the digital divide in education, even in economically developed countries. While these factors also likely affect the perception and use of internet-mediated communicative tools, a discussion of these issues is beyond the scope of this analysis.
3. *Wikipedia* (http://www.wikipedia.org), probably the most well known wiki, is a user-edited online encyclopedia founded in 2001 in which readers make changes and improve the content of the different texts.
4. See Levy and Stone (2006) for a brief discussion in this area.

5. In fact, of all the Web 2.0 technologies, wikis and blogs are arguably the most commonly used Web 2.0 tools in L2 education.
6. These include, for example, pbwiki (http://pbwiki.com), QwikWiki (http://www.qwikiwiki.com), MediaWiki (http://www.mediawiki.org/wiki/MediaWiki), Google Docs (http://www.google.com/google-d-s/intl/en/tour1.html), and wikispaces (http://www.wikispaces.com).
7. As a caveat, access does not necessarily indicate readership.
8. The collaborative aspect of social bookmarking is apparent when one understands that each URL connects the user's page to other users' *del.icio.us* pages who have bookmarked the same URL.
9. In addition, we speculate that through examining the connections behind selected URLs and tags, learners might be more likely to find partners with whom to work on projects closely related to their own interests while also increasing their exposure to, and curiosity about, different topics.
10. To provide a concrete example, by connecting their pages to their blogs, students share their findings and links with the rest of the class, and even a wider community, at the same time that they increase the blog value as a written artifact in the social network. While working in collaborative projects in a wiki, students can easily have access to the shared information to elaborate their project. As the weeks, months, semesters, and years pass by, students will be able to add, delete, and constantly update sources of their interests. Social bookmarking has been little explored in L2 education.
11. 'Pragmatics' addresses the various manners (i.e., linguistic and nonlinguistic) in which meaning is communicated and interpreted in interaction, as well as the sociocultural factors (individual and collective) which influence the communicated and interpreted messages (Crystal, 1997; LoCastro, 2003; Yule, 1996). Interlanguage pragmatics refers to the development of these abilities in a second language.
12. Thorne (2006) advocates for the importance of pragmatics in communicative competency by suggesting a reorientation from a focus on L2 communicative competence to a focus on intercultural competence. This re-orientation emphasizes the critical connection between language and social practice as related to the negotiation of interactional patterns in intercultural communication.
13. For an extensive discussion of these potential benefits, see Sykes (2008).
14. For more information on *Croquelandia* see University of Minnesota Croquet Project (http://croquet.umn.edu).
15. Both Judd (1999) and Cohen (2005) offer instructional methodologies in pragmatics that fit within SIEs. Through different mechanisms, they both suggest the importance of a diversified look at pragmatics and the development of skills for using different pragmatic functions as opposed to teaching chunks or prescriptive formulas.

References

Ahearn, L. (2001). Language and agency. *Annual Review of Anthropology, 30*, 109–137.

Alexander, B. (2006). Web 2.0. A new way of innovation for teaching and learning? *EDUCAUSE Review, 41*, 33–44. Retrieved November 30, 2007, from http://www.educause.edu/ir/library/pdf/erm0621.pdf

Bachman, L. (1997). *Fundamental considerations in language testing.* Oxford: Oxford University Press.

Bardovi-Harlig, K. (2001). Evaluating the empirical evidence: Grounds for instruction in pragmatics? In K. Rose & G. Kasper (Eds.), *Pragmatics in language teaching* (pp. 13–32). Cambridge: Cambridge University Press.

Belz, J. (2003). Linguistic perspectives on the development of intercultural competence in telecollaboration. *Language Learning & Technology, 7*, 68–99. Retrieved March 11, 2008, from http://llt.msu.edu/vol7num2/belz

Belz, J. A., & Thorne, S. L. (Eds.). (2006). *Internet-mediated intercultural foreign language education.* Boston, MA: Thomson Heinle.

Bloch, J. (2007). Abdullah's blogging: A generation 1.5 student enters the blogosphere. *Language Learning & Technology, 11*, 128–141. Retrieved March 11, 2008, from http://llt.msu.edu/vol11num2/bloch/default.html

Brown, S., & Adler, R. P. (2008). Minds on fire. Open education, the long trail, and learning 2.0. *Educause, 43*, 17–32. Retrieved January 25, 2008, from http://connect.educause.edu/Library/EDUCAUSE+Review/MindsonFire-OpenEducationt/45823

Bryant, T. (2006, September). Using World of Warcraft and other MMORPGs to foster a targeted, social, and cooperative approach toward language learning. *Academic Commons.* Retrieved October 6, 2006, from http://www.academic-commons.org/commons/essay/bryant-MMORPGs-for-SLA

Byram, M. (2000). Assessing intercultural competence in language teaching. *Sprogforum, 18*, 8-13. Campbell, A. (2003). Weblogs for use with ESL classes. *The Internet TESL Journal, 9.* Retrieved March 16, 2007, from http://iteslj.org/Techniques/Campbell-Weblogs.html

Canale, M., & Swain, M. (1980). Theoretical bases of communicative approaches to second language teaching and testing. *Applied Linguistics, 1*, 1–47.

Cassell, J., & Jenkins, H. (Eds.). (1998). *From Barbie to Mortal Combat: Gender and computer games.* Cambridge, MA: MIT Press.

Castells, M. (Ed.). (2004). *The network society: A cross-cultural perspective.* Northampton, MA: Edward Edgar.

Cheng, H. (2006). Warning: Adults only. *Wired Magazine, 14.* Retrieved March 11, 2008, from http://www.wired.com/wired/archive/14.04/adults.html

Clark, H., & Brennan, S. (1991). Grounding in communication. In L. B. Resnick, J. M. Levine, & S. D. Teasley, (Eds.), *Perspectives in socially shared cognition* (pp. 127–150). Washington, DC: American Psychological Association.

Cohen, A. D. (1996). Developing pragmatic ability to perform speech acts. *Studies in Second Language Acquisition, 18*, 253–267.

Cohen, A. D. (2004). Assessing speech acts in a second language. In B. Boxer & A.

D. Cohen (Eds.), *Studying speaking to inform second language learning* (pp. 302–327). Clevedon: Multilingual Matters.

Cohen, A. D. (2005). Strategies for learning and performing L2 speech acts. *Intercultural Pragmatics, 2*, 275–301.

Crystal, D. (Ed.). (1997). *The Cambridge encyclopedia of language* (2nd ed.). New York: Cambridge University Press.

de Freitas, S. (2006). *Learning in immersive worlds: A review of game-based learning.* Bristol: Joint Information Systems Committee (JISC) E-Learning Programme. Retrieved March 11, 2008, from http://www.jisc.ac.uk/whatwedo/programmes/elearning_innovation/eli_outcomes/GamingRe port.aspx

Dror, I. (Ed.). (2007). *Cognitive technologies and the pragmatics of cognition.* Amsterdam: John Benjamins Publishing.

Ducate, N., & Lomicka, L. (2005). Exploring the blogosphere: Use of web logs in the foreign language classroom. *Foreign Language Annals, 38*, 410–421.

Elola, I., & Oskoz, A. (2008). Blogging: Fostering intercultural competence development in foreign language and study abroad contexts. *Foreign Language Annals 41*(3), 454–477.

Farabaugh, R. (2007). The isle is full of noises: Using wiki software to establish a discourse community in a Shakespeare classroom. *Language Awareness, 16*, 41–56.

Farabaugh, P., Farabaugh, R., & Freeland, S. (2005, November). *Using wikis in teaching and learning.* Paper presented at the TLT Brown bag, University of Maryland Baltimore County, Baltimore, MD.

Fidalgo-Eick, M. (2006, May). *Blogs in the foreign language classroom.* Paper presented at the annual conference of the Computer Assisted Language Instruction Consortium, Manoa, HI.

Furstenberg, G., Levet, S., English, K., & Maillet, K. (2001). Giving a virtual voice to the silent language of culture: The CULTURA project. *Language Learning & Technology, 5*, 2001. Retrieved March 11, 2008, from http://llt.msu.edu/vol-5num1/furstenberg/default.html

García-Carbonell, A., Montero, B., Rising, B., & Watts, F. (2001). Simulation/gaming and the acquisition of communicative competence in another language. *Simulation & Gaming, 32*, 481–491.

Gee, J. (2003). *What video games have to teach us about learning and literacy.* New York: Palgrave Macmillan.

Gee, J. (2005). *Why video games are good for your soul.* Sydney: Common Ground.

Goodwin-Jones, R. (2003). Blogs and wikis: Environments for on-line collaboration. *Language Learning & Technology, 7*, 12–16. Retrieved March 11, 2008, from http://llt.msu.edu/vol7num2/emerging

Godwin-Jones, R. (2005). Skype and podcasting: Disruptive technologies for language learning. *Language Learning & Technology, 9*, 9–12. Retrieved March 11, 2008, from http://llt.msu.edu/vol9 num3/emerging/default.html

Hymes, D. (1972). Toward ethnographies of communication: The analysis of communicative events. In P. Giglioli (Ed.), *Language and social context* (pp. 21–43). Harmondsworth: Penguin.

Jaschik, S. (2007, January 26). A stand against Wikipedia. *Inside HigherEd.* Retrieved April 4, 2008, from http://www.insidehighered.com/news/2007/01/26/wiki

Jenkins, H. (2006). *Convergence culture: Where old and new media collide*. New York: New York University Press.

Jenkins, H. (2008, January). *What Wikipedia can teach us about new media literacies.* Plenary presented at *EDUCAUSE, Education Learning Initiative*, San Antonio, TX. Available at http://www.educause.edu/Program/13300?PRODUCT_CODE=ELI081/GS01

Jenkins, H., & Squire, K. (2004). Harnessing the power of games in education. *Insight, 3*, 5–33.

Judd, E. (1999). Some issues in the teaching of pragmatic competence. In E. Hinkel (Ed.), *Culture in second language teaching and learning* (pp. 152–166). Cambridge: Cambridge University Press.

Kasper, G. (1997). *Can pragmatic competence be taught?* (Network #6). Honolulu: University of Hawai'i, Second Language Teaching & Curriculum Center. Retrieved November 30, 2007, from http://nflrc.hawaii.edu/NetWorks/NW06/default.html

Kost, C. (2007, May). *Using wikis for a collaborative writing project.* Paper presented at the annual conference of the Computer Assisted Language Instruction Consortium, Texas State University, San Marcos, TX.

Kushner, D. (2006). Good Nintendog! Roll over, Rover. A new breed of games is building deep emotional bonds and rival the best puppy love. *Wired Magazine, 14.* Retrieved March 11, 2008, from http://www.wired.com/wired/archive/14.04/nintendog.html

Lamb, B. (2004). Wide open spaces wikis: wikis ready or not. *EDUCAUSE Review, 39*, 36–46. Retrieved November 30, 2007, from http://www.educause.edu/ir/library/pdf/erm0452.pdf

Lankshear, C., & Knobel, M. (2007). Sampling 'the new' in new literacies. In M. Knobel & C. Lankshear (Eds.), *A new literacies sampler* (pp. 1–24). New York: Peter Lang.

Lantolf, J. P., & Thorne, S. L. (2006). *Sociocultural theory and the genesis of second language development*. Oxford: Oxford University Press.

Levy, S. & Stone, B. (2006, April 3). The new wisdom of the web. *Newsweek.* Retrieved April 4, 2008, from http://www.newsweek.com/id/45976

LoCastro, V. (2003). *An introduction to pragmatics: Social action for language teachers*. Ann Arbor, MI: The University of Michigan Press.

Lomicka, L., Lord, G., Ducate, L., & Arnold, N. (2007, May). *Teaching, learning and collaborating: A foreign language teacher wiki community.* Paper presented at the annual conference of the Computer Assisted Language Instruction Consortium, Texas State University, San Marcos, TX.

Márquez-Reiter, R., & Placencia, M. (2005). *Spanish pragmatics*. New York: Palgrave Macmillan.

McGrath, D. (2004). Equity revisited: PBL and the digital divide. *Learning and Leading with Technology, 32*, 36–39. Retrieved November 30, 2007, from http://www.iste.org/Content/NavigationMenu/Publications/LL/LLIssues/Volume_32_2005_2004_/October_No_2_/October_2004.htm

Mistral, P. (2007). *Second Life* ballet fills the SIM – Linden suggests selling tickets. *Second Life Herald.* Retrieved March 11, 2008, from http://www.secondlife-herald.com/slh/2007/02/olmannen_premie.html

Nardi, B., Ly, S., & Harris, J. (2007). Learning conversations in World of Warcraft. In *The Proceedings of the 2007 Hawaii International Conference on Systems Science*. New York: IEEE Press.

National Summit on Educational Gaming. (2005). *National Summit on Educational Games Fact Sheet*. Retrieved March 11, 2008, from http://www.fas.org/game-summit/Resources/Fact%20Sheet.pdf

Oskoz, A., & Elola, I. (2008) Meeting at the wiki: The new arena for collaborative writing in foreign language courses. In M. J. W. Lee & C. MacLoughlin (Eds.), *Web 2.0-based e-learning: Applying social informatics for tertiary teaching* (pp. 209–227). Hershey, PA: IGI Global.

Prensky, M. (2001). *Digital game-based learning*. St. Paul, MN: Paragon House.

Richardson, W. (2006). *Blogs, wikis, podcasts, and other powerful web tools For classrooms*. Thousand Oaks, CA: Corwin Press.

Roever, C. (2004). Difficulty and practicality in tests of interlanguage pragmatics. In B. Boxer & A. D. Cohen (Eds.), *Studying speaking to inform second language learning* (pp. 283–301). Clevedon: Multilingual Matters.

Rose, K. (2005). On the effects of instruction in second language pragmatics. *System, 33*, 385–399.

Rose, K., & Kasper, G. (Eds.). (2001). *Pragmatics in language teaching*. Cambridge: Cambridge University Press.

Rosenbloom, S. (2006, November 16). Corners: In certain circles, two is a crowd. *The New York Times*. Retrieved March 11, 2008, from http://www.nytimes.com/2006/11/16/fashion/16space.html?_r=1&oref=slogin

Sadler, R. (2007, November 30). Ethics in *Second Life*. Paper presented at the CALL Club, Iowa State University, Ames, IA.

Salaberry, R., & Cohen, A. D. (2006). Testing Spanish. In R. Salaberry & B. Lafford (Eds.), *The art of teaching Spanish: Second language acquisition from research to praxis*. Washington, DC: Georgetown University Press.

Sawyer, B. (2005, summer). Games leaders play. *Threshold*, 26–29. Retrieved March 11, 2008, from http://www.ciconline.org/thresholdsummer05

Second Life Herald. (2006). Retrieved March 11, 2008, from http://www.secondlifeherald.com/slh/2006/01/index.html

Second Life Herald. (2007). Retrieved March 11, 2008, from http://foo.secondlife-herald.com/slh/2007/01/oped_linden_oh_.html

Shamoon, E. (2006). 3BR w/VU of asteroid belt: One man's plan to turn virtual real estate into cold hard cash. *Wired Magazine, 14*. Retrieved March 11, 2008, from http://www.wired.com/wired/archive/14.04/station.html

Slater, M., Antley, A., Davison, A., Swapp, D., Guger, C., Barker, C., et al. (2006). A virtual reprise of the Stanley Milgram experiments. *PLoSOne, 1*, e39. Retrieved March 11, 2008, from http://www.plosone.org/article/info:doi%2F10.1371%2Fjournal.pone.0000039

Steinkuehler, C. A. (2004). Learning in massively multiplayer online games. In Y. B. Kafai, W. A. Sandoval, N. Enyedy, A. S. Nixon, & F. Herrera (Eds.), *Proceedings of the Sixth International Conference of the Learning Sciences* (pp. 521–528). Mahwah, NJ: Lawrence Erlbaum Associates.

Steinkuehler, C. A. (2006). Massively multiplayer online videogaming as participation in a discourse. *Mind, Culture, & Activity, 13*, 38–52.

Steinkuehler, C. (2007). Massively multiplayer online gaming as a constellation of literacy practices. *eLearning, 4*, 297–318.

Sykes, J. M. (2005). Synchronous CMC and pragmatic development: Effects of oral and written chat. *CALICO Journal, 22*, 399–432. Retrieved March 11, 2008, from https://calico.org/p-5-Calico%20Journal.html

Sykes, J. M. (2008). *A dynamic approach to social interaction: SCMC, synthetic immersive environments & Spanish pragmatics.* Unpublished doctoral dissertation, University of Minnesota, Minneapolis, MN.

Tapscott, D. (2000). The digital divide. In *The Jossey-Bass Reader on Technology and Learning* (pp. 127–154). San Francisco, CA: Jossey-Bass.

Thorne, S. L. (2000). Beyond bounded activity systems: Heterogeneous cultures in instructional uses of persistent conversation. In *The Proceedings of the Thirty-Third Hawaii International Conference on Systems Science.* New York: IEEE Press.

Thorne, S. L. (2003). Artifacts and cultures of use in intercultural communication. *Language Learning & Technology, 7*, 38–67. Retrieved March 11, 2008, from http://llt.msu.edu/vol7num2/thorne/default.html

Thorne, S. L. (2006). Pedagogical and praxiological lessons from internet-mediated intercultural foreign language education research. In J. Belz & S. Thorne (Eds.), *Internet-mediated intercultural foreign language education* (pp. 2–30). Boston, MA: Thomson Heinle.

Thorne, S. L. (2008a). Computer-mediated communication. In N. Hornberger & N. Van Duesen-Scholl (Eds.), *Encyclopedia of language and education: Vol. 4. Second and foreign language education* (pp. 325–336). New York: Springer/Kluwer.

Thorne, S. L. (2008b). Mediating technologies and second language learning. In D. Leu, J. Coiro, C. Lankshear & M. Knobel (Eds.), *Handbook of research on new literacies* (pp. 417–449). Mahwah, NJ: Lawrence Erlbaum Associates.

Thorne, S. L. (2008c). Transcultural communication in open internet environments and massively multiplayer online games. In S. Magnan (Ed.), *Mediating discourse online* (pp. 305–327). Amsterdam: John Benjamins.

Thorne, S. L., & Black, R. W. (2007). *New media literacies, online gaming, and language education.* (CALPER Working Paper Series, No. 8). The Pennsylvania State University: Center for Advanced Language Proficiency Education and Research.

Thorne, S. L., & Black, R. (2008). Language and literacy development in computer-mediated contexts and communities. *Annual Review of Applied Linguistics, 27*, 133–160.

Thorne, S. L., & Payne, J. S. (2005). Evolutionary trajectories, internet-mediated expression, and language education. *CALICO Journal, 22*, 371–97. Retrieved March 11, 2008, from https://calico.org/p-5-Calico%20Journal.html

Thorne, S. L. & Reinhardt, J. (2008). 'Bridging activities,' new media literacies and advanced foreign language proficiency. *The CALICO Journal, 25* (3), 558–572. Retrieved May 1, 2008, from https://calico.org/p-5-Calico%20Journal.html

Van Dijk, J. (2005). *The deepening divide: Inequality in the information society.* London: Sage.

Wang, H., Lu, C., Yang, J., Hu, H., Chiou, G., Chiang, Y., et al. (2005). An empirical exploration of using wiki in an English as a second language course. In P. Goodyear, D. G. Sampson, D. J.-T. Yang, T. Okamoto, R. Hartley, & N. S. Chen (Eds.), *Proceedings of the Fifth IEEE International Conference on Advanced Learning* (pp. 155–157). Los Alamitos, CA: IEEE Computer Society. Retrieved April 4, 2008, from http://ieeexplore.ieee.org/iel5/10084/32317/01508634.pdf? arnumber=1508634

Warschauer, M. (2003). *Technology and social inclusion: Rethinking the digital divide*. Cambridge, MA: MIT Press.

Wilcox, L., Allison, R., Elfassy, S., & Grelik, C. (2006). Personal space in virtual reality. *ACM Transactions on Applied Perceptions, 3*, 412–28.

Yule, G. (1996). *Pragmatics*. Oxford: Oxford University Press.

9 Understanding and Working with 'Failed Communication' in Telecollaborative Exchanges

Robert O'Dowd* and Markus Ritter**

Introduction

Telecollaboration refers to the use of online communication tools to bring together language learners in different countries for the development of collaborative project work and intercultural exchange. This type of network-based language teaching (NBLT) covers a wide range of activities and exploits a variety of online communication tools, including email, web-based message boards, and videoconferencing. Apart from the linguistic advantages of engaging learners in authentic language practice with native speakers, telecollaboration is also seen to offer great potential for the development of the skills and attitudes of intercultural competence (Byram, 1997). However, the literature in the area reveals that success in telecollaborative exchanges is far from guaranteed and Kern warns that instead of improving levels of intercultural understanding, 'we find here [in online exchanges] that exposure and awareness of difference seem to reinforce, rather than bridge, feelings of difference' (2000: 256). For this reason, this paper sets out to identify the reasons why online intercultural communica-

* Robert O'Dowd teaches EFL and Applied Linguistics at the University of León, Spain and is also the university's Director of International Training. He has taught English at universities in Ireland, Germany and Spain and has published widely on the application of telecollaboration in foreign language education. He recently coordinated the INTENT project which was funded by the European Commission's Lifelong Learning Programme to support the integration of telecollaboration in European Higher Education (http://www.scoop.it/t/intent-project-news). He is also one of the main developers of the UNICollaboration platform: http://unicollaboration.eu/

** Markus Ritter is a professor in the Department of English at Ruhr University Bochum, Germany.

tion between language learners in such projects often fails to achieve the intended pedagogical goals. Why does online intercultural contact between language students often end in disagreement and misunderstanding? Why is a common outcome of an exchange the confirmation of negative attitudes and stereotypes towards the target culture, when the development of intercultural understanding is one of the central aims of the activity? By reflecting on the answers to these questions, researchers hope to develop a better understanding of what terms such as online intercultural communication and electronic literacy actually involve, while educators aim to improve the structure of their exchanges so they do not lead students to negatively evaluate their experience of contact with members of the target culture.

In the course of the paper, the umbrella term 'failed communication' will be used to refer to cases of telecollaborative interaction which end in low levels of participation, indifference, tension between participants, or negative evaluation of the partner group or their culture. In order to establish an inventory of reasons for failed communication in intercultural online interaction, we will first of all carry out a review of instances of communication breakdown and misunderstanding reported in the literature. Following that, the inventory of reasons for failed communication will be organized into four levels and explained in detail. At this stage, various practical measures are also proposed in order to support teachers in their attempts to deal with problems in their exchanges. Finally, examples taken from a recent telecollaborative exchange will be used to highlight how factors from the different levels of the inventory can contribute to failed communication.

Conflict and Misunderstanding in Online Intercultural Ex-Change: Reports in the Literature

Since the pioneering work in online projects carried out in the late 1980s by the Orillas Network (Cummins & Sayers, 1995; Sayers, 1991) and the AT&T Learning Circles (Riel, 1997), the activity of telecollaborative exchange has grown in importance and is considered today one of the main pillars of online language learning. In the literature on NBLT, a new approach to research into students' use of online networks has seen a shift from essentially quantitative research in networked learning in single classrooms to qualitative studies of interaction between groups of learners in different locations (Kern, Ware, & Warschauer, 2004). These studies have looked at a variety of issues related to online intercultural exchanges, including their contribution to the development of learner autonomy and linguistic competence (Belz & Kinginger, 2003; Brammerts & Kleppin, 2001), the development of online literacy in second language learning (Kramsch, A'Ness, & Lam, 2000; Warschauer, 2000), and the pedagogical structure and design of online projects (Müller-Hartmann, 2000a; Meskill & Ranglova, 2000).

Particular attention has been paid to the reasons for failed communication as an area of further research. A review of the literature reveals that dysfunction in online exchange has been attributed to a complex, often confusing, array of factors related to the students and the sociocultural contexts in which they are operating, the organization and structure of the exchange, and the type of interaction which takes place between the groups in the online environments. It will be argued later that it is often impossible to rely on a single factor to explain an exchange's lack of success; reasons usually include a combination of interconnected factors from different areas.

The problematic area which seems to have received the most attention in this field of research has been the influence of differing sociocultural and institutional factors on the development of exchanges. A major contribution to the field has been the work of Belz, writing alone and together with Müller-Hartmann. They have produced an important body of research on how a wide range of social and institutional factors influenced the outcome of telecollaborative exchanges between university-level foreign-language students in Germany and the US. Belz (2001), for example, shows how the lower social and economic value of German in the US compared to English in Germany led to a proficiency mismatch between partners. As a result, a lower level of fluency in the foreign language meant that American students often wrote shorter emails than the German students. This was interpreted by their partners as a lack of friendliness and motivation and thereby led to negative evaluations of the exchange. Other social and institutional factors which the authors found to influence the exchanges included the misalignment of academic calendars, differences in societal norms with respect to technological access (for more information, see Thorne (2003) on *different cultures of use of the internet* and its effects on telecollaboration), divergent forms of assessment in the respective cultures, and the different physical layout of the universities (Belz, 2001, 2002; Belz & Müller-Hartmann, 2002, 2003).

The work of these authors is complemented by that of Ware (2005), whose qualitative study of an exchange between advanced students of English and German in the US and Germany highlighted the connection between the different uses of linguistic features by both groups in their online interaction, socioinstitutional factors, and low group functionality. Ware found that Americans asked far fewer questions than their partners and also made fewer attempts to establish personal rapport. This type of to-the-point, task-oriented interaction led to what she describes as 'missed communication' between the students and left much of the German group dissatisfied with the exchange. Through the examination of in-depth interviews with members of both groups, Ware identified certain social and cultural factors which determined students' online behavior in each case. The first factor was seen to be the different levels of prior experience with online writing. The American group reported being quite used to using online technologies for communication and learning and was therefore more critical of the technologies than their German counterparts who were found to be more enthusiastic about what was, for them, a novel way of language learning. A second influential factor was the differing social contexts in which each group was operating. The Germans were seen to be more motivated in their language learning than the Americans due to the different status of English and German in their respective countries. The Americans were also found to be much more grade focused than their counterparts. As such, their level of interaction was much more limited than that of their partners who were more motivated by an intrinsic desire to improve their English and make international contacts.

Looking at the Spanish-American context, O'Dowd (2005) reported on the socioinstitutional factors which influenced the development of a Spanish-American exchange based on the Cultura model of telecollaboration (Furstenberg, Levet, English, & Maillet, 2001). Apart from identifying the importance of factors already mentioned by Belz and Ware, including different levels of access to technology and differences in the evaluation requirements at the two institutions, O'Dowd also showed that the negative stereotypical images which each group brought to the exchange about the target culture were likely to influence the levels of motivation and participation of the students involved. Since this particular exchange took place during the academic year 2003–2004, the author found that the ongoing war in Iraq and the complex political relationship between Spain and the US led many of the Spanish students to react negatively to the idea of an exchange with American students and a focus on American materials during class time.

Other research has revealed how individual students' motivation and intercultural communicative competence can have an important influence on the outcome of online partnerships. In reference to motivation, Ware (2005) identified individual differences in motivation as being an important factor in the low functioning of an exchange. In her study, success in the asynchronous exchange required students to spend a substantial amount of time reading and replying to correspondence, and this often clashed with the amount of time students had put aside for such an academic activity. The importance of individual students' intercultural competence is illustrated in O'Dowd's study (2003) of five Spanish-English email partnerships. He found that the essential difference between the successful and unsuccessful partnerships was whether students had the intercultural competence to develop an interculturally rich relationship with their partners through the creation of effective correspondence. This type of correspondence took into account the sociopragmatic rules of the partner's language, provided the partner with personal opinions, asked him/her questions to encourage feedback, tried to develop a personal relationship with the partner, and was sensitive to his/her needs and questions. Fischer's work on high school email exchanges (1998) also highlighted the importance of the students' level of intercultural competence. In this case, he underscored the need for students to bring tolerance and appropriate attitudes of curiosity and openness to their exchanges.

Although surprisingly little research has looked at the relationship between failed exchanges and the methodological aspects of the activity, elements such as task design, the relationship between the teachers in both classes, and the ways in which students are prepared for the exchange have been acknowledged as having a significant influence on the outcome of telecollaboration. For example, in their discussion of a misunderstanding which developed between a German and English student in a web-platform exchange, Ware and Kramsch (2005) suggested that the teachers of both classes could have done more to avoid the breakdown of communication by ensuring that all messages were peer reviewed before being sent to the partner class and by organizing more tightly focused class discussions which would have given the two students in question an opportunity to analyze the messages with the help of their teachers and their peers. Other researchers have also looked at the important role which teachers can play in avoiding or dealing with low functionality and misunderstandings in telecollaboration. O'Dowd and Eberbach (2004) identified various key tasks which confront teachers who wish to exploit the potential for intercultural learning in online exchanges. These included developing students' awareness of how culture and language are interconnected and training learners how to make effective, culturally rich posts on the project's message board. The authors also underlined the need for both teachers to develop a good online working relationship together in order to co-ordinate and reach agreement on the many aspects of the exchange. Finally, in his work on the role of task design in telecollaborative exchange, Müller-Hartmann (2000a) affirmed the need for teachers to be able to identify problematic or provocative correspondence from the partner group which can then be brought into class and discussed in group or as a whole class. The author suggested that it is vital for exchanges to be integrated within the content of the regular classes so students can learn to reflect on and learn from their partners' correspondence.

A small number of texts in the literature argue that low functionality and misunderstandings in online telecollaboration can be explained by an analysis of students' reactions to cultural differences in online communication style and behavior. Despite many claims that the internet is a 'culturally neutral' environment where, in the words of Kramsch and Thorne, many believe that 'native and non-native speakers can have access to one another as linguistic entities on a screen, unfettered by historical, geographical, national or institutional identities' (2002: 85), a small but significant part of the research on online interaction has revealed that, first of all, the internet itself is based on specific cultural principles and values and that, second, users of the internet bring with them their own culturally specific communicative norms and modes of behavior which may or may not be compatible with those of other online users.

An example of this approach is provided by Belz (2003) who showed that the online interaction style of an American student, described as being uncommitted and self-deprecating, led his German partners to dismiss him as someone who was unwilling to engage in debate and confrontation. Similarly, the American student's interpretation of the German's correspondence, which was characterized by directness and categorical assertions, led him to reject them as being rude and aggressive.

In conclusion, it would appear that while there is a growing body of research which attempts to understand why virtual contact between language learners often fails to achieve the intended pedagogic aims, the reasons offered are very diverse in nature and may not serve to give educators a sufficiently broad and comprehensive overview of problematic areas or to illustrate how these are interrelated. For this reason, the following section proposes a structured inventory of factors which may lead to cases of failed communication in online exchanges. Following that, some examples of this phenomenon taken from a telecollaborative exchange will be used to illustrate how these factors are interconnected and influence each other.

Potential Areas of Dysfunction in Telecollaborative Projects: Developing an Inventory

The overview of the literature in the previous section reveals that various problems for successful long-distance collaboration have been identified and described in the past. However, those educators who have had experience with online exchanges are likely to acknowledge that the areas mentioned are not an exhaustive list of challenges. For example, it is evident that the thematic content of the tasks chosen for collaboration is also fundamental for the success of an exchange. In addition, to our knowledge, there has been no attempt to classify such problem areas in some didactically substantial way. Such an endeavor would appear both promising and useful because, in Belz's words, 'one of the most constructive ways to ascertain the developmental path of a particular phenomenon is to study those instances where it is disrupted, that is, those cases where the system fails' (2003: 76). We would argue that by providing a classification of reasons for failed communication, educators can be better prepared for the challenges which await them in their online projects.

Our inventory organizes the reasons for failed communication described in the literature review above (and in our own research) into four different levels. Such a framework is of course a largely idealized display of reality and does not provide a definitive number of reasons. Nevertheless, it is intended to be a step in better understanding the reasons for success or failure in telecollaborative exchanges. Each of the areas in Figure 9.1 will be briefly commented on, whenever possible with reference to relevant research or to data taken from an exchange between Spanish and German university students of English who used English as a lingua franca in their interactions.[1] More examples and findings from a separate exchange will be provided in the next section in order to illustrate how these areas and levels are interconnected.

Moving from an inner to an outer perspective in the inventory shown in Figure 9.1, attention first needs to be addressed to an individual level, the learner's psychobiographical and educational background. Naturally, this perspective entails everything the learner brings into the learning process. We suggest focusing on two areas here that may give rise to setbacks. First, it is the *learner's current level of intercultural communicative competence* (ICC) which should be considered. This construct is well established in the literature and merges skills, attitudes, knowledge, and critical cultural awareness as established by Byram (1997). In the context of online exchanges, learners with little experience in intercultural communication might lack necessary skills of discovery and interaction in order to deal with tasks which involve ethnographic interviewing (see O'Dowd, 2006). Similarly, the simple lack of factual knowledge, also part of Byram's concept of ICC, may lead to misunderstandings in the interpretation of messages from members of the target culture. The example of Katrin,[2] a German student taking part in the exchange with Spanish students can serve to illustrate this point. She reported taking away a negative impression of the partner group for the following reason.

Some of their utterances were quite provocative, for instance concerning the relationship between the USA and Europe. One of the Spanish side wrote that she did not like the USA. To my mind, if someone has an opinion, he or she should substantiate it.

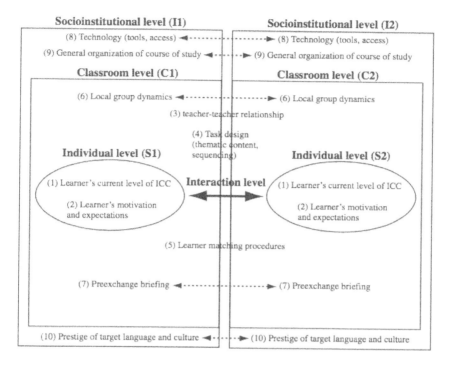

Figure 9.1. Inventory of Reasons for Failed Communication in Telecollaborative Projects

However if Katrin had had more knowledge about the political climate in Spain at the time of the exchange (when the question of the participation of Spain in the second Iraq war had heavily influenced the attitudes of the Spanish student population towards the US), she would have perhaps been more understanding of her partner's statement and would not have reacted to it so defensively.

A second key area at the individual level giving rise to special attention could be summarized as the *learner's motivation and expectations* towards the exchange project. There can be no doubt that the participants' types of motivation and their presuppositions are of great consequence for the success or failure of telecollaboration. In her study, Ware (2005) looked at these two related factors in more detail. One source of tension, she concluded, can be differences in expectations towards a project with regard to grammatical accuracy, message length, or response time. It is perhaps inevitable that there will almost always be differences among learners with respect to how they hope to benefit from an exchange and how much time they are willing to invest in it. However, potential problems can be avoided to a certain extent if both teachers and students are aware of the situation and the expectations of their partners. Extensive contact between teachers before the exchange and introductory writing tasks which involve students telling their distant partners about how they feel about their future work together can go some way to increasing sensitivity to the needs of the other group.

Moving on in the inventory, the classroom (or methodological) level is situated between the individual and the institutional level. Even though such a methodological perspective seems to be the most straightforward field for research, it appears to have received less attention than the other levels. In Figure 9.1, the areas 3, 4, and 5 have been placed at the interface of the two classrooms because decisions in these fields usually have a direct effect on both classrooms. Other areas (6 and 7) influence rather the local classroom situation and will have only an indirect impact on the partner class.

The importance of a good *teacher-teacher relationship* has repeatedly been recognized in the literature. O'Dowd and Eberbach (2004) in their account of a German-Irish exchange stressed the necessity of coordinating the many aspects of such a collaborative project in detail, and Müller-Hartmann (2000b) also looked at the problems which arise in teacher–teacher communication. A first step to deal with this source of difficulty is the awareness that telecollaboration is indeed a form of virtual team teaching that requires thorough consensus on all the facets of the cooperation. Contrary to other team-teaching efforts, teachers involved in online exchanges often do not even know each other face to face and shrink from disclosing all their plans to their partner teacher, a fact that is often made more difficult by the virtual nature of their communication.

The second area at classroom level, *task design*, is one of the domains that involve a profound working relationship between the teachers. Online exchanges are usually arranged around a number of tasks, and their thematic content and sequencing require careful consideration. Teachers are frequently familiar only with the curricular requirements of their local group and have good intuitions what kinds of tasks will lead to positive results in their own teaching contexts. Naturally, there will often be a tendency to try and implement those tasks that are in accordance with their own goals. Finding a compromise in task design that reflects the interests of both groups requires time and openness towards the other side's suggestions. Unfortunately, there is little research to support teachers in the process of answering important questions in the planning of their exchanges: What tasks are particularly suitable for telecollaboration? Are there patterns for sequencing different kinds of tasks that can be recommended? To what extent should student correspondence be written in the target or mother language? (For a description of language use in tandem exchanges, see Appel & Mullen, 2000; for a comparison of language use in the *Cultura* and tandem exchanges, see O'Dowd, 2005.) To what extent should students have a say in the selection of tasks? It is possible that in many telecollaborative projects teachers may be so preoccupied with organizational or technical issues that thematic content often comes only second within the available time frame.

The clash between student and teacher needs in task design was evident in the German-Spanish exchange mentioned earlier. In the end-of-term feedback, all the negative comments made by the Spanish group in reference to the project were in some way related to aspects of task design. One student complained that the topics chosen by the two teachers (based principally on the discussion of newspaper articles and the comparison of student-led surveys) had hindered the development of the online relationships between the German and Spanish students: 'I know that talking about culture could be useful for increasing our knowledge of the world, but neither Germans or Spanish ones will be totally close to one another if we don't talk about hobbies and personal interests.' Another student complained that the fact that the teachers had not corrected language errors before the messages had been posted (another significant issue in task design) had led him to feel he had learned little from the exchange: 'We have made mistakes in our messages, but we don't know what they are. This has been a waste of time.' A remedy for problems in task design may lie in a rigorous process of advance planning and consultation between students and teachers. For example, teachers could distribute preexchange questionnaires to students in all the classes asking them for their opinions on topics that they would like to discuss with their partners. To deal with the issue of accuracy in the L2, teachers could also carry out in-class reviews of their students' correspondence before the messages are actually sent to the partner group.

We suggest *learner-matching procedures* as a third area of potential dysfunction at classroom level. Even though questions of how students can be allocated in virtual pairs or groups seem to be somewhat trivial, it can have a massive effect on the results of the cooperation. Reports in the literature indicate that students are often assigned on a one-to-one basis. As is well known, some of these pairs turn out to be more successful in their interaction than others. The question, then, would be whether to leave these combinations to chance or to consider factors like age, gender, or foreign language proficiency when assigning students. Belz (2001), for example, has shown how a lack of proficiency in the foreign language can lead to students writing shorter correspondence than their partners and that this can consequently be interpreted by their partners as a lack of openness and friendliness. In this context, it is often assumed that telecollaboration takes place between two fairly homogeneous cultures. The literature usually just refers, for example, to a German-Spanish telecollaborative exchange. However, it should not be forgotten that nowadays the composition of groups is usually multicultural. The outcome will be totally different if a student from Portugal, to take an example, happens to spend a term in Germany and is supposed to represent and describe Germany as 'his' or 'her' country in such an exchange. Sometimes pairs or small groups of students are assigned on each side for cooperation. This may be due to institutional constraints (e.g., class size or the number of available computers) but may also be the result of a didactic desire to support negotiation in the foreign language among the members of the local group. Often, groups on both sides are not evenly distributed – one or two students on one side cooperating with three on the other. It is possible that such setups can have negative effects on the interaction between such groups.

As a fourth challenge at classroom level, we propose *local group dynamics*. This is closely related to the one before insofar as it directs attention to the atmosphere in the local class, a facet of cooperation that has repeatedly turned out to be an obstruction in our projects. Naturally, in telecollaborative projects, researchers, as well as teachers, tend to focus on the relationship between members of the two different classes. However, learners in pair or group constellations need to negotiate tasks not only with their online partner(s) but also within their local group. In many university classrooms in Germany, for example, participants have met their fellow students only briefly, and need to agree face-to-face with them on given tasks, formats and deadlines, a process which can turn out to be even more difficult than reaching agreements with virtual partners. Thus, the fact that a major part of the learning process takes place within the local context should not be neglected.

The quality of the *preexchange briefing*, our final aspect at the classroom level, can also be influential on the development and outcome of the exchange. Prior to the actual exchange, learners can be prepared for the stumbling blocks of the cooperation (e.g., technical issues and organizational commitments like response time); factual knowledge about the partners and their background can be provided, or the learners' expectations can be examined and compared to those of the teacher. Preparatory activities and themes should be harmonized to the greatest possible extent to avoid major discrepancies between the expectations and the background expertise of the two groups.

The third level of our inventory in Figure 9.1 focuses on dysfunctions at the socioinstitutional level. This perspective seems to have attracted the most attention in the literature and covers a diverse collection of factors to be taken into account when researching or planning long-distance cooperation. What all these topics have in common is that they pinpoint external areas, often beyond the participants' direct control. We suggest that the following three areas cover the most essential factors that others have put forward or that we have identified as influential in our own exchanges.

The technology itself – the medium by which long-distance exchanges are carried out – and the degree of access to it have an undeniably strong impact on the course of the exchange. Most commonly used communication tools today are probably still text oriented, while video and audio-based tools are gaining in importance (see O'Dowd, 2000, 2006 for examples of the use of videoconferencing in telecollaboration). Nowadays, message boards are usually embedded in learning management systems like *WebCT*, *Blackboard*, or *Moodle*,[3] allowing teachers to provide easy access to other resources and materials related to the exchange. We have found that even supposedly little differences between such systems, or the way they are set up, can have an effect on the exchange. For example, can members attach photos to their names or attachments to their messages? How comprehensible and user friendly are the general layout and organization of the communication tools and forums? Is the learners' view restricted to their partners, or can they read what their classmates have written? One German student made the following comment about the German–Spanish exchange which had been carried out in a *Moodle* platform: 'At the beginning it was confusing because there were so many introductory mails and the names [of the Spanish students] sounded quite similar. In the next week it already got better although you could still hardly remember to whom you had talked before. Hence, I liked the idea to have little pictures beside each name. I also thought it was nice that we took a class picture.'

Apart from the tools themselves, access to them can also be problematic. How natural is the use of online tools in the students' private lives? Do students have permanent out-of-class access to them? Ware (2005) in her study suggested that this external factor can have a significant influence on students' motivation and expectations. It is easy to imagine how limited access and hence shorter messages or a longer response time can lead to misunderstandings between differently equipped partners.

A second area at the socioinstitutional level, the *general organization of the students' course of study*, is meant to cover a variety of circumstances that determine the general context of the participants' schooling or studies. Belz and Müller-Hartmann (2003) identified four instances of how socio-

institutional affordances and constraints can affect German–American partnerships: (a) the misalignment of academic calendars; (b) culture-specific
assessment patterns; (c) differences in the educational backgrounds of each
teacher and the particular aims which they each have for the exchange; and
(d) the differences which exist between both countries as regards student
contact hours and the physical organization of each university. Such differences, the authors warned, can lead to disagreement on the amount of
student work considered appropriate, on the setting of deadlines and on
the functionality of cross-cultural group work. From our own experiences,
two related facets could be added. First, exchanges often bring together
groups following wholly different courses; one group might be enrolled
for a class in cultural studies and intend to focus on intercultural themes,
another group of teacher trainees is primarily expected to investigate the
educational potential of online interaction at a metalevel, while yet another
group envisages the collaboration essentially as a means of authentic language practice. It is easy to imagine how such different academic backgrounds and associated objectives can lead to misunderstandings about task
design and communicative behavior, not only between teachers but also
between students. Second, on many occasions, students as well as teachers act in accordance with a more general teaching and learning philosophy
than is implicitly or explicitly set out at a socioinstitutional level. In some
institutional contexts, for example, there is a considerable amount of freedom in working through a set syllabus, and it is largely the teacher's responsibility to decide what exactly s/he does in a given time frame. His or her
partner teacher, on the other hand, might be under a lot more pressure to
fulfill set requirements and justify the decisions made. Similarly, students'
attitudes can be partly predetermined by such sociocultural differences and
range along a continuum from minimal to total commitment. Again, consequences with regard to reliability or the amount of work that is considered
appropriate are evident.

Finally on this level, attention should be drawn to a well-known phenomenon of any intercultural exchange that might cause dysfunction – the
differences in prestige values of cultures and languages. Any exchange represents a particular constellation of involved cultures in general and languages in particular, and it is beyond question that these constellations can
be a complex source of misunderstandings, feelings of inferiority or resent-
ment. Aspects of cultural stereotyping have been investigated in various
facets in the literature. For example, O'Dowd's (2005) description of a
Spanish–American exchange, mentioned in the previous section, revealed
how anti-American sentiments at the time of the Iraq war in 2004 interfered
with the intended negotiation of cultural meaning between the groups.

The final level of the inventory in Figure 9.1 is the interaction level and refers to the misunderstandings and tension which arise from cultural differences in communicative style and behavior. This aspect of failed communication reflects the focus on intercultural pragmatics of writers such as House who argued that 'an emotional reaction [to cultural differences in communication styles] is often the major factor responsible for a deterioration of rapport and for the mutual attribution of negative personal traits which, in turn, effectively prevent any recognition of real differences in cultural values and norms' (2000: 147). This means that learners often assume that peculiarities in their interlocutors' way of communicating are due to personal oddities while, in reality, they are part of the target culture's communicative style. Examples of this include the different weighting given to small talk by German and English speakers or different attitudes towards indirectness between Spanish and English speakers. Spencer-Oatey (2000) suggested that cultural differences can emerge in communication in various areas, including illocutionary, discourse, participation, stylistic, and nonverbal domains. Although Spencer-Oatey was referring to traditional face-to-face intercultural interaction, it is possible to extrapolate the following issues related to each of these domains in the context of online collaboration.

1. *Illocutionary domain.* What is deemed to be the appropriate use of speech acts in the online interaction?
2. *Discourse domain.* How should the interaction be organized? How should the posts/messages be structured? How much small talk is appropriate? What topics are deemed appropriate for discussion?
3. *Participation domain.* Who should write first and second? How often and how quickly should one reply to the partner's posts? To what extent should explicit reference be made to previous posts?
4. *Stylistic domain.* What tone is considered suitable in the online interaction? Are irony and humor acceptable? What is seen to be genre-appropriate lexis and syntax?
5. *Nonverbal domain.* In a text-based medium, how can students make up for the lack of visual and paralinguistic cues? To what extent should emoticons and images be used to express emotions and content?

All of these areas can have a major influence on the outcomes of telecollaboration. In the German–Spanish exchange, different cultural attitudes to what was considered appropriate participatory behavior (i.e., the participation domain) led some German students to make a negative evaluation of their partner group: 'I doubt if they took it seriously as we did ... they did not always answer our questions and I had the impression that we were the ones who had to make the first move, e.g. creating new topics etc.' The stylistic domain was also seen to be the source of failed communication in this particular exchange. In one group discussion, one Spanish student wrote on the topic of heroes in her country that ... in these days, *El Quijote* by Cervantes has been considered the most important book of humanity.

Her statement, intended as a report of information which the student had read in a newspaper article, was interpreted by her German partners as an arrogant form of boasting about the home culture: 'Is it not quite ignorant, one-sided and rude in respect to other cultures to say this?' Anticipating in advance the exact misunderstandings on the interaction level of an exchange may be impossible, but teachers can take some care to prepare students for these issues by providing them with worksheets containing examples of previous exchanges, showing how misunderstandings occurred due to cultural differences in interaction norms and expectations. Students can be asked, for example, to read through these transcripts and suggest explanations as to what was the intended meaning of the writer and how the text was misinterpreted by the reader.

At this stage, it is important to acknowledge the interrelationship between the four levels of the inventory. For example, it is clear that the learner's motivation and expectations are mutually linked with most of the other fields. Learners' motivation is likely to be high if the chosen technology (e.g., chat) is new and exciting for them in a classroom context, and it is likely to be relatively low if their previous experiences with the technology were ambivalent. To cite a second example, the teacher-teacher relationship and the amount of negotiation between them can have a backwash on the appropriateness of the preexchange briefing, which, in turn, can influence learners' views of what to expect in the forthcoming exchange. Other interrelationships are more subtle, as will be illustrated in the following section.

Sample Data from a Telecollaborative Project

The asynchronous exchange described in this section was carried out in the summer term 2005 and involved students of English at Essen University in Germany and students of German at Macquarie University in Australia. One of the authors was the teacher of the German group and followed the notion of participant observation and action research.[4] The project was run on the *Moodle* platform. Data collection included teacher log books, an archive of all the students' written texts and teachers' messages, written interim and final evaluations by the students, and informal interviews with selected students.

In the eight-week exchange, students worked on four different tasks: (a) an introduction of themselves; (b) the Pope and the media; (c) student life; and (d) typically German, typically Australian? Part of the German students' final assignment was a written evaluation of the whole project, including an appraisal of these four tasks. The students offered generally positive feedback on the tasks, except for the second task (the Pope and the media). Of the 32 students on the German side, 19 were openly dismissive of the task. The intended topic – a comparison of media coverage of a global event – was misinterpreted as an invitation to debate religion.

Students' initial reactions to the second task quickly indicated one source of misconception. German student Sven started his first message as

> Hi folks, our task is about the old and the new pope. I am afraid to say I am not very religious, so what can I say? The only thing I do know is that this non-stop Vatican TV is slowly getting on my nerves.

In his final evaluation (which was addressed only to his teacher), he wrote

> I truly did not like the second topic. Not everyone is interested in the Pope and/or religion. So our messages about this were very short and superficial… This disturbed the rather personal beginning of the exchange. It is definitely not a good choice as the second task for people who barely know each other.

A closer inspection of Sven's reactions testifies to various problem areas. On the teachers' side, the task instruction apparently gave rise to misinterpretation, and teachers' preexchange negotiations were not thoughtful enough to prevent the misunderstanding. Sven, on the other hand, created a causal relationship between his lack of interest and the brevity and superficiality of his messages. Of course, this allows a first conclusion to be drawn about his level of intercultural competence (i.e., his attitudes of openness and curiosity towards his partner's views). His implicit suggestion to do this task at a later stage (when people know each other better) was shared by many students. Leaving aside the fact that his proposal somewhat contradicted his declared lack of interest, it raises the question of the best possible sequencing of tasks. What kind of task – beyond an introductory round – is most suitable for 'establishing cultural identity' (Müller-Hartmann 2000a: 136) and building up a positive working relationship between the exchange partners? The teachers' original intention for the task (media coverage of a global event) had indeed been a gradual start into the exchange. The supposed byproduct, the religious dimension of this task, was clearly underestimated by the teachers and largely impeded the students' interactions. In sum, task design, alongside the students' psychobiographical backgrounds, and the quality of teacher–teacher cooperation led to interaction failures among various members of the groups.

In other cases, though, the analysis is more intricate. The following two examples on the same topic demonstrate that supposedly similar communicative behavior and constellations can result in reasonable success in one case, and open failure in the other. Starting off with an ironic remark about not having heard of the new Pope in the media, Judith and Sandra from Germany then carried on with a fairly blunt declaration that

> the church (at least here in Germany) is not very attractive for young people!

Towards the end of their opening message they took up a piece of information from the introductory round and stated

> We know that you and your brother are active members of the church and we think that church in Australia is more open and lively, isn't it?

The addressed Australian student replied by describing the different churches in Australia but first gave expression to her accommodating attitude.

> First of all I just want to let you guys know that I'm not catholic, so will not be offended by anything you may have to say about the pope.

While here the bluntness of the opening message was somewhat counterbalanced by the partner's forbearance (and maybe the fact that she happened not to be Catholic), in the second example the dialogue developed differently. Amy and Justin from Australia chose a more solemn tone in their opening message, indicating clearly that they considered themselves religious and stressing their active participation in church matters. They then gave thought to the essence of the original task instruction, approaching it in rather academic fashion.

> We are questioning why, that in a time when the topic of religion is a taboo, being suppressed in schools and losing significance in people's lives, that the death and change of the pope was such a large media event.

This time the (indirect) question was not taken up by the two German girls who almost exclusively focused on distancing themselves from church in Germany. In addition, they introduced further controversial topics that they related to the task, criticizing the attitude of the Catholic church towards abortion and homosexuality. Having worked off their list of criticisms, they concluded in a conciliatory way.

> We don't want to offend or influence anyone with views. Looking forward to hearing/reading your opinion.

Again, contrary to the first example, this time the partners' reaction was not as accommodating. Justin basically ignored the vaguely obliging closing announcement of the German students and directly addressed his apprehension with the partners' criticism – and with the issue of abortion in particular. At this point the original task seemed to have fallen into oblivion, and, indeed, the final message of that thread by Vera, one of the girls of the German group, was written in an overly emotional way.

> I, as woman (!!!), do not agree with you. If a woman is raped, she mustn't be forced to bear a child of the criminal! That is what I think! Further more, the woman can be left by the man and then she has got a problem… Bye, Vera

With reference to our inventory, various explanations for the different outcomes of these two examples can be offered. First, at the interaction level, differences in tone (i.e., stylistic domain) are evident, with a more ironic approach in the first case and a more solemn tone in the latter. Also, the personal and direct question in the first example seems to have been more conducive to interaction than the more indirect, academic approach in the second group. Second, differences in learners' individual attitudes and levels of intercultural awareness become evident. While the first exchange is positively influenced by one of the partners' forbearance, in the second group students rather seem to fall victim to their set beliefs about the topic and their lack of tolerance. This is confirmed by the stereotypical explanation that Vera offers in her final evaluation, stating that 'as one could see with the pope task, religion always creates borders and hardly ever does the opposite nowadays'. Third, learner matching happened to bring male and female students together in the second case. It is evident that a topic like abortion which developed out of the original task can lead to gender-related tension. A final reason for failure that is represented in our inventory can be found in the German group constellation. The second girl of that group, who had not made any further contributions to the topic after their first reply, explained in a later interview that she had 'felt uneasy with Vera and her rude style'.

To conclude, this range of reactions and variations in students' communicative behavior can be considered typical of misunderstandings in an exchange and illustrates the interrelatedness between the various disruptive features that we outlined in Figure 9.1. Starting off from a lack of consideration in task design and its thematic content, the majority of the students fall victim to their individual expectations with regard to topic outcome and their insufficient skills in seeing through these conflicts and their genesis. This can be aggravated by local as well as virtual group constellations, which are usually left to chance. Students' specific and culturally influenced verbal behavior, especially when writing in a foreign language, can give rise to further linguistic misinterpretations. All this suggests that to a certain extent one has to comply with the unpredictable and dynamic nature of such exchanges and take the risk of partial interaction failure. However, a more discriminating perspective of potential challenges, both among the teachers and the students, can help to further increase intercultural awareness and the likelihood of satisfying results.

Conclusion

The aim of this paper has been to identify the reasons for failed communication in online intercultural exchanges, to organize these reasons in a pedagogically useful manner, and then to illustrate how these reasons are closely interconnected and influence each other. It is hoped that such an inventory of problematic areas will provide tutors involved in the area of NBLT with a greater understanding of the many complex factors which come into play when students engage in online collaborative tasks with partner learners in distantiated cultures. However, it is important that this inventory should not simply be seen as proposing a path for avoiding cases of failed communication in telecollaboration. In the words of Belz, 'It is very important to understand that these contextually-shaped tensions are not to be viewed as problems that need to be eradicated in order to facilitate smoothly functioning partnerships ... Structural differences frequently constitute precisely these cultural rich-points that we want our students to explore' (2003: 87). Educators interested in organizing telecollaborative projects should therefore have an in-depth understanding of the possible reasons for failed communication and should also possess a battery of techniques and practices which they can use in the course of their online exchanges in order for their students to derive maximum benefit from the exchanges. These techniques and practices could include the following: (a) engaging their students in classroom analysis of a collection of examples of failed communication from a previous exchange: (b) a rigorous approach to communicating with their partner teachers to enable both to understand the sociocultural context in which their partner class is operating; and (c) taking an on-going action research approach to their classes which involves collecting and analyzing online interactions and subsequent feedback from their students.

Notes

1. The research reported here was supported in part by the Junta de Castilla León Project, *Telecollaboración en la enseñanza de lenguas extranjeras.*
2. All students' names in this paper have been changed to preserve anonymity.
3. For more information on the *Moodle* learning management system, see the *Moodle* web.
4. We would like to thank the teacher on the Australian side, Martina Möllering, for her cooperation in this project.

References

Appel, C., & Mullen, T. (2000). Pedagogical considerations for a web-based tandem language learning environment. *Computers & Education, 34*(3–4), 291–308.

Belz, J. A. (2001). Institutional and individual dimensions of transatlantic group work in network-based language teaching. *ReCALL, 13*(2), 213–231.

Belz, J. A. (2002). Social dimensions of telecollaborative foreign language study. *Language Learning & Technology, 6*(1), 60–81. Retrieved August 17, 2005, from http://llt.msu.edu/vol6num1/BELZ/default.html

Belz, J. (2003). Linguistic perspectives on the development of intercultural competence in telecollaboration. *Language Learning & Technology, 7*(2), 68–99. Retrieved August 17, 2005, from http://llt.msu.edu/vol7num2/BELZ/default.html

Belz, J. A., & Kinginger, C. (2002). The cross-linguistic development of address form use in telecollaborative language learning: Two case studies. *Canadian Modern Language Review/Revue canadienne des langues vivantes, 59*(2), 189–214.

Belz, J. A., & Müller-Hartmann, A. (2002). Deutsch-amerikanische Telekollaboration im Fremdsprachenunterricht – Lernende im Kreuzfeuer der institutionellen Zwänge. *Die Unterrichtspraxis/Teaching German, 35*(1), 68–78.

Belz, J. A., & Müller-Hartmann, A. (2003). Teachers negotiating German-American telecollaboration: Between a rock and an institutional hard place. *Modern Language Journal, 87*(1), 71–89.

Brammerts, H., & Kleppin, K. (Eds.). (2005). *Selbstgesteuertes Sprachenlernen im Tandem. Ein Handbuch.* Tübingen: Stauffenburg.

Byram, M. (1997). *Teaching and assessing intercultural communicative competence.* Clevedon: Multilingual Matters.

Cummins, J., & Sayers, D. (1995). *Brave new schools. Challenging cultural literacy through global learning networks.* New York: St. Martin's Press.

Fischer, G. (1998). *E-mail in foreign language teaching. Towards the creation of virtual classrooms.* Tübingen: Stauffenburg.

Furstenberg, G., Levet, S., English, K., & Maillet, K. (2001). Giving a virtual voice to the silent language of culture: The Cultura project. *Language Learning & Technology, 5*(1), 55–102. Retrieved August 17, 2005, from http://llt.msu.edu/vol5num1/furstenberg/default.html

House, J. (2000). How to remain a non-native speaker. In C. Riemer (Ed.), *Cognitive aspects of foreign language learning and teaching* (pp. 101–118). Tübingen: Gunter Narr Verlag.

Kern, R. (2000). *Literacy and language teaching.* Oxford: Oxford University Press.

Kern, R., Ware, P., & Warschauer, M. (2004). Crossing frontiers: New directions in on-line pedagogy and research. *Annual review of Applied Linguistics, 24,* 243–260.

Kramsch, C., A'Ness, F., & Lam, W. S. E. (2000). Authenticity and authorship in the computer-mediated acquisition of L2 literacy. *Language Learning & Technology, 4*(2), 78–104. Retrieved January 17, 2006, from http://llt.msu.edu/vol-4num2/kramsch/default.html

Kramsch, C., & Thorne, S. (2002). Foreign language learning as global communicative practice. In D. Block & D. Cameron (Eds.), *Language learning and teaching in the age of globalization* (pp. 83–100). London: Routledge.

Meskill, C., & Ranglova, K. (2000). Sociocollaborative language learning in Bulgaria. In M. Warschauer & R. Kern (Eds.), *Network-based language teaching: Concepts and practice* (pp. 20–40). Cambridge: Cambridge University Press.

Müller-Hartmann, A. (2000a). The role of tasks in promoting intercultural learning in electronic learning networks. *Language Learning & Technology, 4*(2), 129–147. Retrieved August 17, 2005, from http://llt.msu.edu/vol4num2/muller/default.html

Müller-Hartmann, A. (2000b). Wenn sich die Lehrenden nicht verstehen, wie sollen sich dann die Lernenden verstehen? Fragen nach der Rolle der Lehrenden in global vernetzten Klassenräumen. In L. Bredella, H. Christ, & M. K. Legutke (Eds.), *Fremdverstehen zwischen Theorie und Praxis* (pp. 275–301). Tübingen: Gunter Narr Verlag.

O'Dowd, R. (2000). Intercultural learning via videoconferencing: A pilot exchange project. *ReCALL, 12*(1), 49–63.

O'Dowd, R. (2003). Understanding 'the other side': Intercultural learning in a Spanish-English e-mail exchange. *Language Learning & Technology, 7*(2), 118–144. Retrieved August 17, 2005, from http://llt.msu.edu/vol7num2/odowd/default.html

O'Dowd, R. (2005). Negotiating sociocultural and institutional contexts: The case of Spanish-American telecollaboration. *Language and Intercultural Communication, 5*(1), 40–56.

O'Dowd, R. (2006). The use of videoconferencing and e-mail as mediators of intercultural student ethnography. In J. A. Belz & S. Thorne (Eds.), *Internet-mediated intercultural foreign language education* (pp. 86–120). Boston, MA: Heinle and Heinle.

O'Dowd, R., & Eberbach, K. (2004). Guides on the side? Tasks and challenges for teachers in telecollaborative projects. *ReCALL, 16*(1), 129–144.

Riel, M. (1997). Learning circles make global connections. In R. Donath & I. Volkmer (Eds.), *Das Transatlantische Klassenzimmer* (pp. 329–357). Hamburg: Körber-Stiftung.

Sayers, D. (1991). Cross-cultural exchanges between students from the same culture: A portrait of an emerging relationship mediated by technology. *Cana-*

dian Modern Language Review/Revue canadienne des langues vivantes, 47(4), 678–696.

Spencer-Oatey, H. (Ed.). (2000). *Culturally speaking. Managing rapport through talk across cultures*. London: Continuum.

Thorne, S. (2003). Artifacts and cultures-of-use in intercultural communication. *Language Learning & Technology, 7*(2), 38–67. Retrieved August 17, 2005, from http://llt.msu.edu/vol7num2/thorne

Ware, P. (2005). 'Missed' communication in online communication: Tensions in a German–American telecollaboration. *Language Learning & Technology, 9*(2), 64–89. Retrieved August 17, 2005, from http://llt.msu.edu/vol9num2/ware/default.html

Ware, P. D., & Kramsch, C. (2005). Toward an intercultural stance: Teaching German and English through telecollaboration. *Modern Language Journal, 89*(2), 190–205.

Warschauer, M. (2000). On-line learning in second language classrooms: An ethnographic study. In M. Warschauer & R. Kern (Eds.), *Network-based language teaching: Concepts and practice* (pp. 41–58). Cambridge: Cambridge University Press.

Index

CPSIA information can be obtained at www.ICGtesting.com
Printed in the USA
BVOW06s1231180316

440820BV00002B/2/P

9 781781 793602